Heart Prints

Walking on Holy Ground

Julie Ireland Keene

authorHOUSE®

AuthorHouse™
1663 Liberty Drive
Bloomington, IN 47403
www.authorhouse.com
Phone: 1-800-839-8640

First published by AuthorHouse   10/12/2011

ISBN: 978-1-4670-4321-2 (sc)
ISBN: 978-1-4670-4320-5 (hc)
ISBN: 978-1-4670-4322-9 (ebk)

Library of Congress Control Number: 2011917781

Printed in the United States of America

Any people depicted in stock imagery provided by Thinkstock are models, and such images are being used for illustrative purposes only.
Certain stock imagery © Thinkstock.

This book is printed on acid-free paper.

Table of Contents

Preface

This book is a collection of some of the messages that I've delivered as minister and workshop leader over the past several years. Many people have suggested that I compile these talks into a book, so that is what you're holding in your hands. I don't pretend to be especially wise or enlightened. My primary spiritual goal is to keep expanding my consciousness that I may live and express ever more love and truth. My intention in ministry has always been that I am sharing my journey, hoping that it will be helpful to you in some way. My heart overflows with love and gratitude as I reflect upon the experiences and adventures I've been so fortunate to have along the way. So many have left heart prints in my life and I hope I have also managed to touch others with my own heart prints. The following poem suggested the title for this book:

Heart Prints

Whatever our hands touch we leave fingerprints
On walls, on furniture, on door knobs, dishes and books.
Smudges, showing we were there!
Oh Lord, please, wherever I go today help me leave Heart Prints.
Heart Prints of compassion, understanding and love.
Heart Prints of kindness and genuine concern.
I shall go out today to leave Heart Prints.
And if someone should say, "I felt your touch!"
May that be Your loving touch, Lord, Through me!
May my heart touch my lonely neighbor with a smile,
A worried mother, with peace, a runaway child, with safety,
A homeless person with warmth, and my dear friends, with love.
—anonymous

SECTION ONE
Cosmic Views

"There are a thousand ways to kneel and kiss the earth.
—Rumi

A Grand Design
A Wild Night and a New Road
All Paths Lead to God
And Still I Rise
Balancing on the Razor's Edge
Now is Eternal
Open My Eyes
Our Resurrecting Power
Sweet Mystery of Life
The Circle of Life
The Mystic Path
The Unfinished Symphony
The Wonder of it All
Understanding Jesus
Welcoming the Christ
Who You Truly Are

A Grand Design

"The fabled musk deer searches the world over
for the source of the scent which comes from itself."
—Ramakrishna

Stephen Hawking, the famed scientist and author of a newly released book entitled The Grand Design, talked to Larry King and his guests a few months ago about his new book. Hawking, 68 years old, was diagnosed with ALS 35 years ago. He sits slumped in his wheelchair unable to hold his head up straight and communicates through his computer. He is a professor at Cambridge University in England and highly respected around the world as a brilliant scientist comparable to Einstein.

The premise of his book is that "God may exist, but science can explain existence without the need for God. Theology is unnecessary." Hawking says the grand design can be found in the M theory: "Ours is not the only universe. A great many universes were created out of nothing. Their creation does not require the intervention of some supernatural being or god. These multiple universes arise naturally from physical law."

The bottom line question is what creates physical law and how are universes created from nothing? After the Hawking interview was over, Larry King invited three other guests to discuss the ideas: Leonard Mlodinow (co-author of the Grand Design—a scientist from Cal Tech), a Jesuit priest, Father Robert J. Spitzer, and scientist and metaphysical author Deepak Chopra. Father Spitzer said there is still the problem of "something from nothing, which goes unanswered." He admires Hawking's intellect and accomplishments but points out that he is also a human being capable of oversight and logical errors. Each of the guests had different ways of naming "the nothing." Mlodinow calls it a field of possibilities; Father Spitzer calls it transcendent mind.

I prefer Chopra's explanation: "Nothingness is not an empty void; it's the room of creation. Nature goes to exactly the same place to create a galaxy of stars, a cluster of planets, a rainforest, a human body or a thought. God not only continuously creates universes, he becomes them." We can't find and nail down God with left brain logic and science, but we can certainly investigate, map and explain nature's processes and put our knowledge to good use. However, the transcendent mind and the field of possibilities lie deep within us as our omnipresent spiritual identity. Here is where the philosophers, poets, and metaphysicians go beyond science, while not discounting it." Deepak Chopra said that he agrees with the science in The Grand Design; it's just that there is more to it than what scientists can measure.

The same data can have many different interpretations. We must find the meanings and interpretations that guide our own individual lives. Here, I am responsible for my own thought, my own power of creation. Jesus told us, "ye are Gods" and "what I do you will do and more." What does that mean? We have the power of creative thought and feeling, the power to create Heaven or Hell in our experience. When we take responsibility for our own thoughts and feelings, we see the world in an entirely new light.

A Course in Miracles is helpful because it provides us with a clear and precise method of dealing with ourselves and our ego. It ultimately leads us, if we choose to follow, into a world of unity, love and peace. Larry King asked Hawking what he felt was humanity's greatest danger. His answer: "Human beings are in danger of destroying themselves with greed and stupidity. If we can survive the next 300 years, perhaps we can get out into space."

I can't find the logic in that solution to our problems. If we cannot deal with our greed and stupidity here and now and in the next 300 years, we will simply create more greed and stupidity in space if we manage to live there. In the final analysis, we are still left with the task of dealing with our own consciousness. We all have the task of raising our consciousness to a higher level, leaving hatred, greed, stupidity, prejudice and nonforgiveness behind.

The word repent in the Bible simply means to turn around the other way. So we need to turn from the darkness of ignorance to the light of love and truth. No other person can do our individual work for us. Our help is to be found in the spirit deep within. Like the musk deer we keep searching for our identity and our meaning all over the world when it is right where we are all the time, an integral part of our being.

Here is where teachers and authors such as Eckhart Tolle and David Hawkins and many others can help. Yet, there is no substitute for quiet meditation that takes us into the integral core of our being, which is pure spirit. This is the transcendent mind, the field of possibilities, where we realize our oneness with God. Yes, we are part of the grand design and that grand design is indeed beautiful and awesome beyond measure. It is certainly much larger than any one individual, and yet within us, nearer than breathing, closer than hands and feet. That is why we say God is equally and everywhere present.

Ironically, according to logic and scientific experience with ALS, Hawking should have left his body quite awhile back. Yet, he keeps going and contributing to scientific knowledge. You could say his ongoing ability to think and function is actually quite miraculous. Perhaps miracles can take place in our lives whether we believe in them or not. I have had friends who are skeptics, especially about the idea of reincarnation. I don't fret because I know that sooner or later we will all pass on and if there is more, it will be revealed to us. If not, we won't know the difference anyway!

However, my experience is such that I choose to believe in a transcendence, a higher way, something more, and there is something in me that won't allow me to stop reaching for the stars. I want to not only know about the grand design; I want to be a conscious part of it. How about you? Let us join together in the pursuit of experiencing for ourselves the grand design. I close with a piece from Course in Miracles entitled The Forgotten Song. I feel that song deep within the core of my soul, and I yearn to once more consciously connect with it and help others to do so:

"Listen,—perhaps you catch a hint of an ancient state not quite forgotten; dim perhaps, and yet not altogether unfamiliar, like a song whose name is long forgotten, and the circumstances in which you heard, completely unremembered.—Beyond the body, beyond the sun and stars, past everything you see is an arc of golden light that stretches as you look into a great and shining circle. The circle fills with light before your eyes. The edges of the circle disappear, and what is in it is no longer contained at all. The light expands and covers everything, extending to infinity forever shining and with no break or limit anywhere. Within it, everything is joined in perfect continuity. Nor is it possible to imagine that anything is outside, for there is nowhere this light is not. This is the vision of the son of God; here is the memory of what you are." Let us behold this light in ourselves and in each other, dear friends and celebrate the grand design which encompasses all.

A Wild Night and a New Road

"Dying is a wild night and a new road."
—Emily Dickinson

It is impossible for us to be separate from our source, and since God is life and love, so are we. In truth we are an ageless, birthless, deathless eternal extension and expression of God. However, we suffer from spiritual amnesia, believing we are separate from God and from one another. On the level of human fear and ignorance we believe in birth, death, disease, lack and limitation. We believe our short span here in our current earth suit is "all there is." Once we begin to awaken, we are ready to look at other possibilities. On the human level, expressing as Julie at this moment, I can't know all the places I've been and all those where I will be. Yet, I am sure I'm on a great ongoing adventure, vaster than I can possibly imagine.

At this moment, we're traveling through interstellar space at the speed of 18.5 miles per second—together with the whole planet Earth of course, and with the whole solar system including our sun. The sun itself is a middle-aged star on the periphery of our galaxy—the Milky Way. Each galaxy is made up of myriads of stars, most of which are quite likely to have their own planets circling around them. Information from Hubel tells us there are 50 billion or more galaxies. If only one percent of those planets harbor a technical civilization—and this is a conservative estimate—the universe just may teem with more than 100 trillion civilizations! The concept of no limits to creation definitely boggles the human brain!

For so many centuries we have believed ourselves to be the center of the universe and our limited human capacities the extent of our life. Many people still cling to the way things have always been and still seem to be. But we can't control the universe or stop it from extending itself. Actually, we can't put blinders over our heads and make our small human ego the Reality of ourselves no matter how hard we try. It may take a few thousand years for us to wake, but our destiny is to wake—to remember the truth about ourselves and everyone and everything else: It's all God. It's all Spirit and Spirit is eternal. In truth death does not exist.

What keeps us from embracing the majesty of this truth? Our tendency to stay stuck in limited separation consciousness. Our human ego has a huge stake in keeping us limited and ignorant. When we awaken, the ego disappears into the nothingness it is. The ego—that part of our mind that clings to separateness—does not want us to let go of it. When Paul said, "I must die daily," he meant that his separation consciousness had to die before he could embrace and accept his oneness with God and his eternal identity in God.

This dying daily means releasing the old consciousness right here in the midst of our everyday life. This is where Emily Dickinson's words are appropriate: "Dying is a wild night and a new road." I have a parrot story that illustrates that point. A hunter was in the jungles of South Africa when he ran into an enclave of talkative English speaking parrots. He captured them and sold all but one to a friend who wanted them as a tourist attraction. The hunter took the parrot he kept back to his home in England. The parrot talked every day about how much he missed his buddies and his old home. When the hunter was making plans for his next trip back to Africa, the parrot asked if he would take a message back to his friends who had been captured with him and were still living in cages as a tourist attraction. "Tell them I'm fine, adapting to my cage and content to stay here until I die."

After the hunter delivered the message, the parrots began dropping off their perches, feet up and stiff. The captors opened the cages and threw the "dead" parrots out on a woodpile. The birds immediately revived and flew up onto a high tree branch. The hunter shouted, "You tricked us!" "Yes," replied the parrots. "Our friend sent us a great message: "We had to die in order to be released from our cages." So what's the spiritual message in that? What is our cage? We are caged within the limitations of our human ego until we "die to our false self." Then we are free to fly and travel a new road because we have died to our old ways. It's a wild night and a new road to be born again into a consciousness of our true identity in God.

Oftentimes, people are finally ready to shed old destructive beliefs when they realize their time in their current earth suit is limited. Stephen Levine wrote a helpful book entitled *What If You Had One Year to Live*. He asks readers questions such as, "What would you keep; what would you give up; what would you do differently?" Such questions help broaden our perspective and to more clearly see what is truly important and what is not so important.

Years ago when I was on a Unity trip to Switzerland with my daughter, we visited a small cemetery near the Matterhorn. I've never forgotten the epitaph on the tombstone of a 24 year old man. It said, "I chose to climb." Obviously, mountain climbing can be a very dangerous endeavor and he knew he could possibly lose his current life, but he chose to climb, to take the risk, to do what he was obviously passionate about. We could ask ourselves the question, "Do I choose to climb?" Perhaps not a mountain, but do I choose to climb spiritually higher, to push out the boundaries of my life, to reach for a pinnacle of truth and love?" Of course there are risks in all that, but life is so much more than the number of years we stay here.

It's been said that we can't live fully until we get past the fear of our own death. We must recognize that unless we turn into a body of light and ascend, we will lay aside our current earth suit. The good news is that the soul, the essence of us, cannot die. I must confess that years ago, in my ignorance, I was in such pain that I considered suicide. Now, I realize that it is actually impossible to kill our ongoing spirit, so I have stopped entertaining such thoughts. I just came across this satirical little piece:

"Razors pain you; rivers are damp; acids stain you,
And drugs cause cramps. Guns aren't lawful; nooses give—
Gas smells awful—you might as well live."
Dorothy Parker

A few years ago there was a series of beautiful channeled books by Emmanuel that taught the spiritual truth about so called death. Here are a few quotes: "Death is like taking off a tight shoe. Even when you're dead, you're still alive. You go through the doorway of death alive and there is no altering of the consciousness. It is not a strange land you go to, but a land of living reality where the growth process is a continuation. Life and death should not be considered as opposites. It is closer to the truth to speak of dying as an entrance rather than an exit. If death could be seen as a beautiful clear lake, refreshing and buoyant, then when a consciousness moves towards its exit from a body, there would be that delightful plunge and it would simply swim away."

So, without our fear of dying, we are free to live more fully here and now, free to make the most of whatever time we have in this span. Let's make the most of it so that when our time comes, we leave with few regrets. We do this by dedicating ourselves to embrace and live the highest truth we know. We do this when we refuse to let time and busyness and distance keep us from the essential, which is love for God, our neighbors and ourselves.

This love is not "special" and possessive; it is an experience of unconditional love for all life—what is. Anytime we feel too busy and distracted to live a more expansive life beyond the human ego, we need to remember that it's never too late to make choices in the current moment that can set us free. Seems we have to die daily—sometimes moment to moment—to the human ego and be born anew into a new spirit of love and truth. The only moment we can find God is in this now moment. May you be blessed as you claim the truth of your being in God and live your life to the fullest *today.* Remember—there is only life and you are an eternal part of it.

All Paths Lead to God

"Refuse to be enslaved by the hobgoblin of foolish consistency."
—Ralph Waldo Emerson

There is nowhere else to go, <u>but</u> to God—we live and move and have our being in God—even when we don't realize it. Our true identity cannot be stolen; it is nearer than breathing, closer than hands and feet.

> Truth is within ourselves, it takes no rise
> From outward things, whatever you may believe.
> There in an inmost center in us all
> Where truth abides in fullness; and around,
> Wall upon wall, the gross flesh hems it in,
> This perfect, clear perception—which is Truth.
> A baffling and perverting carnal mesh
> Binds it, and makes all error; and to KNOW,
> Rather consists in opening out a way
> Whence the imprisoned splendor may escape,
> Than in effecting entry for a light
> Supposed to be without.
> —Robert Browning

Simple! All we need do is tune into the Light within and let it shine! So, why isn't it easy? Because we are conditioned to living from the outside in, conditioned to our dream of separation, conditioned to believe we are guilty and unworthy of being host to Divinity. We are all here wandering in our own wilderness while we are already home in Heaven.

I can imagine our ego sense of separation asking itself, "What shall I dream about now? Who shall I be in this dream? What country, what parents, what family, what experiences shall I draw to me in this dream? So, we come in for another go round, another episode in the serial ego drama. Sooner or later we come to the realization that this serial dream is not satisfying—there must be more. We decide we'd rather experience peace, love and joy rather than uproar, separation and depression. We begin to look for answers, each in our own way. Each path looks different, seems different, but the underlying drive is the same—to find and reclaim and wake up to our True Identity in God—to experience the Peace of God.

This life dream can seem like a maze, a labyrinth. Some paths are dead ends, but we can retrace our steps, explore different paths until we find one that leads to the Center, to God, to awakening from the dream. There is not a right path or a wrong path—just different paths—and they will all lead to God in the end. The mystic poet Rumi wrote: "Beyond all ideas of wrong doing and right doing, there is a field—I'll meet you there." We are quick to judge ourselves and others as wrong. We are taught to follow the crowd, to seek approval, to not trust ourselves. William James said: "If you want to go nowhere, follow the crowd."

The more we can come to the center of ourselves, the Divinity in us, even if only for brief moments in meditation or contemplation of truth and beauty, the more courage we have to trust our own guidance, our own path. All too often we are like the characters in this story:

Don't Lose Your Ass.

An old man and a boy and a donkey were going to town. The boy rode on the donkey and the old man walked. As they went along, they passed some people who remarked, "It's a shame the old man is walking while the boy is riding. The man and boy thought maybe the critics were right, so they changed positions. Later, they passed some people that remarked: What a shame, he makes that little boy walk." They decided they both would walk! Soon they passed some more people who thought they were stupid to walk when they had a decent donkey to ride.

So they both rode the donkey! Now they passed some people that shamed them by saying how awful to put such a load on a poor donkey. The boy and man said they were probably right so they decided to carry the donkey. As they crossed a bridge, they lost their grip on the animal and he fell into the river and drowned. The moral of the story: If you try to please everyone, you will eventually lose your ass.

As you may know, my life has not been the standard picture book life; society has not automatically given me its stamp of approval. As a result I have carried around a lot of guilt and shame about how I grew up, my marriages, and my so called unstable life. It has taken me awhile to accept myself and the paths I've traveled. Course in Miracles: "We teach best what we most need to learn." That is what I have been doing for years: teaching myself, and by the grace of God, since we are all One, this teaching has benefitted others as well. I have finally stopped apologizing for my life. I've had some great experiences and grand adventures in the labyrinth dream of this life. We all want the same thing—to awake to our Oneness with God, whether we are conscious of it or not. I'd like to share my journal entry of just a few months ago—The title is Stability:

I have lived a very unstable life—many moves, careers, churches, husbands. I have not been content to remain in one mind set—I am driven—I can only hope divinely driven—to keep moving ahead, to keep digging deeper,—until I am totally wrapped in awareness of God, the Presence of God. And perhaps even then, God will keep me busy going on spiritual errands. God is expansion, unlimited. As a creation of God, am I not made in that image and likeness? It's never too late; I'm never too old. It's been tempting at times to stagnate or even go in reverse. I've tried to get away with it. Sometimes I've felt lazy, not wanting to make the effort of moving ahead—physically, psychologically, or spiritually. Whenever I give in to that, I eventually get literally "blown out" of my rut—out of whatever situation I'm stuck in. I most move on. That has happened in churches and in relationships. I get a chance to forgive, release, bless it and see the growth and good in it.

I have a wonderful friend and fellow Unity minister that I feel is a real soul companion. Helice is stable—that's her path. In her many years of ministry she has served only two churches. She is one of the most loving spiritual people I know. I have often compared myself to her and found myself lacking. But recently I had a liberating insight: We are alike in our deep spiritual commitment, but our paths in the outer world are different—neither one is superior or inferior: It's okay to wander; it's okay to stay put.

A few years ago I interviewed at a fairly large church and really wanted the job. They did not choose me because I had moved around too much. Perhaps they were wise not to select me. The irony is that no one since then has stayed very long in that particular place. I never want to be locked into any situation. If and when Spirit moves me to move, I move. If Spirit says 'stay,' I stay. I'm playing a game of Simon Says with God!

I never want to settle in my inner life. I can't allow myself to think: "I've got it now—I can let my psyche rest." No, there is no rest until I am living in a dynamic consciousness of love, peace and joy. All the guilt and angst I've felt about being unstable has evaporated in the light of realizing and accepting that I have my own unique path, and it's perfectly fine and acceptable. It is what it is, and I bless it. I don't have to carry the donkey over the bridge because someone thinks I should.

Emerson is one of my favorite writers; I believe we are kindred spirits—he said "I will not live outside of me. I will not see with other's eyes; I would be free but cannot be while I take things as others please to rate them. I dare attempt to lay out my own road. Henceforth, please God, forever I forego the yoke of men's opinions. I will be light-hearted as a bird and live with God."

So we must all walk our own path in trust that all paths lead to God. I know the path can be wider and smoother if we invite God, Holy Spirit,—our elder brother and the way shower Jesus the Christ to walk the path beside us. Whatever path you may be walking today, know that God is with you; all you need do is be open to that Presence. You can be sure that you are worthy of that companionship, guidance and instruction. Go to the quiet garden in your mind and put out the invitation. Let's join together in love as we walk our unique paths. Spirit is in each of us; no one is ever left out. All Paths Lead to God. Bless all the paths you've taken up to now. They have led you here and God is here with you.

I'll close with some words of *The One and Only* from our Unity Hymnal:

"I must find my very own path as I go along life's way. Seeking I will find the courage to go further on each day." Please know that God blesses all paths that lead to the mountaintop. And please love and bless yourself as you go along on your unique journey.

And Still I Rise

"Wherever you turn your eyes, the world can shine
like transfiguration. You don't have to bring
a thing to it except a little willingness
to see. Who has the courage to see it?
—Marilynne Robinson

The way onward and upward is ours for the choosing, is ours by the renewing of our minds. When we are ready to awaken, to rise up into a higher dimension of living, we are graced with awakening experiences. Oprah Winfrey devoted many programs to inspirational stories of awakening and overcoming. A while ago a man described his experience of surviving a plane crash. He was seated in the rear of the plane when it crashed; the tail section broke away from the main body. The main body of the plane burst into flames on impact, and the man saw the people trapped and their bodies burning.

But then he saw something like auras or lights departing the bodies from the top of their heads. He noticed that some were brighter than others. This man was not particularly religious, but since this experience he has been motivated to live his life in such a way that his spirit will become as clear and bright as possible.

Another guest on the program was a woman whose face was burned. Even after several surgeries she was so disfigured that it was difficult to look beyond it. Yet, as she spoke and answered Oprah's questions, the beauty of her spirit began to come forth. She is a shining example of the fact that we are so much more than the condition of our body.

Michael J. Fox was interviewed by Larry King and discussed his new book *ALWAYS LOOKING UP: the Adventures of an Incurable Optimist.* His Parkinson's disease is clearly progressing, and Larry asked if he finds it difficult to be in the public eye. Michael's answer was, "Vanity is the first to go, and what I look like and what my body does is not me. In fact I can't be sure what my body is going to do next." All the while it can be observed that he is shaking slightly, that his speech is slower and more disjointed and that his body jumps and twitches and even causes him to involuntarily start to rise up from his chair.

While all this is going on, a strong, loving, courageous spirit shines forth. He refuses to see himself as a victim, and works to help others by being out front and pushing for research to find a cure. He enjoys his life and his family. He exemplifies our theme today, "and still I rise."

This is what Jesus demonstrated for us with his resurrection. We are not a body; we are free as God created us. It is impossible to kill the son of God—and all of us are Sons of God. We are One; we are free in Spirit; we cannot die; we are not a body. Hospice chaplain John Love shared the following: "During hospice visits, I witness the human body in its final hours and minutes before death. During this sacred time, fraud is clearly exposed. While praying with dying people, I recognize that the body is an impostor—the ego's counterfeit shrine to immortality. The body is not real. Only divine Spirit is real."

Jesus tells us in Course in Miracles: "Let us not spend this holy week brooding on the crucifixion of God's son, but happily in the celebration of his release. A slain Christ has no meaning. But a risen Christ becomes the symbol that the son of God has risen from the past, and has awakened to the present. Now is the closest approximation of eternity that this world offers. It is in the reality of now without past or future that the beginning of the appreciation of eternity lies."

A story: A young girl playing in her yard manages to capture a beautiful butterfly. She puts it in a jar and watches it for a long time. She is fascinated by its colors, the delicate tracing in its wings, and the magic of its flight. She wants to keep the beautiful creature forever. As she continues to be enchanted with her prize, her mother comes to see what is so captivating. The mother says to the girl, "Honey, you have to let it go." Reluctantly, the little girl removes the jar's lid, holds it up and the butterfly flies free.

When Mary Magdalene saw Jesus on Easter morning, his first words to her were, 'Don't hold onto me." She had to let go, as we must, in order to experience the free and unlimited teaching of Jesus. We can't keep our own Spirit in a jar or that of others. We need to let go of who we have been, what we have or have not done, and what has or has not been done unto us. In order to fly free we must let go of even our happy past, not clinging to it and insisting that it was better then.

To experience our own resurrection, we must rise up to a new level of life and joy. We must fly out of the jar of confining beliefs. Unless we rise in consciousness, unless we keep walking forward to higher and holy ground, we risk sinking into a quicksand of meaninglessness, depression and despair. We must rise up and bless each eternal moment here and now, no matter what our life circumstances—and trust that the spirit of love and truth is within us, nearer than breathing and closer than hands and feet.

We are constantly unfolding, and we will ultimately reach our destination. As we meet obstacles and we will meet obstacles and challenges here in

Earth School, our mission is to rise up and find a way to go around them, to overcome, to be able to affirm, "And still I rise." We are created with the ability and the deep desire to soar. When we trust that we can rise upon the wings of spirit, when we trust that it is safe to leave our human ego behind as we allow ourselves to be guided and comforted by our indwelling spirit, we do indeed rise above the challenges of the earthbound. We no longer live in a tomb of our own limitation.

Balancing on the Razor's Edge

"If you pour all your energy into one thing,
You're sure to harm the rest of your being
And if you invest it all in profit—
You'll end up losing the whole lot."
—from the Tao Te Ching

Mystic David Hawkins, the author of *The Eye of the I,* reveals a method of calibrating consciousness based on kinesiology. His basic finding is that 78% of the world's population calibrate below the level of integrity. However, the 22% who calibrate higher than that provide a counterbalance that keeps us from destroying ourselves.

Our world right now is seriously out of balance. Politically, environmentally, financially—millions of people have too little and many people have too much. Aware people do what they can in the outer world to balance this, and that is good. However, you and I can begin with ourselves. As we become more balanced, our balanced state influences our immediate environment and extends out into the larger world.

Balance is illustrated by the pendulum. If you pull it 30 degrees to the right, it will swing back 30 degrees to the left. We see this principle operating in ourselves and in life if we pay attention. That's why the idea of depriving ourselves to lose weight does not provide lasting results. I once went on an extreme all protein diet and lost 20 pounds. However, I was so starved for fruits, vegetables and grains, that as soon as I went off this diet, I gained it all back.

It is much more efficient to deal with the body in a balanced manner than to be burdened with the effects of the extremes. The inefficiency of our actions is determined by how many degrees off center we are. When we are off center, we struggle with the opposites. We zig-zag through life instead of walking the straight path. I believe that our experience here in Earth School will be fulfilling to the degree that we stop the zig-zag and find 'the middle way' which is the most direct path of spiritual advancement.

When we sincerely choose the path of spiritual advancement, we often find ourselves skating on the razor's edge. Staying balanced and one pointed in life can be extremely challenging. Yet, the more we do this, the more love, peace, and joy we feel and express. It is all too easy to get lost in the extremes. An example of this is our mood swings. We can all acknowledge that we can have bad moods, dark moods, depressing moods as well as good moods, light-filled moods, uplifting moods.

When we constantly swing from side to side with our moods, our life is not centered. We get caught in the backlash. An effective way to move past extremes is to watch and observe ourselves; to get above and behind the moods—to steer ourselves back to the middle. This is a decision to not participate in the swing. The participation in the swings plays out in the bi-polar person. I think we are all bi-polar to some degree. It's when the pendulum swings to the extremes that it becomes a clinical situation.

Whenever we find ourselves in a place where everything is wrong and the world seems out to get us, a place where we label everything in our past as unfair and hurtful, we can know we are suffering from a case of "stink eye." We are seriously out of balance. The only cure for this is to be open and receptive to higher truth, and then to actually do the spiritual practices and exercises we hear and read about, such as meditation and forgiveness.

Meditation practice is a prerequisite to living in harmony and staying balanced and centered. In the state of meditation the right and left brain functions coordinate and balance. This has been researched and proven at Harvard and other major universities with brain wave testing. My personal experience is that I took giant leaps forward when I began meditating. Instead of pronounced mood swinging back and forth, I began to feel the calm in the center of the storms in my life. My life took a whole new direction and I wanted to share everything I was learning with others.

The good news is that we don't have to live in misery even when life presents us with challenging situations. If we constantly practice the truth we know we can skate on the razor's edge, and when we fall, we can get right back up and keep on skating. Realistically, as long as we are here in Earth School, we will be presented with challenges. Yet, if we face these challenges from a balanced consciousness, we will learn and grow from them and we will keep moving forward.

This is what Jesus was talking about when he said, "Be in the world, but not of it." We are not of the world when we stay balanced and centered. In this state we don't wear ourselves out mentally or physically; we can actually do less and accomplish more. This is what he was talking about when he said, 'for the gate is narrow and the way is hard, that leads to life.' Why is it hard? It is difficult for us because our human ego tendencies rebel against spiritual disciplines.

Our ego believes that the straight and narrow path is a limitation and a bore. That is why skating on the razor's edge feels challenging at first, but once we get into it, we embrace the challenge because we understand that in the end, it leads to our freedom in Spirit. In truth, it is the most expansive, exciting and delightful journey possible! We really get it that we are not human beings having occasional spiritual experiences, but spiritual beings passing through the dream of human experience. If we want to experience a happy dream, we make spiritual awakening our number one priority.

The story of two wolves reminds us that we have the power to choose how we will experience life. A Native American grandfather gives advice to his grandson who comes to him with anger at a friend. The grandfather says: I have struggled with anger and hatred many times. It is like there are two wolves inside me; one is good and does no harm. He lives in harmony with all around him and does not take offence when no offense was intended. He will only fight when it is right to do so, and in the right way.

But, the other wolf-ah! The littlest thing will send him into a fit of temper. He fights everyone, all of the time, for no reason. He cannot think because his anger and hate are so great. It is helpless anger, for his anger will change nothing. Sometimes it is hard to live with these two wolves inside me, for both of them try to dominate my spirit." The boy looked intently into his Grandfather's eyes and asked, "Which one wins, Grandfather?" The Grandfather smiled and quietly said, "The one I feed."

One wolf represents our lower ego nature; the other represents our higher true spiritual identity. One wolf will keep us in turmoil and tragic dreams; the other will walk in the middle way—the way of peace and harmony and balance. So it becomes our responsibility to constantly choose which tendency to feed. It is our spiritual assignment to be part of the 22% of the world's population that rises above the insanity of the world so that we may become beacons of light, so that we may counterbalance the darkness. It is our spiritual assignment to become the observer and the watcher as we walk in the middle way of balance, as we skate on the razor's edge.

So we must ask ourselves if we are ready and willing to dedicate ourselves to transformation. Are we willing to be a beacon of light instead of a carrier of the "stink eye" virus? Are we willing to find the balance? It takes vigilance and commitment, but whenever we are ready, we find that skating on the razor's edge is a delightful & exhilarating experience! The following random passages from the Tao Te Ching are all about cooperating with the natural balance and flow of life:.

The kind of person who always insists
On his way of seeing things
Can never learn anything from anyone.

The great Way is easy,
Yet people prefer the side paths.

If you're not always wanting, you can be at peace.
And if you're not always trying to be someone
You can be who you really are
And go the whole way.

Our soul's assignment is to "go the whole way." We need to stop selling ourselves short and stop getting lost on the side paths. It's time to recognize our true nature as expressions of the living God. It is time to find balance so we can give our best to the world.

Now is Eternal

"You must live in the present,
launch yourself on every wave,
find your eternity in each moment."
—Henry David Thoreau

The wonderful thing about laughing is that we can only laugh in the present moment and that's why it is so beneficial for our emotional and spiritual health. We drop our worries and concerns in that moment when we laugh. Therefore, I'll begin with a laugh for today: One Sunday a pastor told the congregation that the church needed some extra money and asked the people to consider giving a little extra in the offering. Whoever donated the most would be able to choose three hymns.

After the offering was passed the pastor glanced down and noticed that someone had placed a $1,000 check in the offering. He was so excited that he immediately shared his joy with the congregation and said he wanted to personally thank the person who gave the money. A very quiet saintly lady all the way in the back shyly raised her hand and she was asked to come to the front. He told her how wonderful it was that she gave so much and asked her to pick out her three hymns. Her eyes brightened as she looked over the congregation and pointed to the three most handsome men in the room and said, "I'll take him and him and him."

Have you ever seen a now clock? Instead of where the numbers usually are the word "now" appears. Thus to whoever keeps time by this clock, it's always now. And so it is in reality. The problem is that we all have a segment of our mind that could be labeled "monkey mind." Our monkey mind is a traveler who does not want to stay home in the now. It wants to swing back and forth between the past and future while quickly swinging over the present.

There are profound teachings in the Bible that urge us to live in the eternal now: "Take no thought for the morrow, for the morrow will take care of itself. The lilies of the field neither toil nor spin, yet they are taken care of." The Lord's Prayer tells us to pray for our "daily" bread and in the Old Testament the manna from heaven fell each day. And Jesus also taught "nobody who puts his hands to the plow and looks back is fit for the kingdom of God." In Zen teaching it's all about walking the razor's edge of now.

We often look for God and for our good, lo here and lo there, but God and good are to be found deep in our own hearts and minds. We say each Sunday in our prayer for protection: "Wherever I am, God IS," but do we really feel it in the moment or is it just a mindless ritual? I find that it takes focus and commitment to keep focused on right here and right now. The monkey mind wants to constantly lead us on trips to the past and future.

Analise Skarin was an enlightened writer who passed on several years ago. The story is that she was working in her office late at night and her husband found a small pile of ashes the next morning. She writes with authority and wisdom. I'll share some of what she has to say about staying in the present moment: "NOW is as much a part of eternity as all the yesteryears of the past and the great moments of the future. But it is only in the NOW that the powers of eternity are active and of benefit. And it is only in the NOW that one can ever have contact with the great Light of Christ and the Almighty power of God.

The super-conscious (higher Christ Mind) always works in the NOW. When the at-one-ment is established between the conscious and the higher mind one steps into the NOW—the eternal PRESENT. The fulfilling power is always in the NOW. The great living power of the NOW is what Jesus was seeking to reveal when he said, 'take no thought of tomorrow' and when he taught that the fields are already ripe with harvest."

When we wait until our circumstances change in order to savor and enjoy life, we make a great mistake. I've done way too much of that in the past. It can become a habit to save the best for later. There is a story that has been around the internet for awhile that I'll share with you because it is a good illustration of why we don't want to keep waiting to enjoy the good that is already ours. It's called Take Hold of Every Moment:

"A friend of mine opened his wife's underwear drawer and picked up a silk paper wrapped package and said, 'This is not an ordinary package. She got this the first time we went to New York eight or nine years ago. She never put it on because she was saving it for a special occasion. Well, I guess this is it.' He placed the gift box next to the other clothing he was taking to the funeral home; his wife had just died. He turned to me and said, 'Never save something for a special occasion. Every day in your life is a special occasion.' Those words changed my life. Now I do not delay, postpone or keep anything that could bring laughter and joy into my life. Each morning I say to myself, 'This is a special day.' Each day, each hour, each minute is special."

There is a poem, full of wisdom, that I'd like to share. Just so happens that this poem was one of Jacqueline Kennedy's favorite ones—and I do believe that she lived much of the wisdom within it. The main idea of the poem is that we waste our life if we only focus upon our destinations and do not pay attention to what is right in front of us as we go along. The author is referencing the classic epic poem Ulysses which is all about the long journey to Ithaca. This journey symbolizes our own journey through life and the author is urging us to savor the journey while striving to reach the destination.

Ithaca

When you start on your journey to Ithaca,
Then pray that the road is long,
full of adventure, full of knowledge.
Do not fear the Lystrygonians—
and the Cyclopes and the angry Poseidon.
You will never meet such as these on your path,
if your thoughts remain lofty, if a fine
emotion touches your body and your spirit.
You will never meet the Lysgtrygonians,
the Cyclops and the fierce Poseidon,
If you do not carry them in your soul,
if your soul does not raise them up before you.

Then pray that the road is long,
That the summer mornings are many,
That you will enter ports seen for the first time
with such pleasure, with such joy.
Stop at Phoenician markets
And purchase fine merchandise,
Mother of pearl and corals, amber and ebony,

And pleasureable perfumes as you can.
Visit hosts of Egyptian cities,
to learn from those who have knowledge.

Always keep Ithaca fixed in your mind.
To arrive there is your ultimate goal.
But do not hurry the voyage at all.
It is better to let it last for years,
and even to anchor at the isle when you are old,
rich with all that you have gained on the way,
not expecting that Ithaca will offer you riches.

Ithaca has given you the beautiful voyage,
Without her you never would have taken the road.
But she has nothing more to give you.
And if you find her poor, Ithaca has not defrauded you.
With the great wisdom you have gained,
with so much experience,
you must surely have understood by then
what Ithaca means.

—K. Cavafy

To me Ithaca means the ideal, a step higher, and a beckoning light that leads me onward and upward—the poem tells me that while I am moving toward the highest goals and ideals I also need to keep focused on each eternal moment of the journey and to bless each step of the way. As you continue on your spiritual journey, may this day and each moment of every day be filled with the blessings of the Eternal Divine Spirit.

Open My Eyes

"We must find some spiritual basis for living else we die."
—Bill Wilson, founder AA

The wonderful Unity song, "Open my Eyes That I Might See," is a powerful singing prayer, a prayer of surrender to the Divine. It is a prayer that asks God to transform us, to take us beyond old ways of thinking and doing. The first step we all must take if we are going to make positive changes in our lives is to see clearly WHAT it is that needs changing. I once spent some time in a powerful week long workshop where I came away with several nuggets of very helpful healing and growing methods.

One of the questions I learned to ask myself is this: "Am I willing, in a step by step orderly fashion, to take the cover off my structure of knowing and to shine a light upon my most closely held thoughts, beliefs, and opinions?" When we sing and pray the words 'open my eyes that I might see,' we have to be WILLING to see, to have the courage to see what might be quite uncomfortable for us to see. We often avoid quiet time, meditation or exploring our deepest issues in a Journal. We avoid time to just *Be* with Spirit.

Sig Paulson, a poet and Unity minister put it this way in his work entitled:

The Quiet Stretches of the Soul:

For what shall it profit a man if he gain the world
and lose his own soul?
How completely the world lays claim
to us as its own—
How diligently we avoid aloneness.
How eagerly we accept and cling to
the assumed burden
the contrived responsibility
the outworn relationship
the unrelenting task.
Lest, unencumbered,
we make the lonely vital encounter
with our own Inner Self.

My prayer is "Oh, Lord, let me walk the long deep quiet stretches of my own soul with Thee, who alone can transform & set me free!" The song, "Open My Eyes" goes on to ask God to also open our ears, our hearts and our mouths. "Open my ears that I might hear voices of truth thou sendest clear. Open my heart and let me prepare love with thy children thus to share. Open my mouth and let me bear gladly the warm truth everywhere." What an assignment we are asked to take on! It's so much more than to discuss or listen to interesting ideas; so much more than just showing up at church on Sundays. The question becomes, "how willing are we to USE and APPLY the truth we listen to and discuss? Are we willing to have our own encounter with the still small voice of Spirit within? It's been said that without mystical experience, religion is a corpse.

When we sing and pray, open our eyes, ears, hearts and mouths,—we are asking for mystical experiences that will take us higher, move us forward, fill us with love, peace and joy. When we radiate out our uplifted consciousness, we take our religion to a new level of aliveness and spirituality. We cannot pretend to be on an honest spiritual path unless we have the goal to love and forgive everyone, with no exceptions—and this includes ourselves.

When we try to do this on the human ego level, it can be a tremendous struggle. If we can surrender to Spirit and allow Spirit to work in and through us, we can do it. Paul said, "I can do all things through Christ, who strengthens me." The Christ in us IS our only TRUE strength. When we know and live by that principle, we take giant spiritual steps ahead. That's where we want to pray and sing "open my ears that I might hear, voices of truth thou sendest clear." To hear we must be still and listen.

Then the words, "open my heart and let me prepare love with thy children thus to share." I believe that means extending love and forgiveness, seeing beyond all mistakes and errors to the real self of others, the Christ in them. And then, "open my mouth and let me bear gladly the warm truth everywhere." Does this mean preaching and proselytizing? I don't think so It means speaking with love and kindness and being truly helpful, sharing our spiritual path if others are truly interested, but not imposing our ideas on others.

Personally, my life has been uplifted and transformed by the many positive people in my life who may never have spoken specifically about religion, but who embraced me with respect and loving kindness. It is possible to behold the Christ in others without saying, "I behold the Christ in you." That is appropriate in Unity circles, but out there in the world, we use discernment. People respond to our loving and kind words and actions. They may even ultimately ask, "What do you believe, or how can you be so kind and loving?" That's the time to share our specific faith—if and when we are asked. We can open our mouths and bear the warm truth everywhere in all kinds of situations.

I'd like to share a piece with you that has been in my files for awhile. I related to it because it is about a time when people picked up their phones and the operator asked, "Number please." That's the way it was in my growing up years in the small town of Clare, Michigan. After I graduated from high school, I worked for Michigan Bell Telephone and sat in a row with several other operators. When a light in the board in front of me lit up, I plugged into the jack under it and asked, "Number please?" People often called in for the time and information. I don't know where the following story came from or the last name of the man who recounts his experience. But he is sharing some warm truth that illustrates the principles we have discussed today:

The Old Phone

When I was quite young, my father had one of the first telephones in our neighborhood. I remember the polished, old case fastened to the wall. The shiny receiver hung on the side of the box. I was too little to reach the telephone, but used to listen with fascination when my mother talked to it.

Then I discovered that somewhere inside the wonderful device lived an amazing person. Her name was Information Please, and there was nothing she did not know. Information Please could supply anyone's number and the correct time. My personal experience with the genie-in-a-phone-box came one day while my mother was visiting a neighbor.

Amusing myself at the tool bench in the basement, I whacked my finger with a hammer; the pain was terrible, but there seemed no point in crying because there was no one home to give sympathy. I walked around the house sucking my throbbing finger, finally arriving at the stairway. The telephone! Quickly, I ran for the footstool in the parlor and dragged it to the landing. Climbing up, I unhooked the receiver in the parlor and held it to my ear. "Information, please" I said into the mouthpiece just above my head. A click or two and a small clear voice spoke into my ear. "Information." "I hurt my finger!" I wailed into the phone, the tears came readily enough now that I had an audience. "Isn't your mother home?" came the question. "Nobody's home but me," I blubbered. "Are you bleeding?" the voice asked. "No," I replied. "I hit my finger with the hammer and it hurts." "Can you open the icebox?" she asked. I said I could. "Then chip off a little bit of ice and hold it to your finger," said the voice.

After that, I called "Information Please" for everything. I asked her for help with my geography, and she told me where Philadelphia was. She helped me with my math. She told me my pet chipmunk that I had caught in the park just the day before, would eat fruit and nuts. Then, there was the time Petey, our pet canary, died. I called "Information Please," and told her the sad story. She listened, and then said things grown-ups say to soothe a child. But I was not consoled. I asked her, "Why is it that birds should sing so beautifully and bring joy to all families, only to end up as a heap of feathers on the bottom of a cage?" She must have sensed my deep concern, for she said quietly, "Paul always remember that there are other worlds to sing in."

Somehow I felt better. Another day I was on the telephone, "Information Please." "Information," said the now familiar voice. "How do I spell fix?" I asked. All this took place in a small town in the Pacific Northwest. When I was nine years old, we moved across the country to Boston. I missed my friend very much. "Information Please" belonged in that old wooden box back home and I somehow never thought of trying the shiny new phone that sat on the table in the hall. As I grew into my teens, the memories of those childhood conversations never really left me. Often, in moments of doubt and perplexity I would recall the serene sense of security I had then. I appreciated now how patient, understanding, and kind she was to have spent her time on a little boy.

A few years later, on my way west to college, my plane put down in Seattle. I had about a half-hour or so between planes. I spent 15 minutes or so on the phone with my sister, who lives there now. Then without thinking what I was doing, I dialed my hometown operator and said, "Information Please." Miraculously, I heard the small, clear voice I knew so well. "Information." I hadn't planned this, but I heard myself saying, "Could you please tell me how to spell fix?" There was a long pause. Then came the soft spoken answer, "I guess your finger must have healed by now." I laughed, "So it's really you," I said. "I wonder if you have any idea how much you meant to me during that time?" I wonder," she said, "if you know how much your calls meant to me. I never had any children and I used to look forward to your calls." I told her how often I had thought of her over the years and I asked if I could call her again when I came back to visit my sister. "Please do," she said. "Just ask for Sally."

Three months later I was back in Seattle. A different voice answered, "Information." I asked for Sally. "Are you a friend?" she said. "Yes, a very old friend," I answered. "I'm sorry to have to tell you this," she said. "Sally had been working part—time the last few years because she was sick. She died five weeks ago." Before I could hang up she said, "Wait a minute, did you say your name was Paul?" "Yes." I answered. "Well, Sally left a message for you. She wrote it down in case you called. Let me read it to you." The note said, "Tell him there are other worlds to sing in. He'll know what I mean."I thanked her and hung up. I knew what Sally meant. Never underestimate the impression you may make on others. Whose life have you touched today?

So, dear friends, let us keep our eyes, ears, hearts and mouths open to love and truth today and every day. Please know that life is meant to be lived from our Divine Center, our holy, infinite, sacred heart. We are here to extend that heart out into our world. Sometimes it is in very simple and humble ways, and often as in the above phone story, those are just the humble and simple love and caring that is needed.

Our Resurrecting Power

"The greatest tragedy in life is not death,
but what we allow to die in us while we're living."
—Anonymous

One thing for certain is that most of us don't want our zest for living, loving, and laughing to die. And if or when that zest begins to wane, we need to get very serious about changing the situation. In that spirit I'm going to begin with something that I hope will make you laugh, or at least chuckle a bit. I've had it awhile and got it from a site entitled Twisted Jokes, so be prepared. The three stooges have died and are at the pearly gates of Heaven. St. Peter tells them that they can enter the gates if they can answer one simple question. St. Peter asks Curley, "What is Easter?"

He replies, "Oh that easy! It's the holiday in November when everyone gets together, eats turkey, and feels thankful." "Wrong!" replies St. Peter, and proceeds to ask Moe the same question. "What is Easter?" He replies, "Easter is the holiday in December when we put up a nice tree, exchange presents, and celebrate the birth of Jesus." St. Peter shakes his head in disgust and peers over at Larry and asks, "What do you say Easter is?"

Larry smiles confidently and looks St. Peter in the eyes, "I know what Easter is. It's the Christian holiday that coincides with the Jewish celebration of Passover. Jesus and his disciples were eating at the last supper and Jesus was later turned over to the Romans by one of his disciples. The Romans took him to be crucified. He was made to wear a crown of thorns, and was hung on a cross with nails through his hands. He was buried in a nearby cave which was sealed off by a large boulder." St. Peter smiles with delight. Larry continues, "Every year the boulder is moved aside so that Jesus can come out and, if he sees his shadow, there will be six more weeks of winter." (I know it's one of those groaners!)

Now it's time to get serious about the meaning of Easter. It's a time when we celebrate the resurrection and continuing life of Jesus who became the Christ. We celebrate because Jesus demonstrated that nothing of this earth could kill the Reality of him, or the Reality of us, which is Spirit. How can that be? It looks like a whole lot of killing and death going on out there, but all too often we don't recognize what is real and true about ourselves. Although there is a lot of killing and death of earth suits, the particular earth suits we happen to be currently wearing are not who and what we are. Bodies—earth suits—can be killed, but souls cannot be killed. Why?

Our true identity as Spirit is invisible to the eye, but nonetheless the truth of us is totally indestructible, invincible, and eternal. Jesus taught us that what he did, we can do also. Jesus taught that we are all brothers and sisters, and he appeared in this earth in the flesh out of tremendous love to show us the way home. Easter is a celebration of Jesus' demonstration that the Reality of us cannot die.

We make our earth suits so that we may experience what it is like to feel separate from God and from each other. However, in truth we are not separate from God nor from each other; we just believe we are and thus experience the consequences of that belief, which is fear of most everything including God, each other, and death. This is the tomb of spiritual ignorance where we dwell and from which we need to resurrect the Christ of us, the truth of us.

The way out of this predicament is to realize the Christ presence in ourselves and all our brothers and sisters. Jesus, speaking as the Christ said: "I am the resurrection and the life. No one comes to the Father except by me. Does that mean that everyone who is not a Christian will be left out? Absolutely not!

Christ, God individualized within us, includes everyone: Buddhists, Moslems, Hindus—everyone. We cannot gain enlightenment, which is the full awareness and experience of who and what we are, unless we accept and honor that same presence in all others. In that oneness we experience indescribable love, peace, joy and freedom. I heard Ram Dass share the following profound reading many years ago. It was written on a crucifix in 1632 and seems to be God speaking, urging us to wake up and recognize the Truth:

I am the great Sun, but you do not see me.
I am your spouse, but you turn away.
I am the captive, but you do not free me.
I am the captain you will not obey.
I am the Truth, but you will not believe me;
I am the city where you will not stay.
I am your child but you will leave me.
I am that GOD to whom you will not pray.
I am your counsel but you do not hear me.
I am our lover whom you will betray.
I am the victor but you do not cheer me.
I am the Holy Dove whom you will slay.
I am your Life, but you will not name me.
Seal your soul with tears, and never blame me.

So, in our fear and ignorance, we seal our souls with our own tears. We imprison ourselves with our refusal to love our life and everyone in it. And God says, "Don't blame me for your tears. I'm always calling for you to resurrect into the realization and the Reality that you are One with Me and with My Love."

The Good News is that as hard as we may try, we cannot erase the truth of what we are. You and I are now and always have been as God created us, and that can never change. We are birth less, death less, ageless, eternal Spirit, One with God and One with each other. What Jesus, our elder brother and way shower taught us and demonstrated for us is that ultimately the body is temporary, but the Spirit is eternal and indestructible. In that light, we can see that the body is not of great consequence. There is no reason to fear death, because in truth death does not exist. The reason we grieve and resist the loss of the earth suit is that we think it's the total reality of us; thus we fear losing it and mourn over its loss.

The death of the body means <u>only</u> that our soul is finished with its current earth school experience and the soul is ready to move on. We've finished with this movie, this dream, played out whatever we predetermined to play out—and now it's time to move on to our next experience. In truth, we are homesick for the realization of God. We want the full experience of love, peace, joy and freedom that is ours by Divine Right. We will never be satisfied until we experience our own resurrection from our limited earthly ego consciousness and then move on to the ascension—the realization of our original son of God Christ Consciousness. Easter can serve as a reminder that it is possible to move upward in consciousness into our own resurrection from the tomb of limitation. It is possible to ascend into living and experiencing the Truth of our Being—our own Divine connection with the Lord of All.

After Jesus showed himself to his disciples and others, he ascended into the Heaven of Pure Spirit where He is still available to us because in Spirit, there is no time and no space. That's why we can say that Spirit is nearer than breathing, closer than hands and feet. Our goal then becomes living in the Spirit one hundred percent of the time. Last year a woman named Vicky Keike from Costa Rica sent out the following poem to Unity ministers and I would like to share it with you:

Ascension Process

Ascension is actually a realization of entering the oneness of God's wealth,
bypassing the duality of civilization and returning to the One True Self.
Ascension is not about rising anywhere but rather a knowing that you
are there.
It is a divine discovery, deeply profound,
relinquishment of concepts imbedded so sound.
It is in universal faith, with total release of all doubt and
creeping away from the babbling mind that quiet change comes about.
Ascension is elevated consciousness, and no action is required.
It is a complete sacred awareness, which by simply Being is acquired.
Ascension is a prophecy of old, long forgotten when history was told.
It's actually a harmonic cosmic flow, where love and compassion does show.
Ending eons of suffering and strife, and with the cosmos now aligned,
Mother Earth is birthing new life, a sacred contract intricately designed.
Rapidly ascending the Divinity Pole, responding souls no longer fall,
finally understanding their human role, summoned by God's eternal call.
Ascension process occurring now is the destined universal fate.
In peace and unity the Masters bow,
welcoming all to Heaven's Gate.
And So It Is.

Sweet Mystery of Life

"God is pouring Itself through
into expression as individual being.
—Joel Goldsmith

For most of us, there is nothing worse than feeling lost in a foggy sea of meaninglessness, adrift in confusion and uncertainty. Some numb their misery with addictions of all sorts. Others, including me and thee, want something more than just existence on the surface level of physical survival and pleasure.

We want to dig deeper; we want to find love and peace. We want to be involved in the mystery of life and the deeper we get into it, the sweeter it gets. We won't find the complete answer in a single talk or book. Finding the complete answer is a soul's journey toward illumination, and we've been on that journey for hundreds, maybe thousands of years.

The good news is that if God, if illumination, if living the sweet mystery of life is our number one priority, we can come ever closer to the goal of experiencing our oneness with God, and then we will share that consciousness and grace with others. That is illumination; that is coming home to God.

Our journey must begin deep within our very own soul. If we insist on looking lo here and lo there we will stay perpetually lost in that foggy sea of confusion and misery. As Jesus taught us, we must look for the Kingdom of Heaven within ourselves. Thus, deep within ourselves is where we must start on our journey of living the sweet mystery of life.

But wouldn't you just know it? We have an adversary that does everything in its power to keep us from doing the very thing we must do to progress. Who and what is this adversary? It goes by many names: the devil, the ego, the monkey mind, our consciousness of separation, and our fear of losing ourselves if we surrender to God. This adversary works very hard to keep us from understanding that we are spiritual beings with a spiritual home. This adversary wants to keep us earth bound, helpless, angry, frustrated, and separated from our brothers and sisters as a way of preserving itself. I suspect we've all done that to some degree and are still doing it when we forget who we are in truth

However, you are reading this today because you want to move forward, to be inspired to dig deeper. We are all where the prodigal son was when he realized that he would never be happy living with the pigs and eating their food. He decided to rise and go home to his Father. We begin our own journey home by taking an honest look at ourselves and how we've allowed the adversary to rule our lives. We look at the result of our refusal to open our minds and hearts to a higher path. We become willing to see that the so-called sacrifice of our ego habits of judgment and non-forgiveness is not sacrifice at all, but victory and freedom of spirit.

Therefore, the question we must ask ourselves is this: Are we willing to systematically dismantle our old structure of knowing? Our old structures keep us stuck and under the control of the adversary. Of course in order to take down our old structure of knowing, we must look at it honestly and see what it is. It takes honesty and courage to question our most closely held beliefs and opinions. We must be willing to invite the Holy Spirit to walk with us and provide the light on our path. And then we must be willing to surrender the old ways so that we can progress on the onward and upward path.

These are serious issues that we all must deal with if we are going to truly enter into the sweet mystery of life. We need to become mystics, not in monasteries, but in everyday life. Can we say and mean "The peace of God is my One goal? Do we believe that the journey of return to God is the greatest journey possible with the greatest rewards of eternal love, peace, and joy?

To become mystics we must work toward the experience God in our everyday life, which means to go beyond studying about God, learning about God on the mental level. This means keeping the mind and heart stayed on God not just in church or classes or when we pray with our prayer partners, but ALL the time. A mystic is always listening to the still small voice of Spirit, always obedient to instruction and guidance from Holy Spirit. This means adopting God's agenda and surrendering our own (which most likely was given to us by the adversary). Let me assure you that when we sincerely ask for guidance from Spirit, we do receive it.

You know that I love and respect the Course in Miracles and my goal is to use it throughout every day. I have been reading and studying it for over 30 years and it only gets deeper and richer. I constantly discover new depths in it and therefore new depths in my spiritual life. However, by the grace and love of God, there are many routes and many paths that lead to the goal at the top of the spiritual mountain. Please find one that works for you and stick with it.

I love and embrace Unity because it is so lovingly inclusive. But we must remember that we cannot go deeply into our spiritual lives if we just keep exploring the surface of things, continually moving from one thing to another. We need to be committed to daily meditation, prayer, contemplation, which means some kind of spiritual practice. We can be inspired and instructed by the Course, books by Ekhart Tolle, David Hawkins and other spiritual authors and teachers.

However, the bottom line is that we ourselves must do the daily soul work. We must live and experience the things we read about and study. Until we do that, we are not truly on the path; we're taking detours, with the adversary as tour guide. Yet, the true path is ours by Divine Right. Is it your time now to pursue that path? You can participate in the true life of your soul right here and right now in this earth school. That is exactly where God is trying to lead us. The division of Heaven and earth can pass away, leaving only Heaven.

The kingdom of Heaven is within. Let's dig for the treasure there. When the stone was rolled away from the tomb of Jesus, the living spirit of the Christ was released. Just so, we must roll away the stone from our self imposed earthbound limited consciousness so that we may finally be free to embrace the sweet mystery of life, which is our inner Christ and our oneness with God.

In order to experience and embrace the sweet mystery of life we must go within to our interior castle, to the secret place of the most high with prayer and meditation. I leave you with the prayer of St. Teresa of Avila because it so clearly lays out what is required for our progress: "I cross the bridge into the silent bliss of my interior castle. I close the drawbridge and forbid all outside influences from entry into the holy place that is my soul. Here in my castle, I am alone with God. Under God's light and companionship, I discover the depth and beauty of my soul. I embrace the power of prayer. I open myself to divine guidance. I surrender myself to become a channel for grace, healing and service as God directs." (quoted by Carolyn Myss in her book Entering the Castle)

The Circle of Life

"What strange Beings we are!
Sitting in Hell at the bottom of the dark,
We're afraid of our immortality."
—Rumi

Today we're going to look at paradox and extreme opposites that are both true: One: "Life is short; make the most of every minute. Contemplate death and let it teach you to appreciate life." Two: "We have forever; death does not exist." We can learn and grow spiritually by looking at both sides of this coin and seeing the balance in the circle of life and death.

A good exercise for all of us is to find a quiet time to write down what we would do if we knew we had only a year or a month or a week to live. What would we change? What trivia would we let go? This is a good question to ask no matter what our age. Sudden death comes to people of all ages and in all kinds of circumstances. A friend of mine took a walk and while crossing the street she was hit by a bus and killed instantly. My son died suddenly at age nine. We don't consciously know when the current chapter of our life will come to a close.

A great yogi said that every moment of his life he lived as though a sword were suspended above his head by a spider web. If we lived that way, we would not waste time nursing our dark moods and negativity. I was swinging through a mood recently, but stopped and asked myself: "If I died in the next few minutes, would I want to die feeling like this?" Absolutely not! I want to die feeling love and peace, not irritation or frustration. So often we get lost in our emotional extremes instead of staying balanced in the center.

What if we knew this evening would be the last time we saw or talked to our loved ones? We would release any and all little grudges and complaints. We would give them unconditional love, knowing it would be our last time to be with them. How wonderful it would be if we could live like that every moment of every day.

As many of you know, I have a wonderful little dog named Bella. She was nine the end of August 2011, which is middle-aged for her. Her breed lives longer than most, but I am fully aware that our time together will come to an end. My goal is to love and appreciate her to the best of my ability while we're here together. You dog lovers know what I'm talking about. A good question to contemplate is, "Why not try to love everyone as much as we love our dogs?" Bella is so mellow and loving, I call her my God Dog because she teaches me so much about loving. She has the ability to bring me back to center when I'm getting out of balance.

It is vitally important to our spiritual progress to become the Observer, the Watcher, sitting in the center. The observer-watcher has the power to choose to step back, the power to reverse a negative course. This power can be anchored and magnified by spiritual practices such as meditation and regular focus upon higher truths. We can't underestimate the pull of our personal ego dramas. It takes dedication and spiritual strength to stay balanced in our center and not get lost in circumstances. This is what Jesus meant when he taught: "Be in the world, but not *of* it."

Most of us wonder at some time or another how we will react when it's time to face our own death. Ideally we would come to peace within ourselves so that it would not make any difference. How can we do that? We can come to peace by looking at the other side of the paradox: In truth we do have forever because death does not exist. How is this true?

On the personal human personality level, we die. That is mixed news because we bring our unlearned lessons into the next chapter of our ongoing experience of living. Maybe we're another nationality, a different gender and come into different socio-economic conditions. But we bring along the lessons we've set up for ourselves to learn. This is often called our karma. That's why it is so important to pay attention to our lives right here and now if we want to evolve spiritually. Every challenge and frustration is an opportunity to grow.

There is no need to fear death because we are Spirit and Spirit cannot die. We have a capital letter Self that is birthless, deathless, ageless and eternal. When we get in touch with that through our dedicated spiritual practices, we sit back in our balanced center and watch the passing show.

We can live life more fully when we don't fear death, when we can look at it as the transition into a new experience, a transition into the next chapter of our ongoing life. The following story illustrates this attitude: There was a young woman who had been diagnosed with a terminal illness and had been given three months to live. As she was getting her things in order, she contacted her minister and had him come to her house to discuss certain aspects of her final wishes.

She told him which songs she wanted sung at the service, what scriptures she would like read, and what outfit she wanted to be buried in. Everything was in order and the minister was preparing to leave when the woman suddenly remembered something very important to her. There's one more thing she said excitedly. "I want to be buried with a fork in my right hand." The minister looked at the young women, not knowing quite what to say. She gave him her explanation. "Whenever we attend socials and dinners, when the dishes of the main course are being cleared, we often get the instruction, 'keep your fork.' We always know that something good is coming, like velvety chocolate cake or deep dish apple pie, something wonderful and with substance. I just want people to see me there in that casket with a fork in my hand to remind them not to be afraid of dying—the best is yet to come."

So, the balance point is to live fully now without fearing a future death. It's all life. It's all good. One of my favorite spiritual teachers is David Hawkins, author of *The Eye of the I*. He shares what he experienced in the times he was separated from his body and human ego: "For a brief moment as the self disappears into the Self, there is transitory amazement and awe of profound proportion and depth. The death of the self is experienced, and then all is stillness and peace. That the body was ever considered to be "me" seems absurd. All the fears and vicissitudes of life disappear, and now, free of even death itself, there is the remembrance that one always has been and always will be, and that survival was never a problem at all."

I'll close with a piece I often use for memorial services because it illustrates the complete circle of life, which includes our transition into new life: I am standing upon the sea shore. A ship at my side spreads her white sails to the morning breeze and starts for the blue ocean. She is an object of beauty and strength, and I stand and watch her until at length she hangs like a speck of white cloud just where the sea and sky come to mingle with each other.

Then someone at my side says, "There! She's gone!" Gone where? Gone from my sight, that is all. She is just as large in mast and hull and spar as she was when she left my side, and she is just as able to bear her load of living weight to her destined port. Her diminished size is in me, not in her. And just at the moment when someone at my side says, "There! She's gone!"—There are other eyes watching her coming, and other voices ready to take up the glad shout, "Here she comes!" And that is how we go on to our next experience in living, how we travel inside the circle of life. It's all one. It's all life. It's all good.

The Mystic Path

"The most beautiful and profound experience is a mystical one."
—Albert Einstein

Mysticism is an approach to an interior life that seeks to find the holy beyond words and mental concepts. It is to experience the point of Isness in the Allness. True mystics experience the Allness while standing still in the point of Isness. The dictionary describes mysticism as "direct communion with ultimate reality" and "any belief in the existence of realities beyond what we apprehend with the five senses and the intellect."

The question for many here on this "solid" planet earth is "why bother?" The average person lives in the world of the five senses and believes looking for something outside of them is foolish or a waste of time. It is all too easy to get caught up in the human rat race. Lily Tomlin said, "Even if you win in the rat race, you're still a rat." At some point many of us realize that there is indeed something more than the rat race, and we can't rest until we find it.

The experience of the mystic is far beyond the intellect, far beyond thinking. It comes from a living realization of connection with Spirit, rather than the accumulated knowledge of the intellect. Meditation is useful because it is practice in bypassing thoughts, practice in tuning in to the Divine Hum, which must precede the actual experience of transcendence. This experience may last for a second, a minute, a day, or be and "in and out" experience for a long time.

The goal is to actually dwell in conscious communication with God. That's why the master Jesus taught that the Kingdom of God, the Kingdom of

Heaven, is not to be found by looking "lo here and lo there." It is to be located and experienced within ourselves through meditation in "the secret place of the most high"—that place where we implement the biblical advice, "Be still and know that I Am God."

People can be very religious and very intellectual and still miss the mystical experience. This experience can come at any age and any stage as a direct experience of truth, and it is not about following rules or organized religion. It can come to anyone in any organized religion or anyone with no religion. Organized religion is a system of controls. It often obscures the truth by creating its own version of the truth and threatens terrible consequences for those who don't agree.

In fact, many mystics such as Meister Eckart, considered one of the greatest of the Medieval Christian mystics, were charged with heresy by the inquisition. Meister Eckart was imprisoned and died before he could be burned at the stake. It's been said that more mystics were burned at the stake than became saints. Course in Miracles states "The attempt to formalize religion is obviously an ego attempt to reconcile the irreconcilable." In other words it is an attempt to make rigid what is free and unlimited; those two things just cannot be put together and make sense.

The mystic experiences life as an unfolding awareness within himself/herself and realizes that "in Him I move, in Him I live, in Him I have my Being." No language can capture this accurately. God is not a Him or a Her or even a Him and Her combined, although we sometimes address God in prayer as Father/Mother God. God is Spirit, invisible and indivisible. However, even Jesus referred to God as Father, which means source and creator. He accurately said: "Of myself I can do nothing. It is the Father within who does the work." Jesus often acknowledged his powerlessness.

And so must we acknowledge our powerlessness as a human ego if we want to merge with the one presence and power.

We all too often have the notion that we can "use" God to help us obtain what we want on the human level and believe that the ultimate is for us to use God to make our human experience better. And we can do this—it's known as the metaphysical approach, the mental approach. We tell God/The Universe what we want, visualize it, and bring it forth. And it is "the Father's good pleasure to give us the Kingdom." However, this comes after we seek FIRST the Kingdom and trust that everything we need will be added.

We are reminded by mystics such as Joel Goldsmith and Emanuel Swedenborg that the goal is not to use God in this way, but to commune with God through meditation and <u>allow God to use us</u>. In this process, we live by the grace of God, and it is sufficient. Joel taught meditation—communing with God with no agenda, no specific demand—just becoming one with God in conscious realization. This is what he did and this was his method as a healer. If the Catholic Church today would investigate the miraculous healings that were attributed to Joel's consciousness, he would be a saint for sure.

Joel never went into meditative prayer asking for any specific thing or any specific healing. He didn't have to know the name of the person or what needed healing. He trusted that the omniscient God knew what the problem was; Joel saw his part as joining with Higher Consciousness and then the healings took place. He might get a request for help, go into meditation and later find out what the healing was.

He shared an incredible example in a letter to Barbara Mary Muhl, one of his students whom he trained to teach the Infinite Way. She had written jokingly asking him to help her find a good housekeeper. She had six children and was also teaching Infinite Way classes. Here was his response: "Well, I have just had an experience with a new-born baby-paralyzed, deaf, dumb and blind, and within two months, completely restored to normalcy; and a drug baby, that is, one of those born without arms or hands and with deformed feet owing to that German drug that was used for awhile. (Thalidomide) Both arms and both hands have been restored, and the feet have become normal, and so I am sure if the activity of the Christ could bring about such transformations, there is no reason to doubt that it can bring a housekeeper out of the invisible to you."

Now Joel knew and taught that of <u>himself,</u> he did nothing. He simply got his human sense of self out of the way, tuned into the Christ, and let God use him. Of course that was what Jesus did also. And Jesus said, "What I do you can do and even more." And we can if we are willing to be God's instruments, if we are willing to allow God to use us, not the other way around. Joel lived under Grace, enjoyed a prosperous life and traveled the world teaching and healing, all the while trusting God to provide the supply he needed. God cannot use us while we still cling to the human level. We have to be willing to die to it daily so that we might be resurrected into Christ consciousness.

Joel's comment: "Resurrection is an experience which does not come to many. It cannot take place before there is a death (surrendering up the human ego)—and who wants to volunteer for that?" Joel points out that he could not be raised up from the tomb of human ignorance and attachment until his human level consciousness died. He warned that the process of dying is not accomplished with one crucifixion, but an experience of dying daily for a long time. And even then he adds, "It is good to thrust in a dagger to make double sure."

So, the mystical journey is not a humanly easy one. Yet, it is a joyous experience beyond words whenever it is realized. My goal is to live in perfect trust in God's love and grace; I want to deeply know that God is enough—that God's grace is sufficient. In Him we live, move and have our being. The Unity prayer of protection ends with the words, "Wherever God IS, I am, and all is well." This statement takes on a deeper meaning beyond the rote repetition of the words when we actually have a mystical experience of the Presence in meditation and then bring that consciousness out into our daily lives. A powerful prayer and song that has been helpful to me: "Spirit of the Living God, fall afresh on me; melt me; mold me; fill me; use me. Spirit of the Living God, fall afresh on me." So, let us be open and receptive, listening and communing with the God of our being.

I'll close with some mystic wisdom from Course in Miracles:

Lesson 112: I am the home of light and joy and peace. I welcome them into the home I share with God, because I am a part of Him.

Lesson 114: I am the Son of God. No body can contain my spirit, nor impose on me a limitation God created not. I am Spirit.

Lesson 118: Let my own feeble voice be still, and let me hear the mighty Voice for Truth Itself.

Lesson 120: I rest in God today, and let Him work in me and through me, while I rest in Him in quiet and in perfect certainty. Today I lay aside all sick illusions of myself, and let my Father tell me who I really am. I rest in God. I am as God created me.

The Unfinished Symphony

"We claim spiritual progress, not spiritual perfection.
When you fail, just get up, wipe off the blood.
Forgive yourself and move on."
—Barbara Mary Muhl

"The Universe is a *creation,* and not a dead, inexplicable, accidental and meaningless thing. It is a living thing of systems within systems, each with purpose and meaning, each living and capable of developing or degenerating," so Maurice Nicoll teaches in his *Commentaries on The Work.* We are often asleep to higher purpose and meaning because we are entangled in the world of appearances.

Some of us have always known "there must be more than this." Others have not yet been willing to open their minds to see their true situation,—their desperate need for "something more." I consider myself extremely fortunate that I was beaten up by life circumstances early on—there really was no choice except to look for something higher and better. That is why "unfortunate circumstances" bear hidden gifts. Some wallow in self-pity, and I confess that I have sometimes done that. But, by the grace of God, from the time I could first remember anything, I knew I wanted something higher.

Nicoll calls this having "magnetic centre"—something we bring with us as we enter into a new lifetime. Not everyone brings this, and thus their focus is attached to the senses, outer appearances and the mechanical side of life. They think, "Why should I bother with all that? I'm just fine in my mechanical state!" I think that's what Jesus was referring to when he said,

"Let the dead bury their dead." They are not ready to awaken and embrace the aliveness of the Spirit.

I had the realization recently that perhaps a better title for my last book could have been *From Soap Opera to Unfinished Symphony* because there is always more to learn, more to do, more and higher spirituality to embrace. Until we know understand and express the love and truth of our true Being ALL the time, we are not finished. As long as we struggle with fear, anxiety, resentment, anger, distrust, jealousy and all the other negative emotions and attitudes, we can be sure we have more work to do. Unless we are working on ourselves sincerely and passionately every day, we are in fact wasting our time. And we all do our share of that.

We certainly can be out and about enjoying life—our work, friends, activities, and still be spiritually working on ourselves. The big thing is to observe ourselves under all circumstances. We don't need to hide in a closet or go to a monastery—there is more than enough to deal with in the midst of whatever situations we find ourselves in. We just need to notice our thoughts, emotions and reactions to people and events around us. Take an inner photograph of them. We need to think about all this in order to see ourselves as we really are beyond any posturing pose we may show others, beyond whatever mask we wear to impress. We will move ahead in our growth if we dare to look deeply within and get honest as never before.

Sounds like the Twelve Step Program. Actually if we all sincerely started and followed through with the twelve steps, we could not help but progress spiritually and psychologically. Remember that psychological work and healing is part of the spiritual path. These two aspects are just different sides of the same coin. It is not easy to begin looking within honestly. Someone once accused me of thinking I'm so "high and mighty" spiritually—along with a few other things that contained some truth, but were not fun to hear.

There is a fool-proof way to discern whether or not something like that might have some truth in it. Do we become angry, defensive and offended? Or can we be vulnerable and stay centered in love, compassion, and understanding no matter what someone says? My knee jerk reaction was hurt and then anger. I felt very offended! Because I do work on myself every day, I knew I had to forgive and understand and have compassion for the person who attacked me. Okay. So far so good. But there's more.

Truth teacher Maria Nemeth teaches us that we must be willing to take the cover off our structure of knowing and shine a conscious light upon our most closely held thoughts, beliefs and opinions. It is so easy to forget that part. Recently as I was reading my morning chapters of *The Work,* the spirit of truth within me helped me see that indeed I have sometimes come across as a "know it all, and high and mighty." I can recall some conversations where I threw in a sermon whether it was asked for or not. I think perhaps that is an occupational hazard. Looking honestly and clearly at ourselves is hard work.

The lesson for me is to use more discernment when communicating with others. I know that I have been subjected to pontificating mini-sermons in the midst of conversations, and I did not appreciate it at the time either. I am giving this example to illustrate the process of never-ending growth. Our egos can become so proud of our progress that we can become blindsided. The moral is that we cannot take ourselves for granted. The human ego is a trickster and especially loves to trick those of us who preach and teach.

A Course in Miracles provides incredible information, love and Truth. Here is an excerpt from the text Chapter 27: VII: *The Dreamer of the Dream*, last two paragraphs: "Dream softly of your sinless brother, who unites with you in holy innocence. And from this dream the Lord of Heaven will Himself awaken His beloved Son. Dream your brother's kindnesses instead of dwelling in your dreams on his mistakes. Select his thoughtfulness to dream about instead of counting up the hurts he gave. Forgive him his illusions, and give thanks to him for all the helpfulness he gave. And do not brush aside his many gifts because he is not perfect in your dreams. Let all your brother's gifts be seen in light of charity and kindness offered you. And let no pain disturb your dream of deep appreciation for his gifts to you."

We must remember that we are created in the nature of God and we are part of God. The ego refutes that and sees God far away and separate. It wants to be its own God. We make our own world as we experience it, but we did not create ourselves. We have a Higher Power; we are not our own higher power. We must remember that we are a drop in the ocean, but we are not the whole ocean. We have the same properties and have access to the whole ocean, but the moment we set ourselves up as THE ocean, we separate ourselves in consciousness and lose the whole thing. Through the mercy and grace of God, when we wake up and come back to the Truth, Truth and God are waiting for us with open arms.

We separate ourselves from God in consciousness every time we wander into negative territory and embrace it. The sooner we can get back to Truth and "come to our senses," the sooner we will enjoy the experience of love, peace and joy that we so desire. So, dear friends, our symphony of life is ongoing; our lessons and learning are ongoing. Let us walk on together in our journey in love and peace.

The Wonder of It All

"*Miracle* is simply the wonder of the unique
that points us back to the wonder of the everyday."
—Maurice Friedman

Synchronicities are coincidences alive with meaning, and much more than mere "chance." For those with open hearts and minds they are experiences of participation and connection within the cosmic matrix. A link is felt with all living things. There is a holy instant of knowing at a deep level that we are one with God and one with everything in the universe, a holy instant of recognizing our own forever state of grace.

My purpose in sharing "mind-boggling" stories of connection is to boggle the ordinary mind into opening up to greater possibilities. Unfortunately much of our ordinary mind is taken up with fear, distrust and a sense of separation; fortunately we are still free to see and choose a better way, and it's our ultimate destiny to do so. That's why we're in a state of grace forever.

Several years ago, Greg LaVoy, a reporter for the Cincinnati Enquirer, knew that he needed to go out on his own as a free lance writer. He wanted to be free to explore spiritual themes, but he was fearful and dragging his heels. Driving home from work one afternoon the song Desperado by the Eagles was playing. Just before he turned off the ignition of his car, he heard the lines: "Don't draw the Queen of Diamonds; she'll beat you if she's able; the Queen of Hearts is always your best bet."

He stepped out of his car and there at his left foot was a playing card—he turned it over and it was the Queen of Hearts. The next year was an intense inner struggle over the decision to leap into the brave new world of free lance. During that time he found more Queen of Heart cards in very unlikely places: A sidewalk in Cincinnati—a sand dune in Oregon—in a mountain wilderness in Colorado six miles from the nearest trailhead.

He says: "Every time I found another card, the sheer unbelievability of it took another giant step forward. It went far beyond any laws of probability. This was orchestrated by something with Wits!" Greg came to understand that the cards were trying to tell him to follow what his heart was calling him to do—and to get his head out of the way. Eventually he did just that and has done very well. (Science of Mind Magazine article by Greg LaVoy "A Miracle for the Millenium" January 2000.)

It's been said that the mind creates abysses and the heart crosses them. There is a scene in Dante's Inferno in which Dante is not permitted to pass a particular threshold on his journey until he leaves all reason and intellect behind. Of course reason and intellect are useful faculties, but only up to a point. Synchronicities speak directly to the heart and sometimes downright annoy our reason and intellect.

Our challenge is to overcome the cultural conditioning that leads us to reduce life to the ordinary and commonplace where we tend to discount the mysteries we can't understand with the intellect. We are programmed to wake up in the morning and think we must take complete control of our day. We create inflexible mental lists of projects and pursue them with tunnel vision. Yet the "sweet mystery of life" is always available, dancing around the fringes of our consciousness.

What our higher Christ Self already knows and what we need to experience more in our daily lives is that we are not lonely, isolated, insignificant and meaningless creatures, accidently evolved from organic rubbish on a minuscule dot in the vast cosmos. We want to feel linked to all others and to the universe. Synchronistic events give us glimpses into the underlying Oneness.

The following experience of a black pilot during World War II was shared with Jungian analyst Jean Shinoda Bolen after one of her lectures on synchronicity: When he was in training on a segregated air force base in the Deep South, this young man was feeling lonely and isolated. Whenever the black servicemen went into town they experienced intense racial animosity. He felt like a prisoner confined to the base.

One evening he was walking around the base feeling lonely and miserable when he heard singing in the chapel. The choir was rehearsing. He entered the chapel, sat in a back row and listened to the familiar hymns. Then he started thinking about his grandfather, a powerful, loving, protective man, a Baptist head deacon who loved to sing and who had often taken his reluctant grandson to church with him.

The hymn his grandfather loved best came flooding into his mind: "I come to the garden alone." He was missing his grandfather terribly and thinking that he would really like to hear that song. Then he felt a presence and a certainty—he just 'knew' the choir was going to sing it. And in the next moment, the song began. "I Come to the Garden Alone." Tears came up and he felt a tremendous joy and peace. He knew he was being carried and cared for and no longer felt isolated.

Whatever you believe,
whatever you profess,
whatever you doubt or fear or hope for,
there are some things

your heart cannot deny

when you let go

and let yourself know

the wonder of it all.

(From The Wonder of It All by Ralph Marston)

The wonder of it all is that we are spiritual beings in a spiritual universe, governed by spiritual laws. It is safe to trust that as we seek first the kingdom of heaven all else will be added. I think one of the most comforting passages in the Bible is this: "Consider the lilies of the field, how they grow; they neither toil nor spin, yet I tell you, even Solomon in all his glory was not arrayed like one of these. But if God so clothes the grass of the field, which today is alive and tomorrow is thrown into the oven, will he not much more clothe you, O men of little faith? Therefore do not be anxious, saying, what shall we eat? or what shall we drink? Or what shall we wear?—Your heavenly Father knows you need them all. But seek first his Kingdom and his righteousness and all these things shall be yours as well." (Matthew 6: 26-33)

One of my favorite Bible verses is Psalms 42:8: "But each day the Lord pours his unfailing love upon me, and through each night I sing his songs, praying to God who gives me life." The more we can trust this Infinite Spirit and experience it for ourselves, the more we know that we are plugged into the divine and sacred wholistic universe.

I leave you with one more mind-boggling synchronistic event: Steve Roberts is a CNN reporter who told the following story to Larry King. Years ago Steve's grandfather lived in eastern Poland, a part of Russia at the time. He was a humble book binder who fell in love with a rich girl—and she with him. Her family was horrified and sent her away, but before she left, the grandfather assembled a book of poetry, bound it in red leather and gave it to the girl as a remembrance.

Time passed, he married another girl and they immigrated to the United States. Years later, Steve's nephew, his grandfather's great grandson, who is also in the book business, fell in love with a girl from a wealthy and privileged family—and he was disapproved of. By this time, grandfather is dead, but grandmother is still living. The nephew enlists help from his family, asking them to visit the family of the girl he loves so they might be convinced that he comes from a good family, rich in roots and tradition.

During the visit the girl's grandmother was frowning and not open to conversation. However as they begin to discuss the past and where they immigrated from, the girl's grandmother became more interested—"What village? What is your last name again? When did your family immigrate? What was your grandfather's name?"

She excused herself, went into her bedroom and came back with the red leather hand bound book of poetry that had been given her so many years before by this boy's great grandfather. The great grandchildren of the original lovers had fallen in love—and were given the blessing they hoped for. There were no more objections to their marriage. Can you see the wonder of these outrageously improbable mind-boggling events? Will you dare to let go and embrace the wonders the show up in your own life? Remember: "There are some things your heart cannot deny when you let go and let yourself know the wonder of it all."

Understanding Jesus

"I am no greater than you.
I am no greater than any brother
who walks this earth, who ever has, or who shall,
for we are One."
—Jesus
Journey Beyond Words by Brent Haskell

Why has it been so difficult for so many of us to come to an understanding of Jesus? In my own case it was because I could never figure out how it could be that Jesus taught love and yet such horrible things have been done in his name. The Crusades, The Inquisition, the burning of so-called witches, the threatening of those who won't confess Jesus as their personal savior, the condemning of people to Hell—and on and on. Ultimately, I had to leave Jesus behind and go to the Eastern religions and to Transcendental Meditation to find Spirituality. Maharishi Mahesh Yogi, the founder of TM said in a lecture: "It's good to follow your own tradition." I balked at that; I was not relating to the negative things that were done in the world in the name of Christianity.

However, not too long into the meditation process, I was introduced to Unity, introduced to a different way of looking at Jesus. I can't say I turned into a big fan immediately, but my mind was open. I began to see the difference between Jesus and what human egos have done in His name. Jesus tells us in the Course in Miracles: "Not only does the ego cite scripture for its purpose, but even interprets scripture as a witness for itself. The Bible is a fearful thing in the ego's judgment. Perceiving the Bible as frightening, it interprets it fearfully."

Unity teaches love, not fear, does not beat us over the head or threaten. It defines Jesus as elder brother and way-shower, teacher, friend, example. And that is the way Jesus defines Himself. He said, "What I do you can do and more," and "ye are Gods." Jesus teaches us that we are one with God, One with Him, and One with each other. He teaches love and forgiveness. He says that He is the Son of God—and SO ARE WE.! We each have the Christ within us—we just need to awaken to it.

So, it isn't Jesus that is the problem; it is what fear and ignorance have done in his name that is the problem. With this understanding, I can say yes, I love Jesus, although I'm not about to put a bumper sticker on my car that says, "Honk if you love Jesus." Making friends with Jesus has became a heartfelt awakening for me and I especially appreciate the 'laughing Jesus' painting. In that spirit, I'd like to share some Jesus humor with you.

Arguments about Jesus' nationality:
There were 3 good arguments that Jesus was <u>Black:</u>

1. He called everyone "brother."
2. He liked Gospel.
3. He couldn't get a fair trial.

But then there were 3 equally good arguments that Jesus was <u>Jewish</u>:

1. He went into his father's business.
2. He lived at home until he was 33.
3. He was sure his mother was a virgin and his mother was sure he was God.

But then there were 3 equally good arguments that Jesus was <u>Italian</u>:

1. He talked with his hands.
2. He had wine with his meals.
3. He used olive oil

But then there were 3 equally good arguments that Jesus was a <u>Californian</u>:

1. He never cut his hair.
2. He walked around barefoot all the time.
3. He started a new religion.

But then there were 3 equally good arguments that Jesus was an <u>American Indian</u>:

1. He was one with & at peace with nature.
2. He ate a lot of fish.
3. He talked about the Great Spirit.

But then there were 3 equally good arguments that Jesus was <u>Irish</u>:

1. He never got married
2. He was always telling stories
3. He loved green pastures.

But the most compelling evidence of all: 3 proofs that Jesus was a <u>woman</u>:

1. He fed a crowd at a moment's notice when there was no food.
2. He kept trying to get a message across to a bunch of men who just didn't get it.
3. And even when he was dead, he had to get up because there was work to do. And I dare share all this because I truly believe humor is just fine with Jesus.

One of the best explanations of Jesus and his mission on earth comes in the Course in Miracles—<u>Clarification of terms</u> in the <u>Manual for Teachers</u>. A few defining statements:

The name of Jesus is the name of one who was a man but saw the face of Christ in all his brothers and remembered God. So he became identified with Christ, a man no longer, but at one with God. The man was an illusion, for he seemed to be a separate being, walking by himself, within a body that appeared to hold his self from SELF as all illusions do. Christ needed his form that He might appear to men and save them from their own illusions. In his complete identification with the Christ—the perfect Son of God, Jesus became what we all must be. He led the way for us to follow him. He leads us back to God because he saw the road before him and followed it.

He offered a final demonstration that it is impossible to kill God's Son; nor can his life in any way be changed by sin and evil, malice, fear or death. <u>Is He the Christ? O yes, along with you.</u> His brief life on earth was not enough to teach the mighty lesson that he learned for all. He remains to lead us from our hell of separation to the Heaven of Oneness. Walking with him is just as natural as walking with a brother we've always known.

Is he God's _only_ helper? <u>No indeed.</u> The Christ takes many forms with different names until their oneness can be recognized."

So, Jesus, Buddha, Mohammad, Krishna—all of US—are all One—It is the human ego, the sense of separation that splits everything into pieces, separates everything. We are in truth One with God and One with each other. When we experience that rather than just know about it in theory, we are in the realm of mystical experience and unconditional love. That is where we are destined to be. Jesus is not the only path to God. We all have the freedom to find the path that works for us. However, it is good to go deeper into whatever path we follow. It can be a waste of time to keep intellectually learning about different paths, but never truly getting any closer to God and Oneness.

When Jesus said, "I have come that you have life and have it more abundantly," he was not talking about having more stuff, more money, more thrills and chills on the ego level or even more intellectual knowledge. He was talking about going deeper into the experience of God. He was talking about seeking first the Kingdom and trusting that all we need while we're here will be added. In the Course he tells us that we are everything and that we have everything, that the Kingdom of Heaven is within, and the Kingdom of Heaven IS us—the God in us. He tells us to know what we are and to accept our own identity as expressions of God. When we get that, we live abundantly.

On Palm Sunday, the beginning of Easter Week, what is it that Jesus demonstrates to us during this time? We look at it symbolically or metaphysically to see how we can better understand how to better utilize the Truth that Jesus taught. First of all, Jesus rode triumphantly seated on a donkey. The donkey represents our earthly limited nature. Jesus had overcome his earthly nature and rode triumphantly on top of it. The crowd on Palm Sunday recognized him as an embodiment of God—the Christ.

However, the fickle human ego with its doubts and fears, represented by the angry mob who later betrayed him, did not truly accept the Christ. The betrayer of the Christ then and now is the human ego, the sense of separation,—our angry mob of thoughts that believe separation, death and limitation are all we can expect of life. That is how we crucify the Christ in ourselves. However, the meaning of Easter is not in the crucifixion because in spite of appearances, in spite of all the efforts of angry mobs, the son of God cannot be killed. Jesus demonstrated that our human body can be terminated, but our spirit it indestructible and eternal. There is no need to fear.

We forgive the angry mob inside and outside ourselves because, "they know not what they do." And ultimately they cannot destroy the Reality of us—the Christ of us. Jesus says the Course in Miracles is summed up by this simple syllogism: What is Real cannot be threatened; what is unreal does not exist. Therein lies the Peace of God. White Easter lilies represent the innocence of the Christ. But they also symbolize the Christ within each of us that is innocent: The part of us that is Real, Immortal, an extension of the Love of God, an expression of God. When we awaken to this truth, when we experience and demonstrate this truth, we awaken to Heaven here on earth and come to understand that God and Heaven and the truth of our Being are All One.

Welcoming the Christ—Palm Sunday

"The Christ is planted in our consciousness
that we might have life and have it more abundantly;
that the grace of God might fill us
with an infinite abundance of spiritual good."
—Joel Goldsmith

It was Palm Sunday, and because of a sore throat, five year old Johnny stayed home from church with a sitter. When the family returned home, they were carrying several palm branches. The boy asked what they were for. "People held them over Jesus' head as he walked by," his older brother explained. "Wouldn't you know it," the boy fumed, "The one Sunday I don't go, he shows up!"

The fulfillment and satisfaction we feel when we invite our Christ nature into our lives, uplifts our soul. Just knowing about my true identity in Christ, even before I had experiences of it, began to make a positive difference in my life. Much of humanity is bound up in human mortal identity, tuned into trials and tribulations, believing that God is in the sky and no part of them and thus overwhelmed by suffering and despair. The Christ doesn't seem to show up for them.

To welcome and to celebrate the entry of the Christ consciousness into our lives is appropriate. However, the real task before us is to go deeper and deeper into the truth of the Christ of our being until we not only know about it, but feel it, live it, realize it. The challenge for all of us is to hang onto our mountaintop experiences in the valley of everyday appearances when our human lives seem to be falling apart.

I find that I must respect my spiritual path and have faith and trust in it through any and all circumstances. We read in 1ST John 5:4: "The victory that conquers the world is our faith." Hebrews: "Faith is a sure and steadfast anchor of the soul." 2nd Corinthians 4:18: "We look not at what can be seen, but at what cannot be seen; for what can be seen is temporary, but what cannot be seen is eternal." A woman in the crowd around Jesus who had been ill for years had total faith and trust that if she could only touch the hem of his garment, she would be healed, and so she was. Our goal is to have that much desire to touch the Christ consciousness so that we may be healed.

What is healing? What needs to be healed? Healing is restoration and we are healed in body and mind as we allow ourselves to awaken to our true identity and to be restored in consciousness to the truth of ourselves. Jesus, our elder brother and way shower, was so awakened to his true identity that he taught and continues to teach us that our true identity of love can never be destroyed and that death has no power over life.

On Palm Sunday we honor Jesus the Christ who demonstrated the truth of his being and our being. Metaphysically, there is the time when the crowd in our psyche praises and defers to the Christ. But later other parts of our unhealed psyche, out of fear and insanity, would kill or obliterate the awareness of the Christ of us. Of course the good news is that it can't be done.

Some teachings of Jesus regarding the events of his last days in human form on earth appear in A Course in Miracles. "It is not necessary to perceive any form of assault as persecution, because the divinity in us cannot be persecuted. We have perfect immunity, which is the truth in us, and the Divinity of us cannot be assailed. I demonstrated that the most outrageous assault, as judged by the ego, does not matter."

Yet, on our human ego level, we often feel persecuted, victimized and unfairly treated. How can we begin to move past these false perceptions? A question I have found useful is, "What can I learn from this experience?" Sometimes we carry around an experience of feeling victimized for years. Yet at any time, we can choose to see it differently. We can begin to explore what we learned, forgive those involved, realize that our soul set it up in the first place and then begin to bless it all whether it happened yesterday or years ago.

In a recent Oprah program, she talked to a nineteen year old young man who at the age of six had been abused and locked up in a tiny closet for days at a time without food and no opportunity to go to the bathroom. His stepsister ran away from home and when apprehended by police, told them about the abuse of her brother. The boy was rescued and has been living with a loving aunt since then. It is a sad story, but there is an inspirational side of it. This young man, whose drug addicted mother abandoned him and whose father and stepmother were cruel abusers, made a choice. He would not continue to be a victim; his goal would be to be kind and to make others happy.

He wants to be a policeman so that he can help others and work to prevent the kind of abuse he experienced. He had every reason and excuse to act out by taking drugs or getting into other kinds of trouble, but he chose differently. What a lesson for all of us! We CAN CHOOSE to see our problems differently and we can choose how we will respond and live our lives. This is not a new teaching for us, but to see this extreme example of this boy putting it into practice should help us to choose to put our own grievances to rest rather than carry them with us for months and years!

Our ego does not give up its grievances easily; nor does it easily give up its habit of judging by appearances, its habit of making outer appearances its reality. It keeps itself busy with an outward focus; it's addicted to remaining unconscious. That's why it finds prayer and meditation boring and resists it.

Saint Teresa of Avila described how she knew when it was God that was speaking to her. She said, "You will know when God has spoken to you because of three things. One, you are certain of what the words are. You may not get their meaning, but the words are clear. Second thing," Teresa said, "If they are words from God, they will give you a feeling of peace, whether you understand them, or not. Third, 'The words stay with you a long time. Maybe forever.

As I facilitate groups, I sometimes go around the room and ask people to talk about their prayer and meditation experiences. They too often respond by saying, "I don't have enough time." Or "I don't know how to pray". Or "I am not sure God answers prayers." But the most telling answer was, "I am afraid of what God might ask me to do." We sometimes fear surrendering to Spirit because we don't know what we might be asked to do as a result. We just might be asked to give up our grievances and turn them into forgiveness and love.

When we finally do decide to welcome the Christ consciousness into our lives, there is no doubt that change will happen. Our life may unfold in ways we could never have predicted. Yet, we won't make that decision until we have complete trust and realize we are better off than under the guidance and direction of our ego.

Reminds me of the story of the fern and the bamboo as told by someone who was ready to give up hope: "One day I decided to quit. I quit my job, my relationship, my Spirituality—I wanted to quit my life, and I went into the woods to have one last talk with God. "God can you give me one good reason not to give up on my life?" I asked. His answer surprised me. "Look around at the fern and the bamboo."

"When I planted the fern and the bamboo seeds, I took great care of them. I gave them light. I gave them water. The fern quickly grew from the earth. Its brilliant green covered the floor. Yet nothing came from the bamboo seed. But I did not give up on the bamboo. In the second year the fern grew more vibrant and plentiful, but nothing came from the bamboo seed. I did not give up on it.

In the third and fourth year, there was still nothing from the bamboo seed, but I did not quit. Then in the fifth year a tiny sprout emerged from the earth. Compared to the fern, it was seemingly small and insignificant. But just six months later the bamboo rose to over 100 feet tall. It had spent the five years growing roots. Those roots made it strong and gave it what it needed to survive. I would not give any of my creations a challenge it could not handle.

Do you know, my child, that all this time you have been struggling you have actually been growing roots? I never quit on the bamboo and I will never quit on you. Don't judge by appearances or compare yourself to others. The bamboo had a different purpose than the fern; yet they both make the forest beautiful. Your time will come; your destiny is to rise high." After that talk with God, I left the forest and brought back this story. I hope you will see that God never gives up on you.

So we must ask ourselves—are we willing to welcome the Christ into our lives and to continue to trust the results, no matter what the outer appearances? Are we willing to understand that anything and everything we have ever experienced can be used for our learning and growth—for our good? Are we willing to trust that in the end all the years the locusts may have eaten will be restored to us?

A statement from A Course in Miracles encourages us to have faith and trust: "There must come a moment in which you take what you might call a leap of faith. This leap of faith is a choice to go, a choice to move, a choice to become something which you, as yet do not know. This leap of faith will take you home."

Dear Father-Mother God, Yes, we welcome your love and truth into our lives; we accept our true identity and we will have faith in the overcoming Christ of us. We would know and accept that your joy shall lift us up into heavenly realms. Amen.

Who We Truly Are

"It is through knowing who you are not
that the greatest obstacle
to truly knowing yourself is removed.
—Eckhart Tolle

"Nothing can teach you
if you not unlearn everything."
—Rumi

Several years ago a seminary professor was vacationing with his wife in Gatlinburg, Tennessee. One morning, they were eating breakfast at a little restaurant, hoping to enjoy a quiet, family meal. While they were waiting for their food, they noticed a distinguished looking, white-haired man moving from table to table, visiting with the guests. Eventually, the man came over to their table. "Great to have you here in Tennessee," the stranger said. "What do you do for a living?" "I teach at a seminary," the professor replied. "Well, I've got a really great story for you," the white haired man said. And with that, the gentleman pulled up a chair and sat down at the table with the couple.

"See that mountain over there?" he asked as he pointed out the restaurant window. Not far from the base of that mountain, there was a boy born to an unwed mother. He had a hard time growing up because every place he went, he was always asked the same question, "Hey boy, "Who's your daddy?" Whether he was at school, in the grocery store or drug store, people would ask the same question, "Who's your daddy?"

When he was about 12 years old, a new preacher came to his church. The boy would always go in late and slip out early to avoid hearing the question, "Who's your daddy?"'But one day, the new preacher said the benediction so fast that he got caught and had to walk out with the crowd. Just about the time he got to the back door, the new preacher, not knowing anything about him, put his hand on his shoulder and asked him, "Son, who's your daddy?" He could feel every eye in the church looking at him. Now everyone would finally know the answer to the question, "Who's your daddy?"

This new preacher, though, sensed the situation around him and using discernment that only the Holy Spirit could give, said the following to that scared little boy: "Wait a minute! I know who you are! I see the family resemblance now. You are a child of God!" He patted the boy on his shoulder and said, "Boy, you've got a great inheritance. Go and claim it." The boy smiled for the first time in a long time and walked out the door a changed person. Whenever anybody asked him, "Who's your Daddy?" he'd just tell them, "I'm a Child of God." The distinguished gentleman got up from the table and said, "Isn't that a great story?"

The professor agreed that it really was a great story! As the man turned to leave, he said, "You know, if that new preacher hadn't told me that I was one of God's children, I probably never would have amounted to anything!" And he walked away. The seminary professor and his wife were stunned. He called the waitress over and asked her, "Do you know who that man was—the one who just left that was sitting at our table?' The waitress grinned and said, "Of course. Everybody here knows him. That's Ben Hooper. He's the governor of Tennessee!"

The governor spoke about a great lesson we all need to learn: No matter what others may think they know about us, the truth is that each one of us is a child of God. No matter what our circumstances of birth, we are a child of God. I have my own story about that. I was also born to a young unwed mother. In those unenlightened days in Michigan there was a space on the birth certificate that asked: legitimate?—and then a box to check yes or no. I did not see my original birth certificate until I was 18 and applied for a job with Michigan Bell.

Due to the rather harsh circumstances of my life until then, I did not feel particularly good about myself, but when I saw those words—Legitimate? and No! stamped on my birth certificate, it hurt deeply. So, discovering who I truly am beyond labels and circumstances is liberating indeed. That is the truth that sets us free. We start by unlearning what is not true. What is it that we need to unlearn if we want to discover and experience who we truly are? Turns out that we need to unlearn everything that society has taught us about who we are.

We think of ourselves as a body, but we are not our body—we "hang out "in one. To the degree that we make our body our identity, we live in fear of something happening to it. That can be a great distraction from experiencing the peace of God. In truth, the body is simply our current instrument of expression in the outer world. We are more than our emotions, although they may seem to temporarily submerge us. Ideally we learn to observe and understand our emotions and gradually learn to direct, utilize and integrate them harmoniously, but our emotions are not who we truly are.

We have a mind which can be a valuable tool of discovery and expression, but it is not the essence of who we are. Its contents are constantly changing, and often it refuses to obey us; we are more than our intellect. It is not who we truly are. We play a lot of roles, and it's fine to play them as well as we can: parent, spouse, teacher, student, doctor, lawyer, executive, minister, ditch digger, handyman, merry maid—but none of these roles can define who we truly are. We are more than our body, emotions, thoughts and roles.

However, our ego attempts to convince us that we are our body, emotions, thoughts, roles and circumstances. Our ego would have us sacrifice our own true identity in order to find a little separate identity of its own. Yet, that separate identity results in a sense of isolation, loss and loneliness. We deprive ourselves unnecessarily and live in spiritual poverty unless we understand who we truly are and then make it our number one priority to live and express through it. The prerequisite is to unlearn everything that we think we know.

When we can see the ego for what it is, we begin to know who we are not. In the stillness of the now moment we can transcend our identification with the body, with thoughts, emotions, roles and circumstances; we can plunge into the Is-ness, the space beyond and behind it all. This is the peace that passes all understanding; it is a direct experience of Spirit beyond words; it is the revelation that makes us dumb—not ignorant, but speechless and with no content in our minds—just pure awareness of being. Without this direct experience in our lives, we are still on the threshold—outside the door trying to figure out how to get in. The great mystic poet Rumi wrote, "How learned I was before revelation made me dumb."

When we make the peace of God our one goal, circumstances keep going on out there; but we have an inner non-resistance to what happens because we are staying centered in who we truly are—pure spirit, pure love, pure peace and pure joy. We have built our house on the rock—upon a firm foundation that the storms of life cannot shake. We are living in the world but we are not of it.

Eckhart Tolle tells us, "The joy of being, which is the only true happiness, cannot come to you through any form, possession, achievement, person or event—through anything that happens. That joy cannot come to you—ever. It emanates from the formless dimension within you—from Spirit itself and thus is one with who you are." J. Krishnamurti, a great Indian philosopher and teacher, near the end of his more than fifty years of teaching asked his audience: "Do you want to know my secret? It's very simple-I don't mind what happens."

When we know who we truly are, we don't mind what happens, and we can't be turned upside down by what goes on in the world. Circumstances stop having power over us. As we live in the world but not of it, the world is no longer what determines our happiness or unhappiness. We live in the reality of who and what we truly are, which results in a stable consciousness of love, peace and joy. Our true identity as expressions of God is our priceless treasure and who we truly are. Let us go forth and claim our true birthright.

SECTION TWO
Together in Love

"Dare to be Pleasured, Empowered and
transformed by your Divine Heart Center."
—Alec Evason

Messages:

A Reason and a Season

Angels are for Real

The Many Faces of Angels

Living in the Sea of Love

Love is All There Is

Love Never Ends

Love's Demonstrations

Relationships: A Path to God

Remembering My Mothers

Stick With Love

The Loving Eyes of God

The Many Faces of Fathers

Our Divine Mother

Weave Us Together

What Happened to St. Valentine?

A Reason and A Season

"In you is all of Heaven. Every leaf that falls
is given life in you. Each bird that ever sang will
sing again in you. And every flower that ever bloomed
has saved its perfume and its loveliness for you."
—A Course in Miracles

Everywhere we go, we go by Divine Appointment. Our soul has chosen the time and the place and the duration. We are not always conscious of the entire Divine Plan. It looks like the wind blows us one way and another and that we have no choice in the matter. I believe that every experience gives us an opportunity to learn and grow toward the ultimate experience of living in the pure awareness of love.

As we look from the cosmic view we see that the small details of our lives, the comings and goings, the ups and downs, the adventures and misadventures are all part of the learning game of life. The sooner we stop trying to control the world, stop trying to control who comes and goes, stop trying to control who stays and who leaves, the sooner we surrender everything and embrace the love we are, the sooner we will live in the love, peace, and joy of God.

What do we do when we're not manipulating and controlling? Working to have everything go the way we think is best? We relax, release, let go, surrender, give it to God and go around smiling! The more I see my own imagined horror stories for what they are and focus upon the truth instead, the happier I am.

However, on my last Sunday at Garden Park Unity in Cincinnati, Ohio, I could not let the day go by without talking about separations and good-byes. We continually experience separations in one form or another. People make their transitions; they move away, they leave us behind to pursue another path in life; our earth school experiences are fluid and temporary. They are our lessons to be learned from and then we need to release them and move forward. But through it all there is a common thread. That thread is love, the truth of our Being beyond all changes, appearances, and circumstances.

It turns out that when we share loving experiences, we leave heart prints that stay with us always. Our fingers leave fingerprints on what we touch physically, but they can easily be wiped clean. Heart prints are permanent and never forgotten. They open us to the more expansive love of God, which in truth we are. A Course in Miracles instructs us: Teach only love, for that is what you are.

When someone leaves our life for any reason—death, divorce, drifting apart—whatever—the love we shared is permanent and we can bless it. That does not mean that we stay stuck in the past; we need to move on and live in the present. We need to release ourselves and others to be here and now. When I think of the many people who came into my life for a reason and a season but who have now gone on, I still have the heart prints from all those experiences and I bless them. I am richer for all these experiences and I have more to give in the here and now because of them.

It's a good practice to finish business with everyone and everything in the past—to keep the love and learning and then release and free yourself and others to go on. That's why it's so important to acknowledge and express the love and caring we feel for others. Keep your business finished so that if you walk out of a room and drop over, you will have no regrets, no unfinished business. Finishing business with ourselves is also very important.

Walking through life in an unhealed state causes us pain and causes pain for those around us. We must take responsibility for our own thoughts and feelings and when they are harmful, we can know that we can choose again. We can watch our thoughts and feelings and choose to focus on the love instead of fear. There are so many tools and techniques if we will use them. Teachers, books, workshops, classes—we are surrounded with help, but if we are not open to that help, we stay suffering.

It has been said, "There is none so blind as those who will not see." To begin to see, we need the willingness to see, to change, to learn, to move beyond where we are in consciousness. When we are ready, what we need comes to us. The following story illustrates that even in the midst of our resistance, the grace of God in the form of a person who comes into our life for a reason and a season, can wake us up.

This is a true wake up story shared on the internet by Robert Peterson. The events happened several years ago, but he will always carry the heart prints: "She was six years old when I first met her on the beach near where I live. I walk on this beach whenever the world seems to close in on me. She was building a sand castle and looked up, her eyes as blue as the sea. 'Hello,' she said. I answered with a nod, not really in the mood to bother with a small child. 'I'm building,' she said. 'I see that. What is it? I asked, not really caring. 'Oh, I don't know; I just like the feel of the sand.' That sounds good, I thought, and slipped off my shoes.

A sandpiper glided by. 'That's a joy,' the child said. 'It's a what?' 'It's a joy. My mama says sandpipers come to bring us joy.' The bird went gliding down the beach. Good-bye joy, I muttered to myself. Hello pain, and turned to walk on. I was depressed and my life seemed completely out of balance. 'What's your name?' She wouldn't give up. 'Robert,' I answered. 'Mine's Wendy—I'm six.' 'Hi Wendy.' She giggled. 'You're funny,' she said. In spite of my gloom, I laughed too and walked on. Her musical giggle followed me. 'Come again Mr. P,' she called. 'We'll have another happy day.'

The next few days consisted of a group of unruly Boy Scouts, PTA meetings, and an ailing mother. The sun was shining one morning as I took my hands out of the dishwater. I need a sandpiper, I said to myself, gathering up my coat. The ever-changing balm of the seashore awaited me. The breeze was chilly but I strode along, trying to recapture the serenity I needed 'Hello Mr. P,' she said. 'Do you want to play?''Let's just walk,' I answered. Looking at her, I noticed the delicate fairness of her face. 'Where do you live?' I asked. 'Over there,' she pointed toward a row of summer cottages. Strange, I thought, in winter. 'Where do you go to school?' 'I don't go to school; Mommy says we're on vacation.' She chattered little girl talk as we strolled up the beach, but my mind was on other things. When I left for home, Wendy said it had been a happy day. Feeling surprisingly better, I smiled at her and agreed.

Three weeks later, I rushed to my beach in a state of near panic. I was in no mood to even greet Wendy. I thought I saw her mother on the porch and felt like demanding she keep her child at home. 'Look, if you don't mind,' I said crossly when Wendy caught up with me, 'I'd rather be alone today.' She seemed unusually pale and out of breath. 'Why?' she asked. I turned to her and shouted, 'because my mother died!' I thought, my God why was I saying this to a little child? 'Oh, she said quietly, 'then this is a bad day.' 'Yes,' I said, 'and yesterday and the day before and—oh, go away!'

'Did it hurt?' she inquired. 'Did what hurt?' I was exasperated with her, with myself. 'When she died?' 'Of course it hurt!' I snapped, misunderstanding and wrapped up in myself. I strode off. A month or so after that, when I next went to the beach, she wasn't there. Feeling guilty, ashamed, and admitting to myself I missed her, I went up to the cottage after my walk and knocked at the door. A drawn looking young woman with honey-colored hair opened the door.

'Hello, I said, 'I'm Robert Peterson. I missed your little girl today and wondered where she was.' 'Oh yes, Mr. Peterson, please come in. Wendy spoke of you so much. I'm afraid I allowed her to bother you. If she was a nuisance, please accept my apologies.' 'Not at all—she's a delightful child,' I said, suddenly realizing that I meant what I had just said. 'Wendy died last week, Mr. Peterson. She had leukemia. Maybe she didn't tell you.'

Struck dumb I groped for a chair. I had to catch my breath. 'She loved this beach, so when she asked to come, I couldn't say no. She seemed so much better here and had a lot of what she called happy days. But the last few weeks, she declined rapidly.' Her voice faltered. 'She left something for you.' I nodded stupidly, my mind racing for something to say. She handed me an envelope with Mr. P printed in bold childish letters. Inside was a drawing in bright crayon hues—a yellow beach, a blue sea, and a brown bird. Underneath was carefully printed: A Sandpiper to Bring you Joy.

Tears welled up in my eyes and a heart that had almost forgotten to love opened wide. I took Wendy's mother in my arms. "I'm so sorry; I'm so sorry,' I uttered over and over, and we wept together. The precious little picture is framed now and hangs in my study. Six words—one for each year of her life—that speak to me of harmony, courage, and undemanding love. A Sandpiper to Bring you Joy."

Wendy left heart prints in Robert Peterson's life that reminded him of what is truly important beyond the hustle and bustle of everyday traumas and setbacks. Love is the gift that never goes away, that we can carry with us forever. Robert ended his piece with this advice: "Everything happens to us for a reason. Never brush aside anyone as insignificant. Who knows what they can teach us?"

Yes we are all here together by Divine Appointment. We can't always know all the reasons for any one encounter or time spent in any one place, but we can know that we can use every experience and every encounter for good—we can love it and bless it and use it to bring our awareness back to God and the love we are. I'd like to close with the following excerpt from a mystical poet:

A Helper of Hearts

Don't look down upon the heart,
Even if it's not behaving well,
Even in that shape, the heart
is more precious than the teachings
of the Exalted Saints.
If you become a helper of hearts,
springs of wisdom
will flow from your heart.
The water of life will run from your mouth
like a torrent.
Your breath will become medicine
like the breath of Jesus.
Be silent.
Even if you have two hundred tongues
on each hair on your head,
You won't be able to explain the heart.
(author unknown to me)

Angels Are For Real

"No one can fail who seeks to reach the truth.
Angels light the way so that all darkness vanishes,
and you are standing in a light so bright and clear that
you can understand all things you see."
—A Course in Miracles

It can sometimes be challenging for many of us to be open and receptive to things that seem miraculous and extraordinary. We have been trained to believe in so called "solid facts" that are measureable in a laboratory. It seems safer somehow to remain skeptical. However, the further along I travel on this lifetime's journey, the more I realize that all kinds of things are not impossible. Just because my five senses can't discern something does not mean it isn't possible. In fact Reality with a capital R is not solid but invisible to our human eyes, although it may be discerned by the human heart. The poet Rumi advises us: "Sell your cleverness and purchase bewilderment." Not a bad idea! So let's take a look at the miraculous bewildering wonderment of angel appearances.

Angels are an important concept in the belief systems of all world religions,—symbols of beauty, purity, and holiness. Are they celestial beings serving as messengers of God who literally watch over us? The Bible recounts many instances where angels protected, announced, administered, comforted, escorted and gave help to all manner of people. For many, there is no question that angels serve as guides and companions.

Angels are significant elements in Jesus' story from the time Mary was informed by the angel Gabriel that she was to be the mother of Jesus until the end when the soldiers came to Gethsemane to take Jesus away to be crucified. Jesus told those with him not to defend him. He said, "Do you think I cannot appeal to my father and he will at once send more than 12 legions of angels?" I personally believe that angels are the grace of God in action and that they make themselves available and visible to us when we need their comfort and guidance. I could fill a book with many experiences of people who have seen, experienced, and been helped by angels.

There is an amazing book entitled Into the Light by Dr. John Lerma. He is the inpatient medical director for the internationally renowned TMC Hospice, part of the largest medical center in the world, the Medical Center of Houston. He is compassionate, involved with his patients and shares some of their stories and experiences in his book. And lo and behold, all these stories of near death visions and experiences include the appearance of angels. The patients in his Hospice include men, women, and children of all ages. It's amazing how the experiences of a priest, a murderer, a prostitute and an innocent child all include angels.

The Hospice mission is to provide compassionate care and relief from pain so that the transition into the next dimension will be peaceful and pain free. There are no judgments. There is opportunity for people to make peace with their families, arrange for children to be cared for—and take care of any unfinished business which enables them to move on peacefully and easily. Within days of the time for the spirit to leave the earth suit behind, angels and relatives who have passed on begin to fill the patients' rooms with love, light and instructions to release guilt, to forgive themselves and others.

A young woman at the Hospice nearing her death saw angels often and carried on conversations with them. One day her mother witnessed the young woman lifting up her arms and pulling, seemingly from the air, a white six inch feather. She had asked the angel for something so she'd know it would be back, and it gave her permission to reach up and take a feather.

Another patient told Dr. Lerma that the archangel Michael appeared to him and saying that angels continuously work to protect us from ourselves, which helps us continue to have choices and chances to evolve. He also said to never doubt God's angels, that there is nothing we can do that cannot be forgiven and that God understands our individual perceptions of heaven and reflects them back to us. This provides comfort, peace, joy and unconditional love.

I personally embrace the idea that God understands our individual perceptions. I believe that this applies to visions of Jesus as well. Sometimes his eyes are brown and he's dark. Other times, he appears with blond hair and blue eyes. Spirit can and does manifest in any form that we can relate to and recognize. I believe this is the grace of God in action.

Here's an angel story told by the minister of the Marble Collegiate Church in New York. A missionary was on furlough from his assignment in Africa. He was visiting his family in Michigan and while there, he preached a sermon in his home church, which was supporting him and his missionary work. He talked about the small field hospital where he worked in Africa. Every other week he made a two-day bicycle trip to a nearby city to obtain supplies, medicine and cash. On one of his trips he witnessed a fight between two young men. One of them was injured and the missionary went to him and while treating his injuries, told him about Jesus and God's love.

Two weeks later, when the missionary was again in the city, the same young man stopped him and said, "I want to tell you something. After you were here two weeks ago, five of my friends and I followed you to where you were camping by the road. We knew you had money and drugs, and we intended to kill and rob you. But when we approached where you were sleeping, we saw twenty-six armed guards who scared us away." As the missionary was telling his story, a man in the congregation stood up and said, "Excuse me, but I need to interrupt you and ask a question. When was that incident?" The missionary thought a minute and then told him.

The man responded, "On that day, I was going to play golf. But I had a very strong urge to pray for you. It was so compelling that I called a group of people and said, 'Meet me in the sanctuary. We have to pray for our missionary friend.' So we met here and prayed.—Would all of you who were here with me that day stand?" They all stood up. And then they counted the men who were standing—ten, fifteen, and finally twenty-six. I think that demonstrates that angels can assume any form; that the power of unselfish prayer is enormous; and that angels are messengers of God who literally watch over us.

Catherine Ponder in her book *The Prospering Power of Love* gives a technique for contacting angels for very specific help. I have personally used this method and it has been most valuable. It is especially helpful in dealing with people we can't reason with or help in the usual way. Here's the method:

Write out the following sentence fifteen times: "To the angel of____, (can be your own angel or that of another person) I bless you and give thanks that you are bringing about Divine Order and Highest good in this situation AND you are helping me (or another) to overcome this addiction

OR you are helping me(or another) to release inappropriate behavior or relationships OR you are showing me (or another) the way to completely forgive ourselves and others OR you are helping me(or another) establish financial order and prosperity. The point is to write down what *you want the angel to help you or another with.* In the beginning you have affirmed that you are asking for Divine Order and Highest Good for all. Sometimes the answer or help may not come in the form your human level ego may prefer, but it will come as Divine Order and Highest Good—and that you can trust.

Remember that angels are extensions of God Thoughts and God's grace in action. As expressions of the living, loving God we can trust God's love and give thanks for our guardian angels who are always here for us whether we see or communicate with them or not. From A Course in Miracles: "My treasure house is full and angels watch its open doors that not one gift is lost and only more are added. We do not walk alone. God's angels hover near and all about. Love surrounds us and of this we can be sure,—We will never be left comfortless."

Prayer: Dear Father—Mother God: We give thanks for your angels that touch us in limitless, mysterious ways. We cannot comprehend all that you have created to make us mindful of your love and to guide us to truth and light. We give thanks for the angels that help us transform our attitudes, our thoughts and our lives in the direction of wholeness. We give thanks for all the ways you grace us with your Holy Presence. Amen.

The Faces of Angels Among Us

"I believe there are angels among us
Sent down to us from Heaven up above
They come to you and me in our darkest hour
To teach us how to live, to teach us how to give
To light us on our way to love."
—Alabama

Not all angels have wings. Sometimes they show up looking just like everybody else, do what they come to do, and then vanish. Sometimes they are friends or neighbors or even you or me when we are inspired or instructed by the Spirit of God to be truly helpful. I'll share some examples of how angels come to us and demonstrate God's grace in action.

The wise words of Rumi: "Sell your cleverness and purchase bewilderment" apply to an experience I had several years ago that remains vivid, consoling, and bewildering. For quite some time I had been focused on releasing the grief concerning my son Richard's sudden death at age nine. For far too long I had carried the hundred pound weight on my heart and with the help of my dear friend Ione along with spiritual teachers such as Elisabeth Kubler-Ross, Steven Levine, Ram Dass and others, I made great progress. I took care of my unfinished business with him, dealt with guilt over not being a perfect parent, and was able to see the wonderful gift of having this dear loving soul in my life for nine years.

I had always dreamed of Richard in his nine year old earth suit. However, after I had gone through the process of releasing the pain but keeping him close in love, I had a dream of him as a young man. It was a clear 'in my face' dream of him, and he was smiling. I felt that the dream was a sign of release. There was just one thing I still longed for—a real hug—but I knew that could only happen after I made my own transition.

Then one Saturday in July several years ago in Vancouver, Washington, Ione and I were presenting a Dream Interpretation workshop at a Unity church. There was a sign out on the sidewalk inviting anyone interested to stop in and see what it was all about. The workshop was in progress with about 15 people sitting in a circle in the church basement, when a young man walked in. He seemed familiar somehow, and as the minutes passed, I had a sudden realization: "He looks just like Richard in my dream!" Goosebumps appeared on my arms, a shiver ran up my back, and I was in a state of surreal consciousness difficult to describe, but which felt like dreaming and floating.

At the break, I approached the young man and briefly told him about my son, the dream and how he looked like a grown Richard. I didn't even have to ask for the hug; we just naturally embraced as the love flowed. In those moments he shared that he felt the need of mother love because of his own experiences, which he didn't describe. It was almost time for the workshop to resume. He said that he couldn't stay because of other obligations and left—after one more hug.

After the workshop was over, I asked the minister and several people if they knew who this young man was. Everyone answered that they had not seen him before. I was sharing my wonderment with Ione as we were packing up to leave. She said, "Julie, don't you remember what day this is? July 26?" It was Richard's birthday! Somehow my dear son, by the g race of God, had given me a hug on his birthday! Or an angel had appeared in that form—whatever it was, it was a delightful bewilderment.

The following is the story of an angel appearing as a truck driver. A lady was traveling alone on a busy highway in Ohio at dusk when she had a flat tire. She pulled over to the side of the busy six lane freeway without a cell phone, wondering what to do. A semi truck passed and then slowed down and pulled over on the shoulder. The driver walked back to her car and offered to change her tire.

She remembered all the precautions she's been taught. She wrote down the license plate number of the truck and the company name, "just in case." The driver asked for the keys to her trunk, changed the tire and handed the keys back to her. The woman was grateful and offered to pay him, but he refused saying that it was what good Ohio truck drivers do. She asked for his name so that she could write a note to his employer, and he gave her a card with a name and phone number.

When the lady got back to her home state of Florida, she had a T-shirt made that showed an angel in a truck with the words "highway hero" printed under the picture. She sent it to the address on the card and it came back, addressee unknown. She called the number on the card and got a recording saying no such number existed. She called the city newspaper for that town, asked for the editor, explained the dilemma and asked that a letter to the editor be placed in the paper thanking the driver. The editor, who had lived there all his life, said there was no such company in that city.

He further investigated and found there was no such business registered in the state of Ohio. The editor went one step further and called the state motor vehicle bureau to ask about the license and was told no such plate had ever been issued. The upshot is that this man, his truck and the company never existed. So what happened that rainy evening? Was she helped by an angel without wings? She was definitely left in a state of wonder and bewilderment.

Sometimes it's ordinary people such as ourselves that God recruits to be "earth angels." A young man was driving home after a spiritual class at his church. The minister had talked about listening to the Voice for God, The Holy Spirit. The man prayed, "I am listening God; please speak to me." As he was driving home he had a strange thought—'buy a gallon of milk.' He didn't need milk himself and thought, 'God is that you?' He didn't get a direct reply and drove on, but something inside kept suggesting, 'buy a gallon of milk.' So he decided to stop at a convenience store and buy the milk, just in case.

He started home, and as he passed Seventh Street, he again felt the urge—'turn down that street.' He thought that was crazy and drove on, but the thought wouldn't leave him, so he turned around and proceeded down Seventh Street. He drove a few blocks and then felt like he should stop and pulled over to the curb and looked around. Most of the houses looked dark like the people were already in bed. Again he sensed something. "Go and give the milk to the people in the house across the street."

The man looked at the dark house and began to argue: "Lord, this is insane. If I wake these people up they are going to be mad, but I will do this." He walked across the street and rang the bell. A man's voice yelled out, "Who is it? What do you want?" The young man thrust out the gallon of milk and said: "Here, I brought this to you." The man took the milk and rushed down a hallway speaking loudly in Spanish.

Then from down the hall came a woman carrying the milk toward the kitchen. The man was following her holding a baby. The baby was crying and the man had tears running down his face. The man began speaking through his tears. "We were just praying. We had some big bills this month and we ran out of money. We didn't have milk for our baby. I was just praying and asking God to show me how to get some milk." His wife yelled from the kitchen. "I asked him to send an angel with some milk. Are you an angel?" The young man reached into his wallet and pulled out all the money he had with him and pressed it into the man's hand. He turned and walked back to his car knowing that indeed God had communicated with him. He became an earth angel as directed by Spirit.

If you and I will listen, if you and I will dedicate ourselves to sharing the love of God, we won't lack opportunities to be earth angels ourselves. There is more to every situation, every circumstance than we can know on the human level. As we listen to the instruction and guidance of Holy Spirit we will know where to go, what to do, what to say in order to be ambassadors of love here in earth school—and yes, even earth angels.

Most of us have benefitted from the love of God flowing through others, even if they might not think of it that way. I could fill up many pages and give many talks about the people who have been loving and uplifting influences in my life. (And if you'd like to read about them, they can be found in my spiritual autobiography *From Soap Opera to Symphony*.)

I have a homework assignment for you: You might have trouble naming the five wealthiest people in the world, the last five years of Heisman trophy winners, or the last five people who won the Nobel or Pulitzer Prize etc. These people are the best in their fields, not second rate achievers. They may impact the world at large in a positive way, but we can't feel their personal impact upon us.

However, you probably can name some teachers who inspired you in school, three friends who have helped you through difficult times, three spiritual heroes who have inspired you. The people who make a difference in our lives are not the ones with the most credentials, the most money, or the most awards. They are the ones that love and care. They are our earth angels. As we love and care for others and do what we are guided to do, we earn the earth angel designation for ourselves. We become instruments for God's love in action. And in the final analysis, this is our true earth school assignment.

Some words of wisdom and encouragement from Clarissa-Pinkola Estes: "Ours is not the task of fixing the entire world all at once, but of stretching out to the part of the world that is within our reach. Any small, calm thing that one soul can do to help another soul will help immensely. It is not given to us to know which acts and by whom, will cause the critical mass to tip toward an enduring good. To display the lantern of the soul, to show love and mercy toward others is one of the strongest things we can do."

Prayer: Dear Father-Mother God, Sweet Spirit, clothe us now in your sacred presence of peace. Spirit of the Holy One, may you fall afresh upon our awareness—melt our hearts—mold our minds—fill us with your grace. We want to become instruments of your peace and love. We ask for grace and direction that we may become your angels of love, light, comfort and inspiration. We embrace all your sons and daughters, all our brothers and sisters. May we be lifted up as we know, experience and share love. May we fly freely, upward and onward forever and ever in your Infinite Presence. Amen.

Living in the Sea of Love

"God is Love. God is all. We live in a sea of love
while dreaming we are somewhere else."
—A Course in Miracles

Emmet Fox reminds us that there is no problem that enough love cannot cure. I believe that the more we commit to living in a sea of love, the more we can actually feel the light of love in everyday situations of all kinds, the more progress we make toward the goal of living truly free no matter what outer circumstances look like.

When I retired from my ministry in Cincinnati, Ohio, I had a very long drive to Texas. In a small town just inside the state line, a policeman pulled me over and said I was speeding. I didn't think I was, but knew it would be fruitless to argue. Turns out the little town of Timpson, Texas is a well known speed trap. I was cited for going 53 in a 40 speed limit zone. The fine? One hundred and eighty dollars! So, if you ever happen to pass through there, drive slowly! Observing myself, I found that reading and re-reading so much of Byron Katie and her ideas about loving what is, has actually rubbed off on me! I was and am able to shrug my shoulders and say, "it is what it is." Since there is nothing I can do about this, there is no point in being upset.

Now, I am unpacking boxes and getting settled. I thought about postponing my weekly message for another week, but I find that sharing these messages is actually very therapeutic and centering in the midst of the "in process" house settling. It feels good to know that I actually have missed this process. Helps me to know I'm track.

A Course in Miracles reminded me this morning that it is actually impossible to be separated from the love of God and from each other. When we can't feel this, we are having a bad dream. So, the idea is to wake up and realize that we do actually live in love. Love has tremendous power. Many of you have heard of Peace Pilgrim who walked all over the country teaching peace. The only possessions she carried were in her apron pocket. As a penniless pilgrim, she walked until given shelter and fasted until given food. She trusted and loved God and everyone around her. One day when it got cold and she needed something warmer, she found a box of warm clothes under an overpass on the highway.

She made her transition as she walked on a rural road in Indiana in 1981. She had spent 28 years walking more than 25,000 miles all across America. She spoke to thousands of individuals and groups, sharing her message of love and peace. Of course, she had many varied encounters, some with violent and confused people. She survived and thrived because she was very intuitive and sensitive to her surroundings, and most importantly, tuned into and living in the Divine Sea of Love.

One day she was picked up by a young man, and very soon she realized that his intention was to beat and rape her. Immediately she began sending him love. After some conversation, she said: "You know, I'm very tired and I need to rest. I feel very safe with you, so if you don't mind, I'm going to take a nap." The result was that the man did not attack her. Something transformed in him and he decided that she needed protection. He offered to travel with her and help protect her,—which he did for several years.

When we come to the point of living in love, we have let go of our fears and then we are indeed divinely protected. The nightmare of fear and separation is over and we wake up in love, peace, and joy. We can push ourselves, test ourselves and be mindful of the goal of love in all the instances of daily life.

When I was living in Idaho and doing my two mile walk on our country roads, I was put to a test. While walking, I was listening to some tapes by archeologist Maria Gambutus about the goddess culture in central Europe and some of the traditions. It seems that medicine women and healers would milk snakes, (I don't know how one would do this) and green snakes brought particularly good luck and power. In the road ahead, I saw a green snake, and bees were buzzing around the snake as it was trying to get away. Snakes have always been a challenge for me. One day my brother hid behind a tree until I was close to him, and then he waved a snake in my face! I ran down the street screaming for dear life!

But now, I decided to put myself to the test. I actually picked up the little green snake and moved it into some grass on the side of the road! Just for a minute, I was able to do something loving for a snake. That taught me that we do have a choice. We don't have to follow the old patterns. We have so much more power than we know. We are love; we are part of God; it's all God. We can learn to "teach only love,—for that is what we are!"

I invite you to take the love challenge today—to be "in love" with life and with everyone and every circumstance you encounter. Even traffic tickets and snakes! Let us set a holy intention to be an emissary of love, mercy, and generosity to all we meet, both in our mind and in our world. Let us affirm: "Love comes forth to meet me, and in joy we recognize one another."God blesses you and fills this day and every day with love.

Love is All There Is

"The Eskimos have fifty-two names for snow because
It is important to them; we ought to have as many for love."
—Margaret Atwood

Jesus tells us: "You shall love the lord your god with all your heart, and with all your soul, and with all your mind. This is the greatest and the first commandment. The second is like unto it: you shall love your neighbor as yourself." And "By this everyone will know that you are my disciples, if you have love for one another."

Isaiah: "For the mountains may depart, and the hills be removed, but my steadfast love shall not depart from you, and my covenant of peace shall not be removed."

Jeremiah: "I have loved you with an everlasting love."

We cannot separate love from God, nor God from love. In truth we cannot separate ourselves from love and God. We can separate ourselves from the personal experience of the love of God; from our awareness of it, but nonetheless it is always there, nearer than breathing and closer than hands and feet. It is actually a form of insanity to separate our awareness from the love of God when we want love more than anything in the world.

So why do we do it? Our human ego encourages us to continually seek and never find. It lives off negativity, fear and endless drama. We have to learn to choose love—to accept the love of God. Our ego tricks us into believing such things as: I can love myself *after* I lose weight, *after* I get my degree, when I stop losing my patience. I can love you when you get sober, drop your bad habits, clean up your act, stop irritating me. Our inability to see clearly becomes our disability—our handicap—the only way to be healed is to allow God/Holy Spirit/The Christ the Spirit of Truth into our hearts and minds. We all need healing, but we resist giving up our disabilities because we fear we'll have to sacrifice something our ego wants.

This humorous story of Jesus in a bar illustrates the point beautifully:

The bartender was washing glasses when an elderly Irishman came in and with great difficulty, hoisted his bad leg over the bar stool, pulled himself up painfully, and asked for a sip of whiskey. The Irishman looked down the bar and said, "Is that Jesus down there?" The bartender nodded and the Irishman told him to give Jesus an Irish whiskey also.

The next patron was an ailing Italian with a hunched back and slowness of movement. He shuffled up to the barstool and asked for a glass of Chianti. He also looked down the bar and asked if that was Jesus sitting down there. The bartender nodded and the Italian said to give Him a glass of Chianti.

The third patron, a good 'ol boy, swaggered in and hollered,barkeep, set me up a cold one. Hey is that God's Boy down there?" The barkeep nodded, and the guy told him to give Jesus a cold one too.

As Jesus got up to leave, he walked over to the Irishmen and touched him and said, "For your kindness, you are healed!" The Irishman felt the strength come back to his leg, and he got up and danced a jig to the door. Jesus touched the Italian and said, For your kindness YOU are healed!"

The Italian felt his back straighten and he raised his hands above his head and did a flip out the door. As Jesus walked toward the last patron, the good 'ol boy jumped back and exclaimed, "Don't touch ME! I'm drawing Disability!"

Question for ourselves? Do we want to be healed? Do we want the love of God to flow thru our lives or not? Are we willing to pay the price of letting go of our judgments, grievances, and need to control? Are we willing to forgive everyone and everything? If not, we are like the guy in the story, always holding back, always resisting the touch of Spirit. We have to be willing to disrupt our lives, change our lives and be constantly willing to see things differently if we are going to be open and receptive to the love of God. Without the awareness of God's love, we're "drawin' disability!"

The following is a true story of a Vietnam vet, just returning home. He called his parents from San Francisco. "Mom and Dad, I'm coming home, but I have a favor to ask. I have a friend I'd like to bring with me." "Sure," they replied, "We'd love to meet him." "There's something you should know, "the son continued, "He was hurt pretty badly in the fighting. He stepped on a land mine and lost an arm and a leg. He has nowhere else to go, and I want to bring him home to live with us." "I'm sorry about that son. Maybe we can help find him somewhere to live." "No Mom and Dad, I want him to live with us."

"Son," answered the father, "you don't know what you're asking. Someone with such a handicap would be a terrible burden on us. We have our own lives to live, and we can't let something like this interfere with our own lives. I think you should just come home and forget about this guy. He will find a way to live on his own."

At that point, the son hung up the phone. The parents heard nothing more from him. A few days later, however, they received a call from the San Francisco police. Their son had died after falling from a building, they were told. The police believed it was suicide. The grief stricken parents flew to San Francisco and were taken to the city morgue to identify the body of their son. They recognized him, but to their horror they also discovered something they didn't know; their son had only one arm and one leg.

The parents in this story are like many of us. We don't want to deal with people who inconvenience us or make us uncomfortable. We would rather stay away from people who aren't as healthy, good looking, or as smart as we are. But what does Love teach us? To extend our love unconditionally, to love people just the way they are. Jesus was constantly criticized for reaching out to people that were social outcasts. He reached out to people of other cultures and belief systems. He spent time and ate with people that were defiled and hated by others. He chose to keep the high watch of not judging them by appearances or by what they may have done in the past. He chose not to withhold his love; instead he chose to extend his love—and therefore taught us all by his example.

Sometimes find ourselves around family and friends that are different from us. They may have had problems, or they may have a lifestyle that we find hard to accept. They may be of different religion, or none at all. However, we can choose to make a decision for unconditional love. It's not our business to decide who needs fixing; let's just hold everyone in the light of God and trust Spirit to do whatever fixing needs to be done. Most important of all: decide to allow the Christ of love to be born anew in you today and every day. Decide to surrender to the love you are. Stay off spiritual disability.

Love Never Ends

"Throw your heart over the fence
And the rest will follow."
—Norman Vincent Peale

We can trust the love of God for us. "For the mountains may depart and the hills be removed, but my steadfast love shall not depart from you."(Isaiah 54:10) We can trust the love of God and we can trust that same love as our true nature. At Christmastime we celebrate the birth of the Christ child which took place over 2,000 years ago. But the birth of the Christ child here and now within our own hearts brings about the birth of a love in us that never ends and that transcends the way much of the world looks at love.

Let's explore the true spiritual nature of love. It is more than "giving to get," more than expecting others to fill a vacuum in our lives. In truth the kind of love that never ends, the kind of love that comes from our Christ nature is the kind of love that loses sight of separate interests, the kind of love that understands that in the end we don't have separate interests.

Love, like truth and beauty, is concrete. Love goes beyond sweet feelings, sentiment and attachment. Love is a choice, not always a rational choice, but a willingness to keep our hearts open. Love is a willingness to join with others in the healing of our world. Love is the choice to experience life as an equal member of the human family, an equal partner in the dance of life, rather than as a separate soul with separate interests, feeling better than some and worse than others. In each moment we have a choice to make—to see through the eyes of love and unity or of separation and judgment.

A Course in Miracles teaches us that to truly love we must see the innocence in ourselves and others beyond mistakes and errors. Our job is to forgive and love. Once we do this the Course tells us: "All of your past except its beauty is gone, and nothing is left but a blessing." It is our job to "teach only love" for that is indeed our true identity—that is what we are. We can teach innocence and love by our actions or thoughts; in words or soundlessly, in any language or in no language; in any place or manner. We become teachers of God when we see that we have no interests apart from anyone else's. That is love. Even at the level of the most casual encounter, it is possible for people to lose sight of separate interests, if only for a moment.

I'd like to share the following internet story with you:
Breakfast at McDonald's

I am a mother of three and recently completed my college degree. The last class I had to take was Sociology. The teacher was absolutely inspiring with the qualities that I wish every human being had been graced with. The class was instructed to go out and smile at three people and to document their reactions. I am a very friendly person and always smile at everyone and say hello anyway.

Soon after we were assigned the project, my husband, youngest son, and I went out to McDonald's one crisp March morning. It was our way of sharing special playtime with our son. We were standing in line, waiting to be served, when all of a sudden everyone around us began to back away, and then even my husband did. A feeling of panic welled up inside of me as I turned to see why they had moved. As I turned around I smelled a horrible "dirty body" smell, and there standing behind me were two poor homeless men. I looked down at the short gentleman, close to me

& he was smiling. His beautiful sky blue eyes were full of God's Light as he searched for acceptance. He said, "Good day" as he counted the few coins he had been clutching. The second man fumbled with his hands as he stood behind his friend. I realized the second man was mentally challenged and the blue-eyed gentleman was his salvation.

The young lady at the counter asked him what they wanted. He said, "Coffee is all Miss" because that was all they could afford. If they wanted to sit in the restaurant and warm up, they had to buy something. Then I really felt it—the compulsion was so great I almost reached out and embraced the little man with the blue eyes. That is when I noticed all eyes in the restaurant were set on me, judging my every action. I smiled and asked the young lady behind the counter to give me two more breakfast meals on a separate tray. I then walked around the corner to the table that the men had chosen as a resting spot. I put the tray on the table and laid my hand on the blue-eyed gentleman's cold hand. He looked up at me, with tears in his eyes, and said, "Thank you."

I leaned over to pat his hand and said, "I did not do this for you. God is here working through me to give you hope." I started to cry as I walked away to join my husband and son. When I sat down my husband smiled at me and said, "That is why God gave you to me, Honey, to give me hope."

We held hands for a moment and we knew that only because of the Grace that we had been given were we able to give. That day showed me the pure Light of God's sweet love. I returned to college, on the last evening of class, with this story in hand. I turned in "my project" and the instructor read it aloud to the class. As she began to read, I knew that we as human beings, one with each other and one with God, are only truly alive when we are loving one another.

True God Love extends itself; it is not interested in what it can get but in what it can give. It does not see another person's interests as separate. It knows that we all have an equal stake in transforming our world into one of love. Another facet of true God love is this: Love never ends and it is not limited. Love extends beyond physical bodies, beyond so called death. It is natural to miss the presence of a loved one's physical body, the loss of the ability to call on the phone or share a meal or just be physically close.

However, the truth is that we are not separated from the spirit of that loved one. I am as close to my son Richard who left his body years ago as I am to my two other children who are still here in Earth School with me. The truth is that we are not our bodies; we are free with the freedom of spirit. The Truth is that we are all dressed up in earth suit costumes—our naked truth is that we are spirit—eternal, ageless, and one with God.

The highest use of our body, our earth suit costume, is to use it to communicate love to one another. Whether we realize it or not, we are always communicating either love or fear, either oneness or separation. We choose each moment what it will be. It can be very difficult to realize that everyone, with no exception, is a beloved child of God. Jesus said: "Inasmuch as ye do it unto the least of these, my brethren, ye do it unto me." When we get angry at anyone for any reason, we need to remember we are really angry at God disguised in an earth suit. To mistreat anyone is to mistreat God. And because we are an equal part of God, we are also mistreating ourselves. If we could truly learn this lesson beyond it being just a mental exercise, we could save thousands of years of useless suffering.

When I first more consciously began my spiritual journey, I listened to a recording of Ram Dass over and over again. In this recording he read a piece that was found on a Norman Crucifix dated 1632. He read it reverently and it obviously was a great teaching for him. At the time I respected that, but I could not quite get it. Now years later, I'm beginning to understand the point, not just in my head, but in my heart.

It is all about the truth that God is present here and now and you and I and everyone around us is an expression of that same God. Perhaps a flawed expression, but still an expression that can help us learn to love unconditionally if we will simply "throw our hearts over the fence" and trust that all else will follow. God is reminding us in this reading that too much of the time we forget our Spirit, our God Self and turn away from its expression in those around us:

> I AM the great Sun, but you do not see me;
> I am your spouse, but you turn away;
> I am the captive, but you do not free me;
> I am the captain you will not obey.
> I am the Truth, but you will not believe me;
> I am the city where you will not stay;
> I am your child, but you will leave me;
> I am that God to whom you will not pray.
> I am your counsel but you do not hear me;
> I am your lover whom you will betray;
> I am the victor, but you do not cheer me;
> I am the Holy Dove whom you will slay.
> I am your Life, but if you will not name me,
> Seal your soul with tears, and never blame me.

Closing Prayer:

Dear Father, Mother God: May we learn to see and appreciate your presence in everyone without exception. May we truly see past all disguises, mistakes and errors to Your Presence in All. May the Christ continually be born anew in our hearts. We open our hearts and invite you in; we embrace your Presence in ourselves and in all those we encounter. We are grateful for your Grace. Amen.

Love's Demonstrations

"When someone knows the song of your soul,
They sing it back to you when you have forgotten."
—A Course in Miracles

Quite awhile ago I received a heartfelt email request from a dear friend whose family member had just made her transition. I received permission from Rick to share his email and his prayer request. All too often we get caught up in thinking love is all about earth suits and how we show up in them. It is so much deeper than that. It is two souls coming together to share love and support, and it does not always look exactly like we might imagine. I will let Rick's letter speak for itself and ask you to keep him and his wife Dana and extended family members in the light of your thoughts and prayers:

Dear Julie, I don't recall if I ever told you much about my nephew Tony and his partner Melissa. Tony just turned 40 this past March and I think Melissa was around 33 or 34. They met about 10 or12 years ago at the community college where they were both students. Melissa fell and although she had numerous health problems died quite unexpectedly early Wednesday morning. My older sister Ruth and her first husband adopted Tony when he had just turned three from an orphanage in Korea.

He was blind and only knew 17 words in Korean. He had been dropped off at a police station within the first few days of his birth and brought to the orphanage. When I first met him he had been in America for around three months. He was still learning to swallow. Apparently at the orphanage the children were never sure when, how often or how much they might eat.

As a survival mechanism they would pack their cheeks, not unlike a chipmunk, to save some food for later. Tony's lack of both sight and height, he's about 4'7," are most assuredly from malnutrition. Ruth wanted to adopt a child that would not have a chance, and so she did. Armed with a masters in special education and being blind herself she was much better equipped than most to raise such a child.

Tony has grown to be a sweet loving man. Melissa saw his sweetness. These two are truly the embodiment of someone for everyone. They began dating. Melissa had her own problems. She had genetically short heel cords which did not allow her heels to touch the ground and could only walk for very short distances up on her toes on her own. She used a wheelchair and despite surgeries, none successful, she became essentially wheelchair bound.

Other health issues surfaced and eventually Melissa had a pain pump placed in her body. Although this brought her some comfort it also brought more surgeries. In the last few years Melissa spent way too much time in hospitals and nursing homes. She was also losing her sight and was unable to read even large print although she could see to travel and was a pretty good cook.

Eventually Tony and Melissa got an apartment together which they shared for several years. It is in a building designed for handicapped individuals and the rent is based on a percent of income. They would have married but in just another of our maddening regulations, the nation which screams family values, would have cut their benefits by about a third. That's hard to do when you're just getting by.

They put together a rewarding life with each other. As my sister Barb said, Melissa really seemed to "get" Tony. She noted that she saw more love in their relationship than most couples she knew. So often those who are different in our society are not seen. This is sometimes by choice sometimes by circumstance, not Tony and Melissa.

He was the power and she was the guide as he pushed her in her wheelchair. They went about their life going to the grocery store, the mall, the movies, a game room, restaurant and out and about. They had many friends in their building and would have game nights or people over for dinner. Despite all of their inconveniences as a couple they truly prevailed in living a life that all of us can admire. I worry about Tony. Not just for his loss but for all of the changes. Melissa was a great money manager, Tony not so much. Melissa was the cook and nutritionist, Tony the junk food junky; she was his lover, his friend, his partner.

My heart is in pieces. I'm just so sad over this state of affairs. At this point in our lives we've all lost parents and friends, and in your life Julie, even a child. I cannot imagine the heartbreak. My sister Barb said that this is the one time where she just really wished she could go back in time and change this. I take some consolation that Melissa is no longer in pain. And I like to believe she will go on to new and better circumstances.

Please say a prayer for Melissa and for Tony, and for my sister Ruth and her husband Jim who invested so much in caring for both of these sweet souls, for Barb a loving and caring aunt, for my brother Steve who I am sure is quite saddened as well and for Dana who always treated them both with an open heart, kindness and respect. Thank you.

It is obvious that Tony and Melissa knew the soul song of one another and sang it back to each other if ever they forgot. I have been thinking quite a bit lately about reincarnation and soul choice. Perhaps these two souls came together to demonstrate how beautiful love can be regardless of what challenges the earth suit may have. I'm not going to add more to this beautiful sharing and request. It speaks eloquently for itself.

Dear Father Mother God: We see Melissa safe and secure and at One with you in spirit. We see Tony being guided and directed, supported and loved; we see his soul advancing; we see him true to his soul song and open to the ongoing vision and love that Melissa will always share with him. We bless him and ask that all his extended family and friends receive Your comfort and peace. Amen

Relationships: A Path to God

"In each human being there is a meeting with the Divine.
That intersection is the human heart."
—Coleman Barks

Have you ever had a thought like this? "If I didn't have to deal with these turkeys, my life would be just fine?" Or: "You don't have to be a cannibal to get fed up with people?" Someone once defined Christians as those who love God and hate other people. Our basic challenge here in earth school is to deal with people!

Jesus said the supreme commandment is "to love God with all your heart, soul and strength and to love your neighbor as yourself." It's easy to feel holy and pure in isolation, on spiritual highs. The challenging task is to bring love into our everyday encounters. Earth school is a laboratory where we are called upon to prove, demonstrate, and live what we say we believe.

If we want to work with our relationships as a pathway to God, we must include all encounters with others, as well as our relationship with ourselves. It is important to pay attention to what we're thinking and feeling and learn to notice when we are coming from love and spirit and when we're coming from fear and ego. We start by recognizing ego for what it is, a sense of separation from God and from one another. Ego wants to keep us trapped in lower levels of consciousness. It wants to blame those around us for our unhappiness or discomfort, and it pretends to seek love while believing it is nowhere to be found. Breakthroughs come when we begin to take responsibility for the way we feel, when we begin to realize that we set up the experiences that we take as real!

The human ego tends to categorize and establish pecking orders. It dehumanizes outcasts, misfits, and anyone who is "down and out." Yet, Jesus taught us; "Inasmuch as ye do it unto the least of these, my brethren, ye do it unto me." That statement is true because we are one with the Divine in us, one with the Christ in us and one with everyone else. There is only *one* presence and power. We say the words, but do we really live by them? We might want to ask ourselves: "Was I rude to God when he/she waited on me?" "Did I ignore God when he/she asked for food?" Do I judge God when he/she makes mistakes on the human level?" Ernest Holmes reminded us that "Our love must be expressed for all people! Most of us are afraid to love that much because we can't conceive of a love that includes all."

Where can we start? Start here and now with a person that bugs you or irritates you. Begin in your mind to visualize that person in pink love light. Although you may not feel differently right away, practice the visualization and watch your attitude and your relationship change. That person is part of God just as much as a wave is part of the ocean. There are no exceptions.

The next challenge is to continually seek to support and encourage others, beginning with those nearest and dearest to you. Some of the greatest success stories in history have followed a word of encouragement or an act of confidence by a loved one or trusted friend. Had it not been for the confident wife of Nathanial Hawthorne, the world might not have been enriched by his literature.

Nathanial was heartbroken when he went home to tell his wife Sophia that he was a failure and had been fired from his job in a customhouse. She surprised him with an exclamation of joy. "Now," she said triumphantly, "You can write your book!" He replied, "But how can we live while I'm writing it?" To his amazement she opened a drawer and pulled out a substantial amount of money. "Where on earth did you get that?" he exclaimed. "I always felt you were a man of genius," she told him. "I knew that someday you would write a masterpiece. So, every week, out of the money you gave me for housekeeping, I saved a little bit. So here is enough to last us for a whole year." From her trust and confidence came one of the greatest novels of American literature, *The Scarlet Letter.*

We cannot love totally and open heartedly unless we become as little children. We can't hold back. Again Jesus taught: "Unless ye become as little children, you can't enter the kingdom of Heaven." We must be pure hearted in our loving, as pure hearted as the little boy in this true story told by Dan Millman:

"When I worked as a volunteer at Stanford Hospital, I got to know a little girl named Liza who was suffering from a rare and serious disease. Her only chance of recovery appeared to be a blood transfusion from her five year old brother, who had miraculously survived the same disease and had developed the antibodies needed to combat the illness. The doctor explained the situation to her little brother and asked the boy if he would be willing to give his blood to his sister. I saw him hesitate for only a moment before taking a deep breath and saying, 'Yes, I'll do it if it will save Liza.'

"As the transfusion progressed, he lay in a bed next to his sister and smiled, as we all did, seeing the color return to her cheeks. Then his face grew pale and his smile faded. He looked up at the doctor and asked with a trembling voice, 'Will I start to die right away?' The little boy had misunderstood the doctor; he thought he was going to have to give his sister *all* of his blood." This is certainly an incredible and concrete example of being willing to lay down our life for our brother.

Conditional love says, "I'll love you IF you please me, IF you do what I think you should do, IF I approve of your actions." Unconditional love is a beautiful thing. It says," I love you whether you please me or not, whether you do what I ask or not, whether I approve of what you do or not. I distinguish the essence of you from your human actions and mistakes, and thus I love you unconditionally."

At the same time, it is important to establish appropriate boundaries with others. We can love unconditionally and at the same time not allow others to abuse us physically, verbally or emotionally. We can love while removing ourselves from harmful situations. We must learn to honor the divinity in ourselves and to love and respect ourselves as much as we love and respect others. It is possible to separate actions from the essence of the soul.

Finally, it is never too late to learn from our relationships. We can go back and forgive, release, heal, and extend unconditional love, even after someone has dropped the earth suit and passed on into their next experience. In the end it is impossible to progress spiritually without cleaning up our relationships with others. It is equally important to deal every day here and now with the opportunities to love that come to us. The following is a wonderful example:

Too often we feel alone. But there is always someone ready to take our hand. A tired overworked nurse escorted a tired young man to her patient's bedside. Leaning over and speaking loudly to the elderly patient, she said, "Your son is here." With great effort, his unfocused eyes opened, then flickered shut again. The young man squeezed the aged hand in his and sat beside the bed. Throughout the night he sat there, holding the old man's hand and whispering words of comfort.

By morning's light, the patient had died. In moments, the hospital staff swarmed into the room to turn off machines and remove needles. The nurse stepped over to the young man's side and began to offer sympathy, but he interrupted her. "Who was that man?" he asked. The startled nurse replied, 'I thought he was your father!" "No, he was not my father," he answered. I never saw him before in my life." The nurse then asked, "why didn't you say something when I took you to him:" The young man explained, "I realized he needed his son and his son wasn't here. And since he was too sick to recognize that I was not his son, I knew he needed me." (from a subscriber to Positive Daily Inspiration, a Rev.Chris Chenoweth online ministry.)

Mother Teresa reminded us that nobody should have to die alone. No one should have to grieve alone or cry alone either. Or laugh alone or celebrate alone. We are made to travel life's journey hand in hand. There is someone ready to grasp your hand today. And someone hoping you will take theirs. This is how we can use our encounters and relationships to awaken to the presence and power of God, right where we stand. God is love; we are not separate from God; therefore, in truth, we are love. Our task is to embrace and to express the truth and the love of the divinity in us, nearer than breathing, closer than hands and feet. Let's go forth and love our way to enlightenment.

Remembering My Mothers

Safe passage, pilgrims of the spirit.
Peace be with you on your way back home.
You are in my heart as you travel nearer.
Safe journey; now your work is done.

—unknown

It has been over twelve years now since both my Mothers made their transitions. One mother, Ruth, was my birth mother who was no doubt traumatized by the situation around her pregnancy with me; she was only 15 when I was born. I was raised by my maternal grandmother until I was nine; then I was adopted. My new mother—Mama Mary and my new family provided the stability I desperately needed, although there would be challenges later there as well.

But on this Mother's Day weekend, I want to pay tribute to all mothers and specifically to remember with love my own mothers. In many ways I actually had three mothers if I include the grandmother Florence who raised me (sporadically) until I was nine. I felt love from each of them and I have always loved each of them. Wise teachers have pointed out that we are all one big family and that sometimes we receive the nurturing we need from those outside our birth families. I have noticed over the years that this is so. I have had close friendships with many people who have been like family to me. I suppose on some deep level I have related to them as surrogate mothers and fathers, sisters and brothers.

I truly believe that we choose our parents and our circumstances in between our earth school lives. And we sometimes ask, "Why in the world would

I have chosen these difficulties?" There is a two part answer that makes sense to me: 1) because we are balancing our karmic debts 2) because we set up the circumstances to create an opportunity to express forgiveness and unconditional love. It has been healing for me to use my own journey through difficult circumstances to help others.

It seems that it is the very specific souls with whom we need to finish business that often form our birth families. The result is that many people do not experience that perfect Hallmark family. The challenge is to understand, love and forgive with the idea that our circumstances were and are exactly as they are supposed to be. We can go on from where we are now to make changes if we so choose. I love the idea that "it's never too late to have a happy childhood." Why? Because we can understand and forgive, love and re-parent our child.

I have mothered my own inner child, Julie May, all the while growing in understanding and forgiveness, which all comes together as unconditional love for myself and my mothers and extends out into a large circle of love for all others as my extended human family. I think this is what Jesus was urging us to do when he said: "Love one another."

I have not been a perfect mother myself, but I have never faltered in my love for my children. I have made mistakes to the degree that I was unhealed at the time I made those mistakes. I have come to understand that being unhealed is exactly how and why everyone, including parents, makes mistakes which can hurt those close to them. It turns out that the majority of humankind is in dire need of psychological and spiritual healing.

We have choices to make. We can make it our business to find the help we need to heal in order to get to a place of understanding, love and forgiveness. Or we can just muddle along in an unhealed state which only ultimately hurts ourselves and those around us. I invite you on this Mother's Day weekend (or at any time) to think about what needs healing in regard to your mother and to send love and blessings to her, whether she is still here or on the other side. It's never too late to take care of the business of love and forgiveness.

If you have already healed those issues that need to be healed regarding your mother, you are blessed. If more healing needs to be done, the time is always right to work on that. If she has gone on, of course you will miss her, but know that the soul is ongoing. You have been with her before and probably will be again. I miss my mothers and wish I could just pick up the phone and call. However, I can remember them with love, and this remembering with love is another kind of call that reaches out and embraces them wherever they are. Please remember that you too can always reach out and finish business and embrace your own mother wherever she may be.

Stick With Love

"I have decided to stick with love.
Hate is too great a burden to bear."
—Martin Luther King, Jr.

We can't deny the ugliness of war, murder, and outrageous cruelties of all kinds, not to mention disease, accidents and natural disasters. When we try to figure out the "why" of it, it's too much to wrap our mind around. Many people become cynics and live in anger and bitterness. I have been there myself, and I understand the frustration of it all.

Ultimately the questions become, "what can we do about the darkness? Is there a way to stay sane in an insane world? How shall we live?" Writers, philosophers, saints, religious leaders and just about everyone else has tried to unravel the answers to these questions.

Many years ago Father James Keller founded the order of Christopher's—a group of spiritual optimists. He is most remembered by the following two statements. "Better to light one little candle than to curse the darkness." And "A candle loses nothing by lighting another candle."

Although we cannot single handedly wipe out darkness, we can light our own candle, and we can pass on the light we have. I believe that our Earth School assignment is to love and to do good where and how we can. In spite of the magnitude of hatred and darkness which the media highlights, there is even a greater magnitude of everyday goodness, caring, kindness, helpfulness, and yes even love.

Turns out we have a choice. We can become mired in the darkness and curse it, or we can choose to stand in the light and pass it on. Most of us have our dark and challenging times when we need help. There are those times when we need to be givers and at other times gracious and grateful receivers.

At this time in Tallahassee I am grateful for the support and for the welcome. At the same time I rejoice that I might be helpful—to give aid and comfort to those who want spiritual support and guidance here in Tallahassee and everywhere my internet ministry travels. A Course in Miracles says giving and receiving are one and the same. I believe that is true. I'd like to share the following story:

The Whale: If you read a recent front page story of the San Francisco Chronicle, you read about a whale entangled in a spider web of crab traps and lines. She was weighted down by hundreds of pounds of traps that caused her to struggle to stay afloat. She also had hundreds of yards of line rope wrapped around her body, her tail, her torso, and a line tugging in her mouth. A fisherman spotted her just east of the Farallon Islands (outside the Golden Gate) and radioed an environmental group for help.

Within a few hours, the rescue team arrived and determined that she was so bad off, the only way to save her was to dive in and untangle her. They worked for hours with curved knives and eventually freed her. When this whale was free, the divers say she swam in what seemed like joyous circles. She then came back to each and every diver, one at a time, and nudged them, pushed them gently around—she was thanking them. Some said it was the most incredibly beautiful experience of their lives. The guy who cut the rope out of her mouth said her eyes were following him the whole time, and he will never be the same. May you, and all those you love, be so blessed and fortunate to be surrounded by people who will help you get untangled from the things that are binding you.

Let us all accept the help we need when we get so tangled up in life that we cannot go it alone. And also let us all be ready and willing to help others who are tangled up in their life and cannot go it alone. Remember: a candle loses nothing by passing along its own light. We lose nothing by passing along our own light; on the contrary we are blessed, nourished, and rewarded in ways we could never predict. The golden rule never goes out of date or style: "Do unto others as you would have them do unto you." We can't lose if we stick with love.

The Loving Eyes of God

If, for even one moment,
you can look at someone with the eyes of true love,
you'll know those eyes are not yours.
Those are the eyes of God looking out through you.
—Michael Singer

It is a challenge for us to totally accept the statements: God is love. God is all there is. Love is all there is. We have been programmed to believe that God is a judge and we'd better watch out for His punishment. We've been taught that we'd better always put ourselves first in this dog eat dog world. We'd better be a competitor in every arena we find ourselves in; if we come out on top, maybe we can find peace and happiness.

When I was a little girl, I was neglected sexually abused and left alone a lot. Yet, somehow I knew that God was good, that I was good, and that life would get better. Through a lot of ups and downs I still hung on to that belief. But at the same time I picked up some error thinking. From listening to soap operas on the radio, I picked up the belief that if I found the perfect man to be with, life would indeed be beautiful.

I found a wonderful guy that I fell in love with right away, but he had a problem my 18 year old mind believed I could fix with enough love. He was an alcoholic. So I prayed to God in the form of bargaining, "Please God made him stop drinking. I'll love him and be a perfect wife and mother."

Nothing changed, so I became angry with God and started to dwell upon the unfairness of life. This was played out further by the death of our oldest son, the serious illness of the second son, and my husband's affair that resulted in her pregnancy. They woke me up in the middle of one Saturday night (of course they had been drinking) and gave me the news.

I was 29 years old with a high school education and a hateful bitter attitude. So where was the truth of God is love; God is all there is; love is all there is? It was definitely buried and covered over. The truth was and is always there, but I was blind to it. "There is none so blind who will not see." We abandon the love and grace of God when our fears, ignorance and bitterness take us over and rule our life. However, the good news is that the love and grace of God never abandon us.

Even through all the anger and bitterness, I was a reader, a seeker, always looking for answers. Why do people do what they do? Is there any sense to life? What is it for? Even in the midst of just trying to survive and take care of my children, I asked these questions. I had to experience a number of trials and tribulations before I opened to the answers, before I finally opened to the love and grace of God. Yet, it did not eliminate earth school challenges. We'll continue to have them as long as we're here. But I learned to see and handle them in an entirely different way—the spiritual way, the way of a higher viewpoint.

The Bible tells us: "Seek and ye shall find; knock and the door shall be opened; ask and it shall be given." This does not mean ego seeking, knocking, and asking, because the ego's aim is to seek and never find. It means sincere spiritual seeking; it means becoming humble enough to admit that "on the human level my life is unmanageable and I need help." It means being willing to heal and forgive the past and move on.

It means the willingness to put spiritual teachings into practice in our everyday lives.

Fortunately, the grace and love of God keep surrounding us even in the midst of our confusion. Right in the middle of mine, my brother Will inspired me to start college. He was doing it while working and supporting his family, and I opened my mind to the possibility for myself. At the age of 36, I finished college with a master's degree and started teaching at Ferris State University in Michigan.

My life definitely changed for the better, but I still had much to learn. The bottom line is that the grace and love of God never leaves us. We can shut it out, turn our backs, ignore it and go down our accustomed paths of misery, but nonetheless it is always there, right in the midst of our triumphs and our disasters, ours for the accepting.

There is one prerequisite: we must stop judging and blaming ourselves and others, which means we must forgive ourselves and others. Judgment and non-forgiveness are like dark blinders over our eyes that keep us from seeing the light of truth about ourselves and our brothers and sisters. Judgment and non-forgiveness pit us against each other, and because we are one in Spirit, we only attack ourselves.

The following words are about a turnaround in consciousness: "The God I understood was one I couldn't and wouldn't accept as my God. In my willfulness, I rejected hearing any notions of other concepts of God. When I began to make the connection between my healing and another way of understanding God, shifts of incredible proportions occurred in my thinking, my emotions, my very being. I was amazed that although I had so vehemently rejected God, God had never rejected me.

I always had some connection with the God that is the love deep inside me, but I had never realized what it was. The Loving Presence had been calling to me and available to me always. As I allowed myself to accept that love and to develop a trusting relationship with it, other forces in me—guilt, shame, fear, anger—lost power. Slowly I began to realize that life's events were not to be taken personally.

Energy spent on blame was wasted. Energy spent on forgiveness was life-giving. I snipped away at the ties that bound me to past hurts, disappointments, and error thinking. I began to grow into a person who could be fully present to my gifts, my joy, my inner peace, and my loving nature. I became free to be me." (unknown author)

Course in Miracles reminds us: "Heaven is the natural state of all the sons of God as He created them. Such is their reality forever. It has not changed because it has been forgotten. Forgiveness is the means by which we will remember. Through forgiveness the thinking of the world is reversed. The forgiven world becomes the gate of Heaven, because by its mercy we can at last forgive ourselves. Holding no one prisoner to guilt, we become free.

Acknowledging Christ in all our brothers, we recognize His Presence in ourselves. Forgetting all our misperceptions, and with nothing from the past to hold us back, we can remember God. Beyond this, learning cannot go. When we are ready, God Himself will take the final step in our return to Him."

Prayer is an important piece of the puzzle in the journey which will take us back to the memory of the Loving Presence. We have misunderstood the true purpose of prayer. We have believed that prayer is asking for special favors. I asked God for special intervention in my marriage and it did not happen; therefore I became bitter and lost faith. When we pray from the ego viewpoint of wanting something, we pray amiss.

Spiritual progress comes when we surrender to the will of God, and pray "thy kingdom come, Thy will be done." We begin to pray for divine order and highest good; we trust that God knows what is best; we trust that God does not play favorites,—that what is best for one is also best for the other, no matter what it looks like on the human level.

The highest form of prayer is meditation and contemplation—just "hanging out" with God with no agenda other than to tune into love and peace. One of my favorite affirmations from A Course in Miracles is this: "I will be still and let the earth be still along with me. And in that stillness we will find the peace of God. It is within my heart, which witnesses to God Himself."

I will close with two poems of wisdom by Kabir, a mystical poet with a divine sense of humor. He was born in India in 1440. He says, "The thirsty fish in the water needs serious professional counseling!" Yes, we hunger for God, Love, and Truth when we are already swimming in it!

The Smart Dogs Ran Off
I sat one day with a priest who
expounded on the doctrine of hell.
I listened to him for hours,
then he asked me what I thought of all he said.
And I replied, 'that doctrine seems an inhumane cage;
no wonder the smart dogs ran off!

What Kind of God?

And what kind of God would He be
if the vote of millions in this world
could sway Him to change the divine law
of love that speaks so clearly
with compassion's elegant tongue,
saying, eternally saying: all are forgiven.
Moreover, dears, no one has ever been guilty.
What a God—what a God we have.

What better thing for us to do than to spend time hanging out with the Divine Presence in prayer? When we do that, we make space for the loving eyes of God to look at our world through our eyes, and we are blessed beyond measure.

The Many Faces of Fathers

"Remember *only* the *loving thoughts* that you gave
in the past and the *loving thoughts* that were given to you."
—A Course in Miracles

Over one hundred years ago Mark Twain wrote: "When I was a boy of 14, my father was so ignorant; I could hardly stand to have the old man around. But when I got to be 21, I was astonished at how much he had learned in seven years. Father's Day often brings up mixed emotions for us. Perhaps your father has passed on, or you may feel the pain of your father's inadequacies, mistakes or abandonment. You may feel that you yourself have been less than a perfect father;—and that's probably true, because on the human level no man is a perfect father.

An important lesson I've learned in my own life is that many people have experienced what seems like harsh lessons concerning parents who were not capable of skillfully meeting their needs. At a deeper level, we are all "wounded children" to some degree. How should we handle that? What can we do about it? Personally, I never had a human "loving father" experience this lifetime. Living in various homes and sometimes in foster care, then adopted at age nine by a sexually molesting and alcoholic father, that ideal model was just not there for me. That set up a dramatic dysfunctional life for many years that I describe in my spiritual autobiography, *From Soap Opera to Symphony*.

How did I manage to heal and get on with my life and ultimately live in love peace and joy? The recipe for that is one that works for anyone who will use it. We must realize that "on the human level our lives are unmanageable and we need help." The help we need comes from a higher level that can help us to heal psychologically and provide a clear direction for us to follow, and that level is spiritual. Components of that are "seeing the big picture"—we choose our parents and the circumstances that will help us awaken to our true spirit before we enter this Earth School dimension. We are not victims and never have been, although it often feels like it in the middle of our distress.

Another crucial component is forgiveness of those father figures who through their own ignorance, fear, and wounding, were not healed enough to provide the love and support we needed. I can testify that forgiveness is possible. We do need to remember there is a difference between forgiving and condoning. We can forgive without condoning the action. We certainly don't condone cruel or unskillful behavior; we separate the actor from the action. We just keep peeling the onion skins of our hurt and anger and at the same time ask Holy Spirit to help us forgive and ultimately send love. It is the way to peace and freedom for ourselves.

After I found the Unity teachings and began to pray to Father-Mother God, I saw that I had access to a perfect father—the father God within myself. Because of that, it was possible for me to realize that I have always had all the father love I could possibly ever need—pressed down and running over! In truth, we all have the Father love of God.

Also, by the grace of God, loving human beings can offer healing fatherly experiences that strengthen us along the way. A truly loving experience, no matter how brief, can sustain us for a lifetime. The following story illustrates that point: During World War II, a young Jewish boy was separated from his family and his parents were put to death. The boy was shown no kindness as he was brutalized, worked, and starved. At the end of the war he sick, emaciated, and wandering around in a daze.

On the day of liberation, he was befriended by a group of soldiers who gave him rations and an American flag. One touched his shoulder and spoke encouraging words, hugged him, and told him where to go in the camp to get help. That five minute incident changed that boy's entire life. He eventually immigrated to the United States and decided to become a counselor of disadvantaged and troubled youth. Why? Because he remembered those five minutes of kindness that changed his life. Perhaps stored in your own memory bank are incidents, however brief, of loving kindness extended to you.

It is healing for us to embrace whatever love and kindness that comes into our lives, from whatever source, and build on that. The next step is to become an extender—a giver of love and kindness wherever we are. Those American soldiers probably had no idea of the impact they had on that boy's life, and we may not know what specific impact we may have as we extend love either. However, it is important to let our love light shine. We can never know how our own fathering or mothering of another might positively impact a soul who desperately needs it. Fathering and Mothering does not have to be dependent on biology or even on raising a child; it's a matter of being willing to extend the love of God.

Dear friends, you and I have the capacity to extend love to warm the hearts of others. If you didn't have a good parenting experience, why not reach out and become a Big Brother to a boy who desperately needs it or a Big Sister to a girl whose life could be changed by some loving kindness and attention? It could be just the healing experience you need. You cannot reach out and help another without helping yourself in the process.

Try the following visual prayer: See yourself in a circle of golden light with a male being—Jesus the Christ, an angel, or any sacred figure with whom you are comfortable. Be aware that this Being is filling your body, mind, and soul with infinite love, kindness and respect. Absorb all the feelings you ever wanted to receive from your earthly father. See your earthy father's errors dissolving in the Light. Realize that the love and kindness you are now receiving from a higher source will never be taken away from you. Relax and allow healing of any and all lack of parental love. You can freely forgive because you now have all the love you could possibly ever need or want. You are whole and complete in the love of Spirit and ready to share that love with your world. And so it is. God is blessing you now and always.

Our Divine Mother

"I find God in me, and I love Her; I love Her fiercely."
—Ntozoke Shange

I'd like to begin today with a little mother humor most of us can relate to:

My Mother taught me LOGIC: "If you fall off that swing and break your neck, you can't go to the store with me."

My Mother taught me MEDICINE: "If you don't stop crossing your eyes, they're going to freeze that way."

My Mother taught me ESP: "Put your sweater on; don't you think that I know when you're cold!'

My Mother taught me how to meet a CHALLENGE: "What were you thinking? Answer me when I talk to you! Don't talk back to me!"

My Mother taught me HUMOR: "When that lawn mower cuts off your toes, don't come running to me!"

My Mother taught me about GENETICS: "You are just like your father!"

My mother taught me about ROOTS: "Do you think you were born in a barn!"

My Mother taught me about the WISDOM OF AGE: "When you get to be my age, you will understand."

My Mother taught me about ANTICIPATION: "Just wait until your father gets home!"

My Mother taught me about JUSTICE: "One day you will have kids, and I hope they turn out just like you. Then you'll see what it's like."

Now for a little more serious piece concerning motherhood entitled, When You Thought I Wasn't Looking:

When you thought I wasn't looking, I saw you hang my first painting on the refrigerator, and I wanted to paint another one.

When you thought I wasn't looking, I saw you feed a stray cat, and I thought it was good to be kind to animals.

When you thought I wasn't looking, I saw you make my favorite cake for me, and I knew that little things are special things.

When you thought I wasn't looking, I heard you say a prayer, and I believed there is a God I could always talk to.

When you thought I wasn't looking, I felt you kiss me goodnight, and I felt loved.

When you thought I wasn't looking, I saw tears come from your eyes, and I learned that sometimes things hurt, but it's all right to cry.

When you thought I wasn't looking, I saw that you cared and I wanted to be everything that I could be.

When you thought I wasn't looking, I looked and wanted to say thanks for all the things I saw when you thought I wasn't looking. (anon)

On Mother's Day we honor the <u>noble ideal</u> of Motherhood. Many mothers here in earth school live up to that noble and loving ideal. However, many mothers are unhealed and unable to live up to the loving and noble ideal. Perhaps for most of us, it's some of both. We do the best we can to the degree we are healed and centered at any given time. What matters most is the love we give or receive that dissolves the memory of the less than loving times.

I found that even just a brief interlude of love and kindness is powerful enough to erase many of the sins of omission and commission that a mother might make. In spite of foster care and being left alone at too early an age, I did receive enough motherly love from several sources to give me a deep seated feeling that I was indeed loved in spite of all the challenging circumstances.

As a mother myself I certainly had many unhealed issues when my children were young; nonetheless, they knew I loved them very much in spite of my distractions. Seems like we are given the opportunity to forgive and be forgiven. It has been transforming for me to find the spiritual path and find spiritual answers to some of the mysteries and misfortunes of life.

First of all I believe we choose our parents even when the idea seems ridiculous. Why would we choose misery? The answer: to learn and grow and to take care of our karma. We can't know what our relationships have been in past lives, but we can be sure that those in our lives now are here for a reason and that we have had a past relationship with them. We are here to heal whatever needs to be healed so that our souls may progress.

We all have a Karmic Bank, which is the sum of our previous life experiences, conscious and unconscious. Stored in that bank is the memory of all previous life thoughts and behaviors. We are drawn to those experiences here in earth school that provide us with opportunities to balance our account. These experiences have been described as "our needle." I sometimes think of it as a Prod or a Cosmic Goose.

A person or a thing acts as the needle that pricks us to provide lessons for us. The needle is the "stumbling block" that we actually need for our spiritual progress. "We usually are born to our needle, give birth to our needle, or marry it." (Barbara Mary Muhl) So, if we can see our difficulties with a parent as something that can push us forward, something that can help us learn compassion, forgiveness and unconditional love, we free ourselves from the sense of being victims.

The good news is that when we are on a sincere spiritual path and communing with the Christ Spirit, though study, meditation, and daily practice, we are on a path of love and forgiveness that can quickly erase our karmic debts. This is known as Grace. There are two ways to deal with Karma: pay it—or dissolve it with the realization of Christ consciousness, which is Grace.

We often pray to Father-Mother God. God is pure Spirit, pure Love, neither male nor female, but expressing the love of Perfect Parent. We do have a Divine Mother (and Father) who constantly love and care for us no matter what we happen to be experiencing on the human level. We are One with God, One with that perfect parent; it is only our human ego sense of separation that keeps us from the experience of constant love peace and joy.

Once we connect with our Divine Mother, we can experience perfect mother love that will heal any lack of human mother love we might have felt previously. We need to come to the understanding that mother, father, sister, brother are all roles we play and have played, and that behind the roles our unchanging spirit has always resided. We have played many roles in many lifetimes, but when we realize and express who and what we are in Spirit, we are free.

We read in Mark 3: 31-35: And Jesus' mother and his brothers came; and standing outside they sent to him and called for him. And a crowd was sitting about him and they said to him, 'Your mother and your brothers are outside, asking for you.' And he replied, 'Who are my mother and my brothers?' And looking around on those who sat about him, he said, 'Here are my mother and my brothers!'

You and I are one in the family of God. We are sons and daughters of the living, loving God. Jesus speaking as the Christ said, 'Inasmuch as ye do it unto the least of these, ye do it unto me.' In other words we need to wake up not only to our own identity in God, but to wake up to that same identity in others as well. We all can hide behind many veils of fear and ignorance, but we cannot alter the truth of our oneness with God.

In the final analysis, we need to love and nurture one another in whatever role we are called upon to play. It's been said that sometimes our true family does not grow up in the same household. Once we recognize the assignment to "love one another," it is not so important where we receive human love. It is important that we extend love and keep our hearts and minds open and receptive to receiving Divine love. We need to know and trust that our Divine Mother-Father God is always with us and loves us unconditionally.

Love and Light are Reality and are mightier than hatred and Darkness. In fact hatred and darkness dissolve in the presence of Love and Light. Our safety lies in becoming a radiating center of divine love and light. So let us honor and send love and light to all mothers today, the unhealed as well as those who more closely match our ideal of motherhood.

It is important to remember that we can send love and light to those mothers who have made their transition and gone on to their next experience. Take a moment now to form a mental picture of your mother or someone who has acted as a loving mother whether here or on the next plane of existence and say to them: I bless you; I forgive you for all errors of omission or commission; Please forgive me for my errors of omission or commission; I love you and give thanks for you.

Let us pray: Dear Mother-Father God—our Perfect Parent and True Source of all life: We open our hearts to you and let your love flow freely, to heal and bless us and everyone in our lives. May we radiate and extend your love to all those who share planet earth with us. May we awaken to the realization of your love, now and forevermore. Amen.

Weave Us Together

"Synchronicities are miracles of a sort
because they offer us the gift of astonishment.
—Greg LaVoy

Whenever we feel that God is eluding us—whenever we stretch and strain to find a faraway God—we are like a fish in the ocean who wanders far and wide looking for water. It's swimming in the very water it is searching for, but does not realize it. We are like that fish looking far and wide for God when we are already swimming in the ocean of God's love life and delight.

In order to break through the barrier of ignorance that separates us from the realization of who and what and where we are, we need to be willing to stretch our minds and hearts to so that we can see and absorb the wondrous synchronicities and miracles that surround us. The unified universe signals us that we are an integral part of it and One Unity. What do these signals look like? When facts, statistics, and common sense say it could not happen and it does—that's a synchronicity signal that we do live in a grand design, a great tapestry of love and oneness.

The lyrics of the song <u>Weave</u> explain that we are many textures, many colors, each one different from the other, but that we are entwined with one another in one great tapestry. I'd like to share some synchronicity signals that I and others have received in the hope that you will be motivated to look into your own life experiences and see the signals that have been sent to you in the past and continue to be sent to you as you move through your life.

I have a needlework piece that I picked up in Michigan several years ago that is a prized possession. Why? Here's the story. My mother used to live in St. Louis, Michigan. One summer when I was visiting from Idaho (while on tour with my friend Ione) I wanted to also visit with a friend who lived there and who was in graduate school with me. Pat is a woman who loves to explore garage sales, and she asked if I would come along with her this particular Saturday so that we could have fun and a good visit at the same time. I am not a particular fan of garage sales and never go on my own, but I wanted to see Pat, so I agreed to go with her.

She had a newspaper that advertised the sales in St. Louis and the surrounding area, so off we went. In the afternoon we'd covered a lot of territory and were getting tired, but Pat wanted to check out a couple of places in nearby Mt. Pleasant, which is a little larger and the home of Central Michigan University, our alma mater. This whole area of central Michigan included Clare, where I grew up after I was adopted, and Rosebush, where I lived and brought up my children their first few years.

When we arrived in Mt. Pleasant, Pat picked out an ad at random from the newspaper. She thought that the address was in a good neighborhood and she might find some nice bargains. We went in. I had not purchased anything all day (Ione and I were traveling in a motor home without a whole lot of extra room). However, I was poking around in back of this garage and saw a needlework, picked it up and put it back down, saying, "I do this myself and have far more than I can hang already." Pat said, "The frame itself is worth more than the three dollars,—and maybe your mother would like it." So I decided to buy it. When we went to pay, I recognized the lady up front collecting the money and introduced myself. As I was paying for the needlework, she said, "Oh, that's one of Bernice Morrison's pieces." And I asked, "Did she ever teach third grade in Rosebush?" And she answered, "Yes, and she's standing right over there; she's my neighbor."

I went over and talked to the woman who had been my son Richard's third grade teacher. He died the summer after he finished the third grade, so she was his last teacher. Mrs. Morrison remembered Richard and the year that she taught him. "Actually, I was working on that needlepoint that year. We were studying birds," she told me. The needlepoint also just happens to be the tree of life, which represents ongoing life. This was another one of those times that Richard found a way to say "Hi. I'm OK Mom."

What were the chances of all that happening statistically? I just happened to be in the area the day of the sale. Pat and I decided at the last minute to go to Mt.Pleasant with no plan of which house to check out. It was the only day of this particular sale. I bought the needlework on a "whim" not knowing it would have any particular significance. The lady taking the money just happened to mention that it was the work of Bernice Morrison who just happened to be there to talk to me. I don't think all that was an accident.

Sig Paulson, minister at Unity Village Chapel for many years was also a poet. The following poem captures the essence of how Spirit moves through our lives:

Dances From God

Love is not a clod; it does not plod through life.
It dances and prances and romances!
Love not only thinks, it winks
at life and its creatures.
Love laughs as it heals,
as it forgives, as it frees,
as it unfolds all who are open
to its ecstatic energies.

I believe my experience that long ago day in Mt. Pleasant, Michigan was a wink from God and a loving signal from my dear son. Here's another heart and mind stretching story: "A woman and her grown daughter were also very good friends. They lived near one another and saw each other often. In between visits they talked on the phone. When the daughter called her Mom, she always said, "Hi Mom, it's "Me." And the mother would say, "Hi Me, how are you doing today?"

Then the daughter died without warning from a brain hemorrhage. It took considerable faith for the parents to just keep going. The parents decided to donate their daughter's organs so at least some good could come from such an otherwise tragic situation. In due time the parents heard from the Organ Retrieval Group telling them where their daughter's organs went. No names were mentioned, of course. About a year later the parents were forwarded an anonymous letter from the young man who received their daughter's pancreas and kidney telling them what a wonderful difference it had made in his life. And since he could not use his own name, he signed the letter—Me." Just coincidence? Probably not.

Oprah had a couple on one of her shows about miracles. This couple had endured much. Their three young children, two boys and a girl—had been involved in a car accident and killed. The couple were so despairing that they actually considered suicide. However, they made a decision to live and a pact to stay together and move forward with their lives. Exactly two years after the accident, the wife delivered triplets—two boys and a girl. They are doing fine and look and act much like the siblings who had gone on. What are the chances of all that?

I invite you to watch for synchronicities in your own life, and give those around you the gift of sharing them. Let's make a decision to expand our horizons, to push beyond narrow ways of seeing. We need to know that all the odd pieces of our lives do fit together into a plan that only could have been created by a higher power. As we gain more perspective, we see that the whole tapestry of our lives begins to form a Divine Pattern.

The poet Rumi says: "If God said, Rumi, pay homage to everything that has helped you enter my arms, there would not be one experience in my life, not one thought, not one feeling, not any act, I would not bow to." Remember we are like the fish in the ocean; we are swimming in a sea of God, a sea of grand design. God is all around. God loves us; in that love God dwells within and around us. God's love is not a thought He sends us, but Divinity that dwells within us. We are safe and secure in the mind and heart of God, and that will always be so—whether we're here in Earth School or in Spirit beyond.

What Happened to St. Valentine?

"The day will come, after we have harnessed the energies
of space, wind, tides and gravity, that we will harvest the
energy of love. And for the second time in the history of
the world, we will have discovered fire."
—Tiehard de Chardin

Valentine's Day is a wonderful day because there is nothing more important to us than to love and be loved. I thought it might be interesting to trace the roots of this day. It began in the third century with an oppressive Roman emperor and a humble Christian martyr. The emperor was Claudius II, and the Christian martyr was Valentinus. Claudius had ordered all Romans to worship twelve gods, and he made it a crime punishable by death to associate with Christians. Valentinus was dedicated to the ideals of Jesus Christ and not even the threat of death could keep him from practicing his beliefs. He was arrested and imprisoned.

During the last weeks of Valentinus' life a remarkable thing happened. Seeing that he was a man of learning, the jailer asked whether his daughter, Julia, might be brought to Valentinus for lessons. She had been blind from birth. Julia was a pretty young girl with a quick mind. Valentinus read stories of Rome's history to her. He described the world of nature to her. He taught her arithmetic, and told her about God. She saw the world through his eyes, trusted his wisdom, and found comfort in his quiet strength.

"Valentinus, does God really hear our prayers?" Julia asked one day. "Yes, my child. God hears each one," he replied. Julia said: Do you know what I pray for every morning and every night? I pray that I might see. I want so much to see everything you've told me about! "God does what is best for us if we will only believe," Valentinus said. "Oh, Valentinus, I do believe," Julia said intensely. "I do." She knelt and gripped his hand. They prayed together. Suddenly there was a brilliant light in the prison cell. Radiant, Julia cried, "Valentinus, I can see. I can see!" "Praise be to God!" Valentius answered.

On the eve of his death, Valentinus wrote a last note to Julia, urging her to stay close to God, and he signed it, "From Your Valentine." His sentence was carried out the next day, February 14, 270 A.D., near a gate that was later named Porta Valentini in his memory. He was buried at what is now the Church of Praxedes in Rome. It is said that Julia herself planted a pink-blossomed almond tree near his grave. Even today, the almond tree remains a symbol of abiding love and friendship. (shared by Rev. Chris Chenoweth in *Positive Daily Inspirations*)

Unfortunately, much of the world's interpretation of love is love to get, love to fill up emptiness, to escape loneliness and boredom. This is known as conditional love, special love. In contrast are relationships based on unconditional love, where the love of God is freely extended. Out of this comes Holy Relationships which are unconditional and radiate and extend the love of God. Conditional love says, I'll love you *if* you do what I say, *if* you give me what I need, *if* I don't get tired of you, *if* you made me happy, *if* you make me look good, *if* you support me. This describes the special relationships of the human level ego.

I made the great mistake that many make; I thought that love must be returned in just the form I wanted and expected. After the painful experiences that led up to my divorce from the father of my children, I was hurting, angry and scared. A friend's wise words changed everything. "Just go ahead and let your love flow—love the heck out of him—no matter what he did or what he does. Just let yourself love; your pain comes from shutting off the flow of love." I started doing that and felt tremendous relief.

Love frees, does not bind. It loves with open arms and open hands. It loves all who cross its path and does not expect anything in return. Love is its own reward. As we allow the unconditional love of God to express through us, new horizons open up before us. We experience life in a new open hearted way. We discover that ultimately, love is the only satisfying emotion there is.

This kind of love has requirements and the major one is forgiveness. Obviously we can't hold a grudge and love purely and unconditionally at the same time, nor can we live in the past and future. Life and love happen right here and right now in front of our nose. We must stand before what **is** with an open heart. Just like heat melts ice, Divine love melts discord. Emet Fox said: "There is no difficulty that enough love cannot conquer." I'll share a humorous story that illustrates how pseudo—love is carved up, conditional and given out less than whole heartedly.

A man walks out to the street and catches a taxi. He gets into the taxi, and the cabbie says, "Perfect timing. You're just like Frank was." <u>Passenger</u>: "Who?" <u>Cabbie.</u> "Frank Feldman. He's a guy who did everything right all the time. Like my coming along when you needed a cab, things would happen like that to Frank Feldman every single time."

<u>Passenger:</u> "There are always a few clouds over everybody."

Cabbie: "Not Frank Feldman. He was a terrific athlete. He could have won the Grand Slam at tennis. He could golf with the pros. He sang like an opera baritone and danced like a Broadway star and you should have heard him play the piano. He was an amazing guy." Passenger: "Sounds like he was something really special."

Cabbie: "There's more. He had a memory like a computer. He remembered everybody's birthday. He knew all about wine, which foods to order and which fork to eat them with. He could fix anything. Not like me. I change a fuse, and the whole street blacks out. But Frank Feldman, he could do everything right." Passenger: "Wow. Some guy then."

Cabbie: "He always knew the quickest way to go in traffic and avoid traffic jams. Not like me, I always seem to get stuck in them. But Frank, he never made a mistake, and he really knew how to treat a woman and make her feel good. He was the perfect man! He never made a mistake. No one could ever measure up to Frank Feldman."

Passenger: "An amazing fellow. How did you meet him?" Cabbie: "Well, I never actually met Frank. He died. I'm married to his widow."

This poor cabbie married a woman who obviously does not love him unconditionally. Constant comparing is not love. On the other side of the coin, here's a story with a different slant: "When I was a little boy, my mom liked to make breakfast food for dinner every now and then. And I remember one night in particular when she had made breakfast after a long, hard day at work. On that evening so long ago, my mom placed a plate of eggs, sausage and extremely burned biscuits in front of my dad. I remember waiting to see if anyone noticed!

All my dad did was reach for his biscuit, smile at my mom and ask me how my day was at school. I don't remember how I answered him that night, but I do remember watching him smear butter and jelly on that biscuit and eat every bite! When I got up from the table that evening, I remember hearing my mom apologize to my dad for burning the biscuits. And I'll never forget what he said: "Baby, I love burned biscuits." Later that night, I went to hug Daddy good night and I asked him if he really liked his biscuits burned. He wrapped me in his arms and said, "Your Momma put in a hard day at work today and she's real tired. And besides—a little burnt biscuit never hurt anyone."

Some people I know go about helping others quietly and without any desire for recognition. They give a gentle touch, have intuitive understanding of other people's needs, and express love and compassion without fanfare. Surely it is love—love of God flowing through them as love for humankind. Let us try to see others as individualized expressions of the One God. Let us see physical bodies as the visible form that holds the invisible Spirit. The love we extend to another, first flows though us to strengthen and inspire us. What better gift could we give to each other than the very love out of which we—and all life—are created?

I invite you to close your eyes for a few moments now for a closing visualization and prayer. Bring to mind a person or situation that is currently challenging you. See the person, the challenge, and yourself in a circle of golden love and light. Then, invite into this circle Jesus the Christ, an angel, or any light being you feel comfortable with. Just soak up the energy of light and love. See it melting any discord or misunderstanding and replacing it with unconditional love and understanding. Sincerely ask for an open heart to receive Divine Love and Divine Order and Highest good for everyone involved. Feel the Light and Warmth. Give Thanks that as we ask in faith believing, our prayer is answered.

Let us determine to be an ambassador of Divine love. Every bit of love we extend to the world helps to raise the consciousness of all. It feels so much better to love than to be fearful or negative. Let us pray that our existence is not a desperate search for love, but that love and joy become a light <u>in us</u> that shines and <u>extends out</u> into our world.

SECTION THREE
Walking Through Our Storms

"If you knew who walks beside you on the path
you have chosen, fear would be impossible."
—A Course in Miracles

A Dream of Wild Horses

Rev. Julie Keene

"The very softest thing of all can ride like
a galloping horse through the hardest of things."
—Tao Te Ching

I once saw an artistic film called "A Dream of Wild Horses." It consisted of several horses running along a beach, manes and tails flying in the wind, running fast and free. Those horses were definitely unfettered and free. In truth, you and I are as free as those wild horses on the beach, but we don't know it. Every since we decided to separate ourselves from continual awareness of God, we often live in a dream world of fear, and as a result, build a psychological fortress around our free spirit that we believe will keep us safe but instead keeps our true spirit imprisoned.

The price we must pay to become free is to muster the courage to venture out from our fortress. Then we have a chance to take an honest look at our real problems. We can do this right where we are without changing any outer circumstance. Michael Singer's book *The Unthethered Soul,* is a refreshing and clear map that shows the way to step outside our usual viewpoints. He says: "Basically, you recreate the outside world inside yourself, and then you live in your mind. [You] use your mind to buffer yourself from life instead of living it." (page 23)

So let's take a look at what we're doing. We are certainly familiar with the voice in our head that is constantly narrating our life for us. It never shuts up. We're driving ourselves down the road of life, but we have a back-seat driver who is constantly talking to us about what is good, bad, and scary,—it's constantly judging and yakking about what is going on out there. That voice is never content. Even when good things are happening, it worries and strategizes about how to hold on to the experience. It always has a problem with something. And our soul's predicament is that we lose ourselves in our so-called problems.

I had an interesting experience while driving to Florida with a friend. We were driving through Atlanta on a Saturday morning, and I was at the wheel because I'd driven through several times before and felt quite confident. Well, something happened and I got off on an exit instead of following I-75. Immediately my problem oriented voice kicked in, and I said out loud, "Oh crap! Here we are in the middle of this city and the problem is that there's never a gas station or anyone to ask about getting back to the freeway." I was upset.

Then my friend and spiritual sidekick said, "Now Julie, it doesn't have to be a problem. It's not a problem unless you make it a problem. It's just fine." That was like a splash of cold water in a lunatic's face. I settled down—what a novel approach! I didn't have to make it a problem. Almost immediately we saw a U-Haul rental business ahead on our right and there were men standing around. We pulled into that driveway, asked directions and were given simple directions back to the freeway.

That experience stays with me because I have a tendency to get disturbed and perturbed about such minor things. The lesson I took from that is: "I don't have to make it a problem!" That idea can be extended into all kinds of situations in our lives. The voice in our head jumps on every little thing in an attempt to make it a problem. The voice in the head is an aspect of the ego and the ego loves problems because through them it generates fear, anxiety, self-righteousness and then feeds on those things. That keeps us from actually experiencing the free and unlimited Being we truly are.

We can begin to free ourselves by self-observation. We can begin to watch ourselves and what we're doing. The good thing about my experience in Atlanta was that almost immediately because of my friend's prompting, I saw what I was doing and decided to turn it around. I stopped listening to the upset voice and looked at the situation in a new light. I separated from my own drama enough to see it another way. I could see what I was doing and decided to stop it.

We all have that capacity to become the Watcher of what we are thinking and feeling. We have thoughts and feelings, but that is not who we are in truth. We are the Watcher behind it all—pure consciousness, a Higher Part. From that Centered vantage point we can observe our personality with all its strengths and weaknesses. We all have that capacity to become the Watcher of what we are thinking and feeling. We have thoughts and feelings, but that is not who we are in truth. We are the Watcher behind it all—pure consciousness, a Higher Part. From that Centered vantage point we can observe our personality with all its strengths and weaknesses.

In *The Untethered Soul*, Michael Singer calls that ego personality our inner roommate and we're locked in there with a maniac! He points out that our inner roommate can ruin anything we're doing at a moment's notice: "It could ruin your wedding day, or even your wedding night. That part of you can ruin anything and everything and it generally does. You buy a brand new car and it's beautiful. But every time you drive it, your inner roommate finds something wrong with it. The mental voice keeps pointing out every little squeak, every little vibration, until eventually you don't even like the car anymore. Once you see what this can do to your life, you are ready for spiritual growth. You're ready for real transformation when you finally say, 'Look at this thing. It's ruining my life. I'm trying to live a peaceful, meaningful existence, but I feel like I'm sitting on top of a volcano. At any moment this thing can decide to freak, close down, and fight with what's happening . . . My life is a mess just because this thing that lives in here with me has to make a melodrama out of everything.'"(page 18) Can you imagine your inner roommate as actually a person outside of yourself?

What can we do to free ourselves from this bully that won't shut up and leave us alone? The question becomes,—"do I want to be free?"—"do I want to be healed?" If so, choices have to be made; effort has to be made. We cannot be spiritually lazy and experience our soul's freedom at the same time. If we want to be as free as those wild horses on the beach, we must "put on the whole armor of God," leave the enclosed fortress and do what is ours to do to progress on the spiritual path.

Let's talk about the choice we always have. We can choose to listen to the voice of Holy Spirit instead of the ego, also known as our crazy roommate. What does that mean exactly? It means that we don't jump on every fearful and negative thought and run away with it. Imagine a beautiful round ball of light deep within yourself. This light is stable, our Higher Self, the voice for God, the indwelling Holy Spirit that knows its identity as one with God. If we practice listening to this voice, we will eventually become capable of standing back and watching life unfold while blessing it all. In truth we are totally safe and secure in the mind and heart of God. When we can feel the truth of this, it is possible for us to just watch and bless life as it shows up rather than getting caught up in ego dilemmas.

It's important to remember that to observe and watch ourselves does not mean to judge ourselves. It just means to see clearly what we're doing. Laying guilt upon ourselves is just another road to nowhere. No need for guilt. Just turn around and decide to go the other way. That is the true meaning of repentance—we just stop what we're doing, turn around and go the other way. We can make that decision. We can choose to see it differently. We can choose to move toward the light. The good news is that sooner or later, we will so choose. That is our destiny. We can play around with our crazy roommate inside the defenses of our ego fortress for as long as we want, but ultimately we'll decide to put on a suit of spiritual armor and free ourselves.

The following is an autobiographical story by the author of The Little Prince, Antoine de Saint-Exupery. He was a fighter pilot who fought against the Nazis and was killed in action in World War II. He previously fought in the Spanish Civil War against the fascists and wrote this story entitled The Smile, based on his experience of being taken prisoner. He was captured and thrown into a jail cell, and quite certain, because of the contemptuous looks and rough treatment he received, that he would be executed soon. In spite of that threat he was able to allow the spirit within him to smile at another person, right in the face of death. And then the miracle of freedom became his:

"I was sure that I was to be killed. I became terribly nervous and distraught. I fumbled in my pockets to see if there were any cigarettes which had escaped their search. I found one and because of my shaking hands, I could barely get it to my lips. But I had no matches; they had taken those. I looked through the bars at my jailer. He did not make eye contact with me. After all, one does not make eye contact with a thing, a corpse. I called out to him 'Have you got a light, por favor?' He looked at me, shrugged and came over to light my cigarette. As he came close and lit the match, his eyes inadvertently locked with mine. At that moment, I smiled. I don't know why I did that. Perhaps it was nervousness, perhaps it was because, when you get very close, one to another, it is very hard not to smile. In any case, I smiled.

In that instant, it was as though a spark jumped across the gap between our two hearts, our two human souls. I know he didn't want to, but my smile leaped through the bars and generated a smile on his lips, too. He lit my cigarette but stayed near, looking at me directly in the eyes and continuing to smile. I kept smiling at him, now aware of him as a person and not just a jailer. And his looking at me seemed to have a new dimension, too. 'Do you have kids?' he asked.

'Yes, here, here.' I took out my wallet and nervously fumbled for the pictures of my family. He, too, took out the pictures of his ninos and began to talk about his plans and hopes for them. My eyes filled with tears. I said that I feared that I'd never see my family again, never have the chance to see them grow up.

Tears came to his eyes, too. Suddenly, without another word, he unlocked my cell and silently led me out of the jail, quietly and by back routes, out of the town. There, at the edge of town, he released me. And without another word, he turned back toward the town. My life was saved by a smile."

This story speaks of those moments when souls bypass human insanity and thus recognize each other. Whenever the distracting fearful voice in the head falls silent under the influence of the centered, true Self, the stage is set for a miracle of love. Yes, the very softest of things—just a smile—can ride like a galloping horse through the hardest of things.

All or Nothing at All

"In our devotion to God, we must be willing to surrender
even life itself to know eternal truth."
—David Hawkins

It's interesting to note how much passion and commitment we can gather up for our favorite sports and games. Long ago, when people cursed and beat the ground with sticks, it was called Witchcraft. Today it's called golf. It's easy to see that if success is to be gained in golf or any sport or skill, we have to give it some time, attention and passion. We go through periods of frustration and discouragement, but we know we need to keep on keeping on and when people care enough, they succeed. However there is another ingredient that is needed and that is good direction. Here's an internet story that illustrates that:

"As a bagpiper, I play many places. Recently I was asked by a funeral director to play at a graveside service for a homeless man. He had no family or friends, so the service was to be at a pauper's cemetery in the Kentucky back country. As I was not familiar with the backwoods, I got lost and, being a typical man, I didn't stop for directions.

I finally arrived an hour late and saw the funeral guy had evidently gone and the hearse was nowhere in sight. There were only the diggers and crew left and they were eating lunch. I felt bad and apologized to the men for being late. I went to the side of the grave and looked down and the vault lid was already in place. I didn't know what else to do, so I started to play.

The workers put down their lunches and began to gather around. I played with my heart and soul for this homeless man with no family and friends. And as I played Amazing Grace, the workers began to weep. They wept, I wept; we all wept. When I finished I packed up my bagpipes and started for my car. Though my head hung low, my heart was full. As I opened the door to my car, I heard one of the workers say, "I never seen nothin' like that before and I've been putting in septic tanks for twenty years." Apparently I'm still lost—it's a man thing.

Actually being lost is a human thing. This guy certainly had talent and passion, but failed to accomplish his mission because his human ego wouldn't allow him to ask for direction. If we are going to succeed in our spiritual goal of attaining the mind that was in Christ Jesus, attaining the goal of living and demonstrating the love, peace, and joy of God, we need all the help we can get. And we certainly need to give it our passion and commitment—and then be willing, wise and humble enough to ask for instruction, guidance and direction.

All that sounds reasonable doesn't it? So why do we have such a struggle with it? Someone once advised: "Take a big leap; you can't cross a chasm in two small jumps." If we are to succeed in progressing on our spiritual path, we have to be willing to take some big leaps. It's also been said, "The Spirit is willing, but the flesh is weak." Put another way: Our higher Self is willing but the human level ego is a very fearful and resistant, and its mission is to sabotage us every step of the way.

If we are too afraid to take big leaps—make big commitments with passion, wisdom, direction, and follow through—we're going to end up in the gap—the chasm of no man's land. We set ourselves adrift spiritually, give our ego the control and wander around in confusion and wonder why life is so difficult.

So the question becomes, "what can we do about it?" There are many helpful things we can and must do. However, in order to receive help in crossing the chasm of our human ego which is our sense of separation from God and from one another, we must be open and receptive to instruction and guidance and then be willing to follow directions.

Course in Miracles: "What is this dream world except a little gap perceived to tear eternity apart and break it into days, months, years? And what are you who live within the dream world except a picture of the son of God in broken pieces, each one concealed within a separate and uncertain bit of clay? It is the Holy Spirit's function to take the broken pieces and put them into place again. There is no middle ground. Either there is a gap between you and your brother, between you and God—or we are One." It is all or nothing at all!

I've found that an important place to begin to climb up out of the chasm is to realize that any and all of our so called failures, mistakes, and discouragements can be used for good. We start by realizing that we are not victims, that we have the power to choose to use it all for good. But we have to be willing to make our connection with God our first priority. Jesus said, "Seek ye first the Kingdom of Heaven and all else will follow."

Sounds simple, but we resist because we're afraid we might have to give up all the human pleasures and goals. When I started meditating I was told that I didn't need to be concerned about giving up things—that as I raise my consciousness the desire for things that no longer serve me will gradually fade away. The requirement was commitment to meditate regularly every day—and as I felt better and better, I became more and more passionate about doing it. Now years later, it's true that many of the things that used to be important to me have faded away and my clear and passionate number one priority is my connection with Spirit. And I am willing to give it my all and I'm willing to go to Spirit for guidance and direction.

I still have human level issues and temptations and we all will have as long as we're here in human form. We still have to be diligent and vigilant—passionately focused upon our spiritual development. We live in a sea of mixed consciousness which hypnotizes us and entices us to believe the world is out to get us and that we are victims of people and circumstances. One of the first big necessary leaps for us to take is over this chasm of ignorance.

Michigan poet Theodore Rilke wrote: We have no reason to harbor any mistrust against our world, for it is not against us. If it has terrors, they are our terrors; if it has abysses, these abysses belong to us. If there are dangers and difficulties, we must try to bless them, for we cannot know what work these conditions are doing inside us."

God—Life—Spirit cannot forget us; we are held in Its hands, no matter how it seems. It's time to "Put on the whole armor of God"—jump across the chasm and leap into the loving consciousness of Spirit. It's time to stop being afraid of giving our all to our spiritual life—because if we don't, we have nothing. I'll close with one of my favorite poems. I heard Jean Houston recite this powerful poem years ago at Unity Village when I was a ministerial student. It applies to all of us today.

A SLEEP OF PRISONERS

The human heart can go to the lengths of God.
Dark and cold we may be, but this is no winter now.
The frozen misery of centuries breaks, cracks, begins to move
—The thaw, the flood, the upstart spring.
Thank God our time is now
When wrong comes up to face us everywhere, never to leave us
Until we take the longest stride of soul men ever took.
Affairs are now Soul Size. The enterprise is exploration into God.
It takes so many thousands of years to wake,
But will you wake, for pity's sake?
—Christopher Fry

Daily Life as Temple and Religion

"Is not religion all deeds and all reflection,
and that which is neither deed nor reflection,
but a wonder and a surprise ever springing in the soul,
even while the hands hew the stone or tend the loom?"
—Kalil Gibran

It's been said that the eternal is curled up in the here and now. It's difficult to realize that every moment of every day is just as important as all the others. It's a habit for many of us to "hold our breath" psychologically between highlights, or during work hours, or while doing mundane tasks. It's easy to tune out and close our hearts and minds, waiting for the next high or more interesting event. That's how we manage to sleepwalk through too much of our lives.

A dilemma we all deal with is our tendency to congeal—to stiffen—to set limits for ourselves and to stay in them. All the wonder and zeal fades in the midst of the daily grind. The question is, how do we keep from sleepwalking? How do we stay awake, aware, always moving forward discovering ever new and expanding consciousness within ourselves?

A man went up to the top of a mountain, threw open his arms and asked God to fill him. God answered: "My son, I am always filling you, but you keep leaking!" Truth is, we are always full of God life and energy, but that awareness too often leaks out as we go about our daily business.

As we examine the lives of people such as Brother Lawrence, Saint Francis, and Saint Teresa of Avila, we see that they made their daily lives their temple and their religion. They kept a close and running dialogue with God, making God an intimate everyday part of their lives. They knocked on Spirit's door every day—and they were not afraid to talk back to God on occasion.

One stormy night, St. Teresa of Avila was traveling along a rutted road in an old ox cart. She held the reins of two oxen as the cart bumped over the muddy Spanish road. At one particularly loud burst of thunder and a close lightening strike, the oxen sped up in panic. A wheel caught in a deep hole and St. Teresa was thrown off the cart, landing face first in the mud. She knew she was supposed to thank God for everything, but she was having a hard time with this one.

Then she heard the voice of Jesus: "Be not dismayed, only strengthened, by adversity. I offer this experience only to my most faithful friends." She wiped mud off her face and thought a minute and replied: "Maybe that's why you have so few!" Yes, even saints have their moments, and we can fully expect to have ours too. Making our daily life our temple and religion does not mean that we'll not have to face the appearances of everyday life—the disturbances of our own dark unhealed places. We are here in Earth School because we have work to do.

Life takes on a whole new meaning when we see our difficult experiences for the lessons and opportunities for growth they offer us. When we see difficulties in that light, we keep ourselves from becoming congealed. We congeal when we confine ourselves to living in the framework of what we already know. Living by the rules and regulations of our human ego and sleepwalking between highs and lows is the very opposite of making daily life our temple and religion. When we are open and receptive to instruction and guidance from Spirit and then follow that instruction and guidance, our daily life can become an exciting adventure in exploration and growth. Mystical magical moments become part of our ongoing process. No boring moments exist in the truly spiritual life!

Our everyday experiences take on deeper meaning when we begin to see every experience as a holy one, every encounter as a holy encounter. We behold the Christ in ourselves and others. The Course in Miracles reminds us: "When you meet anyone, remember it is a holy encounter. As you see him you will see yourself. As you treat him you will treat yourself. As you think of him you will think of yourself. Never forget this, for in him you will find yourself or lose yourself."

Brother Lawrence practiced the Presence in the midst of everyday chores, and we too must learn to practice the Presence in every circumstance. It involves more than just belief and faith. We can believe and have faith and never get out of our chair. We must go into action in thought, word, and deed and apply the principles of the truth we know. Application is everything. Otherwise it is like reading a book about playing the piano. Unless we practice, we won't learn to actually play. We need to make God contact every day if we want to live a truly expanded spiritual life. We can't do this by just reading books.

Many of us love reading all kinds of spiritual literature, and it helps us. Yet, in the final analysis, if we don't incorporate the material and make use of the spiritual tools, we remain in a congealed state of consciousness. An artist puts brush and paint to palette; a dancer moves the body and practices the routines; a musician picks up his instruments to practice. It is not helpful to our soul growth to sit back and philosophize without applying our knowledge each day.

Alan Watts reminded us that the purpose of music is not to get to the end of it or to see how fast a piece can be played. The purpose is to enjoy each note for itself just as it is played. Can we learn to enjoy each moment of our daily life as it plays itself out—without trying to stop it or rush ahead to the next thing?

Of course, it is difficult for us to do that during darker challenging times. However, the more we learn to embrace and bless all the lessons and challenges, the higher we climb in consciousness. Butterflies need time to grow and develop in the cocoon so that they will be strong enough to make the necessary effort at the end to climb out of it. Just so we need every experience in our own cocoon of challenges so that we can develop the spiritual muscles that will take us to a higher level of consciousness.

I remember years ago when I was minister full time in Tallahassee. The church was growing incredibly fast and there was much to do. I remember one day on my way to visit a dear lady in a nursing home, my energy was very low and I felt like I could not make it through the remainder of the day. At that point, I began to talk to my elder brother and way shower, Jesus the Christ. "Please ride in this car with me, walk with me, stay with me while I visit the nursing home, and please stand in the pulpit beside me." And because Spirit is always nearer than breathing and closer than hands and feet, I experienced the spiritual strength and support I needed. A favorite saying from Course in Miracles: "If you knew who walks beside you on the way you have chosen, fear would be impossible."

I invite you to experiment by asking Spirit to be with you everywhere you go today. Make Spirit your Siamese twin and see what happens. Of course all this is much smoother if you meditate every day. There is no wrong or right way to meditate; what matters is that you get your human ego out of the way and that you actually <u>feel and experience</u> the higher power, the divine hum, the higher self, the God in you, the Christ in you that is your hope of glory. Some form of tuning into Spirit at a deep level every day is essential to a serious spiritual life. Gibran advises us, "Let your visit to the temple of the invisible be for naught but ecstasy and sweet communion."

A devout woman named Virginia developed a life threatening cancer. She had a vision of seeing herself healed and her x-rays normal. Then for a period of six months, she began to see in her peripheral vision, Jesus walking with her. Ultimately, she was healed. After her healing, the vision of Jesus began to fade and finally was gone altogether. She was distraught and concerned that she was being abandoned. She had made a prior commitment to do a presentation in front of the congregation at her church. She walked out onto the platform and began to speak.

When she raised her eyes to look into the congregation, she saw the face of Jesus the Christ super-imposed on the faces of everyone. Can you imagine? St. Paul reminded us of "Christ in you, your hope of glory." Virginia's vision of the face of the Christ upon all the faces in the crowd is a vision you and I can seek to have for ourselves. We say rather off-handedly at times, "I behold the Christ in You." In fact there's a song with that title in the Unity hymnbook. Our job is to make beholding the Christ, the divinity in others, a spiritual priority in our daily lives. Yes, that includes the boss, the obstreperous child, the client, the mate or whoever may misunderstand us. That is making daily life our temple and our religion.

Here are a few lines from The Prophet by Kahlil Gibran concerning religion: "Who can separate his faith from his actions, or his belief from his occupations?—And he to whom worshipping is a window to open, but also to shut, has not yet visited the house of his soul whose windows are open from dawn to dawn.—Your daily life is your temple and your religion.—And if you would know God, be not therefore a solver of riddles. Rather look about you and you shall see Him playing with your children.—And look into space; you shall see Him walking in the cloud, outstretching His arms in the lightning and descending in rain.—You shall see Him smiling in flowers, then rising and waving His hands in trees." Yes, God is blessing us every day; we just have to open our hearts and receive.

Do You Want to be RIGHT
—or HAPPY?

"Here lies the body of William Jay
Who died maintaining his right of way.
He was right, dead right as he sped along.
But he's just as dead as if he'd been wrong."
—unknown

The Course in Miracles asks the question, "Do you want to be right, or happy? Unfortunately, much of the world would rather be right! But, we can make our own choice. Many wise teachers proclaim that a state of unconditional happiness (happiness through right and wrong, good and bad, thick and thin) is a path to enlightenment. That seems ridiculous at first. That's all I have to do, be happy? Okay! I'll sign up for that! However, there is another word here that I might have overlooked—unconditional. How might that affect the proposition? That means I have to be happy no matter what happens out there! Well, that's another story!

As I was walking my dog Bella this morning, I had an opportunity to work with this idea. I am an ardent advocate of people picking up their dog's poop, but of course not everyone bothers to do it. So, I'm walking along and noticing a pile and a certain annoyance rises up within me along with the conviction that of course, I'm right about this. About then I remembered the theme of this talk and realized that I had a choice, and I made it. I would not tune into my "rightness and judgment" about the pile of dog poop because I did not want to spoil my happy and serene walk with Bella.

We usually believe that we can be happy only when things are right "out there" and in alignment with what we want. The right job, the right relationship, plenty of everything we want—ah yes, THEN we can be happy! Even so much of our New Thought teaching is about manifesting what we want. Nothing wrong with that, but so often we get what we want and that does not satisfy us either. Actually the human ego can never "get enough"—it is always going to want something more, and it is always going to find fault with something. Therefore if we're going to be happy, it can't depend on our making sure the "right" things appear in our outer world.

An ad came over the internet recently advertising a new "natural" mood enhancing product. It did a great job of describing our emotional struggle with life: *Beep—beep—beep! You know the sound of your alarm clock going off again. Tired, sluggish, worn out from the day before and suddenly it's time for the daily grind again. Life is tough and once you become an adult it doesn't get any easier. There are tough days at work, hectic family time, and missing out on friends. It can be tough to stay happy and upbeat with the challenges that life throws at you. Are you unable to focus? Do you ever feel unhappy? Our LIVING HAPPY natural product empowers you to live a better, more successful life.*

What this ad seems to be telling us is that we do indeed have "good reasons" to be unhappy, but that we can bypass it all with just the right pill. Yet, even with a pill, life and the world often fail to line up with what we think we want at any given time. Sometimes, it IS necessary to take medication. It's just that if we want to awaken to our true spiritual identity, we can't stop there. We may be tempted to stop psychological and spiritual work because we don't want to face and heal the real issues in our life. That can seem like just too much effort! Yet, if we will keep pushing our growing edge, the rewards we reap will be worth it.

My goal is to find a way to accept all of life—the good and bad, the right and wrong,—and deal with my soul's responsibility to wake up to the joys of the Spirit. Mother Teresa had a poem on the wall of her home for the poor in Calcutta. It's widely known as the ANYWAY poem. The idea is that no matter what anyone says or does, we love them anyway, do good anyway. This is great advice and we could add another line to the piece. No matter what anyone says or does, <u>be happy</u> anyway!

A few years ago I played a song called "Don't Worry, Be Happy" over and over in the cassette player in my car,—wonderful spiritual advice from Bobby McFerrin. It reminded me to take responsibility for myself whether things seemed right to me out there or not. Whenever we try to make anyone or anything outside of ourselves responsible for our happiness, we end up feeling frustrated and disillusioned. I know this is true because I tried to make people and events in my own life responsible for my happiness. Of course it never works for anyone.

We all need to develop enough spiritual understanding and strength to stay open and loving and to let go of having to be right. I have never known a happy person who insists on being right all the time. To have to be right demonstrates that one ego is battling for supremacy over another ego, or that a group of egos is battling for supremacy over another group of egos. We see this in Politics and in War.

It is possible to decrease the prominence of our ego as we stand firm in happiness. This is possible because underneath the melodrama, uproar and ignorance of our human ego lives, there is the truth of our being. A story illustrates this point: Many years ago in the East a band of monks came together to plan a way to save their priceless treasure, a Golden Buddha, from the invaders they knew would soon conquer them. They decided to plaster the Buddha with layers of clay; the plan worked and the invaders didn't recognize the statue as being valuable. Years passed, the invaders left, but the people had forgotten about the true Buddha hidden under the clay. Then one day after a particularly heavy rain, a young monk saw a shimmer near the Buddha's foot and began to peel away the clay. As more and more gold became exposed, others joined him and soon the priceless treasure, the gleaming gold Buddha was revealed in all its glory.

We all have a priceless treasure within ourselves that we cover up with the clay of unhappiness and self-righteousness, which is the "I'm always right" syndrome." A good starting place for the spiritual journey is to know the priceless treasure we are and possess: The Presence of God within us, nearer than breathing, closer than hands and feet. The precious treasure of love, peace, joy, and happiness will reveal itself as we release everything else, including the need to be right. The treasure is waiting for us to claim it. Fortunately, help is available.

Whenever we make spiritual advancement our first priority, all the books, teachers, tools and techniques present themselves to us. Whenever we are ready the right and perfect teacher appears with the right and perfect message for us at that time, a message that will point the way to our own inner treasure. So let us keep our hearts open to love and open and receptive to the instruction and guidance of the Holy Spirit. This is facilitated by our use of the master tool of meditation in the silence. As we grow in consciousness, we drop the need to be right on the human level. We begin to agree with The Course in Miracles that on the human level, we don't know our own best interests.

If we can choose to keep expanding our love and forgiveness; if we can keep the inner Watcher on duty; if we can listen for the Voice of the Holy Spirit, the Voice of the Golden Buddha inside ourselves, we will be happy and we will progress. We will be happy <u>because</u> we have moved past the need to be right. We will understand that being right does not prove our worthiness. We're fine just as we are, right or wrong.

Edwin Markham offered a great piece of advice to us whenever we are tempted to insist that we're right: "He drew a circle that shut me out—called me heretic, rebel, and a thing to flout. But love and I had the wit to win; we drew a circle that took him in." Our job, if we are serious about happiness, is to keep drawing circles that include everyone, right or wrong.

In that state we are ready to truly enjoy and celebrate life. Biblical prophets tell us, "do not be grieved, for the joy of the Lord is your strength." (Nehemiah) And "For you shall go out in joy and be led forth in peace; the mountains and the hills before you shall break forth into singing and all the trees of the field shall clap their hands." (Isaiah)

We won't feel the *need* to be right once we realize that we are *actually happier* when we don't *have* to be right! Let's give up the struggle and choose to live, love, laugh and be happy: Walk in the rain, smell flowers, blow bubbles, build sand castles, act silly. Dance, trust the universe and smile a lot. Choose to laugh, play and be happy wherever you are!

Drinking From My Saucer

"I have a sufficiency of enoughness;
Any more would be a super abundance."
—unknown

A tombstone was recently discovered with just the person's name and the epitaph: "Thanks for everything." Meister Eckhart said: "If the only prayer you say in your whole life is 'thank you,' that would suffice." It's difficult to be sad and grateful at the same time, so it certainly pays off to have an "attitude of gratitude." Gratitude is not so much in things and events as it is in ourselves. A Yiddish proverb declares: "To a worm in horseradish, the whole world is horseradish." Turns out that when we can be grateful for everything and love what is, the world transforms into a joyous place. I love the philosophy in the following poem:

Drinking From My Saucer:

I've never made a fortune
and it's probably too late now.
But I don't worry about that much
I'm happy anyhow.
And as I go along life's way,
I'm reaping better than I sowed.
I'm drinking from my saucer
'Cause my cup has overflowed.

Haven't got a lot of riches,
and sometimes the going's tough.
But I've got loving ones around me,
and that makes me rich enough
I thank God for his blessings,
and the mercies He's bestowed.
I'm drinking from my saucer
'cause my cup has overflowed.

Chief Tecumseh: "When you rise in the morning give thanks for the morning light. Give thanks for your life and strength. Give thanks for your food and for the joy of living. And if perchance you see no reason for giving thanks, rest assured the fault is in yourself."

To be grateful, we need to look at what we have, rather than what we don't have. It's been said that happiness does not depend upon what we can hold in our hand; it depends on what we can hold in our heart. It is not based on what we can get, but rather on what we can give. On the first Thanksgiving Day in 1621, the colonists invited the Indians to join them to celebrate and give thanks for the harvest; being thankful meant having enough to share. According to historian H. U. Westermayer, the pilgrims dug seven times more graves than huts they built for the living. Yet, they set aside a day for Thanksgiving.

Jesus reminds us in the Course in Miracles: "You are everything & you have everything." How and why can this be true? Spirit is the basis of everything; our true identity is pure spirit, one with God. Therefore we do have everything that matters, everything that is truly real. Again from the Course: "God Himself has left no gift beyond what you already have (you have it all right now)—nor has he denied the tiniest blessing. Gratitude to God becomes the way in which He is remembered, for love cannot be far behind a grateful heart and thankful mind. God enters easily into a grateful heart and a thankful mind, for these are the conditions of your homecoming." Coming home is entering into the consciousness of God's love, peace and joy.

Radical Thanksgiving is to give thanks for everything, no matter what it looks like: When there is something we don't' know, we can be thankful: we have just discovered an opportunity to learn.—When difficulties come our way, we can be thankful that we are put in a position to grow and become stronger.—When we run up against our limitations, we have just discovered where we can make improvements.—When we make a mistake, we can give thanks for it because we will more clearly remember what not to do next time.—We can give thanks for the setbacks because we can learn and grow from them. They are valuable because they impel us to persist and endure.

Whenever we think of someone who in the past or present has seemingly harmed us or who we have seemingly harmed, here's an idea that can turn it around. Say to yourself and the other person in your mind: "Thank you for doing to me all that you have done. Forgive me for doing all that I have done to you. Why in the world should we give thanks to someone who has harmed us? The answer: So we can learn forgiveness and so we can learn what is real and eternal in us—what is real and eternal is our Spirit—and it cannot be harmed. Again from the Course in Miracles: "What is Real cannot be threatened; what is unreal does not exist—therein lies the Peace of God." A closing Apache blessing:

May the sun bring you new energy by day.

May the moon softly restore you by night.

May the rain wash away your worries.

May the breeze blow new strength into your Being.

May you walk gently through the world

and know its beauty all the days of your life

Give Yourself an Attitude Adjustment

"Two men look out from the same bars;
one sees the mud, and one the stars."
—Frederick Langbridge

An attitude adjustment is moving from a sour point of view to making a decision to be at peace, a decision to look at the situation from a new viewpoint. It is living the serenity prayer and knowing "It IS what it IS.' We can check out our attitude by noticing what tune we're playing in the background of our mind. Is it serene, upbeat, lively? Or sad, dissonant funeral music? Is the soundtrack from <u>Jaws</u> or from <u>The Sound of Music</u>? The good news is that we can change our inner tune from sad and frustrated to happy and serene with an attitude adjustment.

A humorous story about a change of attitude: The chief executive of a large company was very successful because of his energy and drive. However, he had an embarrassing weakness. Each time he was called into the president's office to make his weekly report, he wet his pants! The president was a kind man and advised that he see a urologist at company expense. But the following week, his pants were again wet. "Didn't you see the urologist?" asked the president. "No, he was out. I saw a psychiatrist instead, and I'm cured," replied the executive. "I no longer feel embarrassed!"

The more we make it a habit to adjust our attitudes, and the more we decide for peace, we build a sturdy spiritual and psychological platform from which to live our lives. When something disturbing happens, as it is sure to do in Earth School, our automatic response will be to choose peace instead of uproar and drama. William James said "The greatest revolution of our generation is the discovery that by adjusting our inner attitudes, we can change the outer aspects of our lives."

We can benefit from an attitude adjustment whenever we find ourselves stuck in the mud of anxiety and worry, or feeling unfairly treated, judgmental, or jealous. All these toxic emotions are a poisonous cocktail, a recipe for misery and unhappiness—a recipe for useless, unnecessary suffering! And we all do our share of it. Many of us go to chiropractors when we need an adjustment in our body—back, neck, spine etc. When we need an attitude adjustment, we need to make God, Holy Spirit, Presence,—whatever you want to call it—our spiritual chiropractor. Spirit's adjustments work every time!

However, we have to begin by being completely honest with ourselves: Do we want the peace of God or are we addicted to upset, drama, and unhappiness? This should be a no brainer—of course we want peace! Then why don't we experience it more of the time? We are conditioned by the world to listen to the wrong voice, the voice for separation, drama, lack and limitation instead of the voice for love, peace, and joy.

We become fascinated with our own drama and upset; and then stress takes us over until it becomes very difficult to see beyond it. Stress causes more stress; it multiplies itself like a virus and we can become submerged in our own negative attitude. We're stuck and feeling helpless. Bernard Jordan, the author of The Laws of Thinking says: "Worry constipates the manifestation of Spirit."—and—"Worry is meditation in the wrong direction." Ekhart Tolle calls worry the "babbling noise machine in our head."

We desperately need to find a way to get past all this. That way is attitude adjustments that call upon the voice of Spirit, always nearer than breathing, closer than hands and feet. Yes, God is always right here and now pouring blessings upon us; all we need do is to be open and receptive to this guidance and direction. We don't really have any legitimate excuse to be miserable!

To establish ourselves in an oasis of peace, even through the storms and challenges of life, takes commitment. I have found the following tools and techniques to be of help to me—but only to the degree that I make a commitment to use them consistently: Regular prayer and meditation, inspirational reading, Journaling, waking mantra, coming back to the present moment, and monitoring and observing my thoughts and feelings so that I don't wander too far off track.

When Ekhart Tolle was on public television he left us with the following question: "Can I be in the space for what is happening in this moment and not demand that it be different?" We create so much misery for ourselves by demanding that things be different. We need to stop resisting what is. We need to bless it whether it is a large or a small matter.

A few years ago my peace was challenged during a cruise with my friend Helice. At a certain point I became aware that I had failed to zip a compartment in my jewelry bag and discovered that a valuable ruby ring was lost. I felt some panic and anger at myself for being so careless. This ring had sentimental value. It was given to me in Hawaii by my dear ex-husband Joe. I quickly came to the realization that it was gone and that there was nothing to be done about it. IT IS WHAT IT IS. So, I made an attitude adjustment and decided to accept what happened and to bless the ring on its way. I hoped that whoever found it would enjoy it and be blessed by it. I had enjoyed it for several years, so I decided to bless and release it. I reminded myself, "In the grand scheme of things, this is a small matter, just a material thing.

Now for an example of what can happen when we give ourselves an attitude adjustment and release all outcomes to spirit. Several months after the cruise, I got my jewelry container out of the closet to get ready for a few days vacation. As I was putting jewelry into it, I felt a funny lump. There was nothing visible, but I turned the bag every which way and discovered a slit in the top and a big space that ran the length of the bag. The lump was in that space—and it was my ruby ring!

But, what about larger issues, bigger adjustments such as loss of loved ones through death or divorce, or job losses, monetary losses? Most of us have ideas about how our lives "should" unfold. My picture book was happily ever after with a perfect husband, perfect children and a Leave it to Beaver lifestyle. In reality, my life has been everything but that. Divorces, death of one son, handicap of another, all kinds of uproar and drama, but with lots of good thrown into the mix as well. I have enjoyed success as teacher and minister, wonderful loving friends, a great relationship with my son and daughter. I can honestly say I love my life. All of it.

I have learned to embrace my mistakes and craziness and to learn from it all. In fact, the dramas and traumas I experienced propelled me toward the search for answers to life—and by the grace of God I have found many of them. I feel incredibly blessed to be able to share my journey and to use my experience to help others. It is also a blessing that in doing what I do I don't have the luxury of wandering off the path for long. I owe it to God, to you, and to life to be accountable. I have learned to be ready and willing to make attitude adjustments as I move through the circumstances of my life. I have come to realize that every drama and trauma has made me a more compassionate and understanding person, so I can bless it all. It all adds up to one big attitude adjustment that has been a work in progress over the years.

Huge adjustments can take time. Yet we need to know that by the grace of God they don't need to take as much time as we think. A woman named Emily Perl Kingsley wrote to Ann Landers a few years ago to describe the experience of raising a child with Down's syndrome. Here's what she wrote: "When you're going to have a baby, it's like planning a fabulous vacation trip to Italy. You buy some guidebooks and make wonderful plans: The Coliseum, Michelangelo's 'David, the gondolas in Venice. It's all very exciting. After months of eager anticipation, the day finally arrives. You pack your bags and off you go. Several hours later, the plane lands. The flight attendant says, "Welcome to Holland.""

"Holland?!" you say. "What do you mean, Holland? I'm supposed to be in Italy. All my life I've dreamed of going to Italy!" But there has been a change in the flight plan. The plane has landed in Holland and there you will stay. The important thing is that they have not taken you to a horrible, disgusting, filthy place full of pestilence, famine and disease. It's just a different place. So you must go out and buy new guidebooks, learn a whole new language. You will meet a whole new group of people you would not have met in Italy.

Holland is slower-paced, less flashy than Italy. But after you've been there for a while and you catch your breath, you look around and you begin to notice that Holland has windmills, tulips and Rembrandts. But everyone you know is busy coming and going from Italy, and they all brag about what a wonderful time they had there. And for the rest of your life you will say, "Yes, that's where I was supposed to go; that's what I planned."

The pain of the loss of that dream is significant. But if you spend your life mourning the fact that you didn't get to Italy, you will never be free to enjoy the very special and lovely things about Holland.

This moving testimony is all about attitude adjustment; accepting and blessing what cannot change. Most of us at some time have found ourselves in a situation where we least expected to be. Yet I believe our soul has programmed the whole thing. We can't know this consciously, but we are following our soul's plan. Our challenge and our opportunity is to keep our attitude adjusted so that we bring Spirit into everything we do, every hour of every day, through triumphs AND disasters,—that is the way to profound peace—and our soul's ultimate plan for us. Let us trust that our Highest Good can be found in whatever circumstance we may find ourselves. It's been said: "Every moment you are peaceful and happy is a gift to the rest of the world." May we all learn to accept our Earth School assignment, whatever it happens to be. Course in Miracles tells us that God loves a happy learner. So let us make whatever attitude adjustments it may take to enjoy this beautiful life and to live it with a pure heart and a peaceful mind.

One of my heroes is Mattie J. T. Stepanek, who went to live in Heaven at age 14 a few years ago. He was born with a rare form of muscular dystrophy and spent much of his life in pain, in hospitals and in a wheelchair. He wrote poetry from the time he was three years old and dictated it to his mother. All of Mattie's books of poetry made the New York Times bestseller list. In spite of his pain, he always had a smile on his face and love in his heart for everyone. He felt very close to God and trusted that he would see his previously deceased siblings in Heaven. I believe he was a teaching angel in a little boy's body.

In *Journey Through Heartsongs*, the end of a poem entitled Heartsong reminds us that: "Everyone in the whole wide world has a special heart song. If you believe in magical musical hearts, and if you believe you can be happy, then you too will hear your song." Mattie's life is an example for us all to follow. May we listen for our heart song in whatever circumstances we find ourselves. If we listen for our heart song and truly hear it, we will be ready and willing to make attitude adjustments and to become "happy learners" as we travel through our journey of life.

In Times Of Radical Change

Worry is like a rocking chair;
It keeps you busy, but you don't get anywhere."
(anon)

We might as well give up the idea that we are immune from radical change. What we need is to know that we can survive and thrive in the midst of it. I grew up in the forties and fifties and I confess that my mind boggles at the rate of current change. Spiritual teacher Jean Houston says that the whole planet is on a fast track; evolution feels speeded up. She calls it Jump Time.

The theory is that evolution is slow and steady and then at times seems to mysteriously speed up; radical changes occur, and everything jumps to a new level. It is not enough for us to sit back and worry while wringing our hands and declaring, "What is the world coming to?" We each must take responsibility for adding love and light to the world; we must turn away from despair and darkness, no matter what our current painful experience may be.

Fortunately, we have been left road maps, by enlightened beings such as Jesus, Buddha, Krishna and many others. We can study these maps, but we can't stop there. We've got to travel the road ourselves or we will stay stuck in a stagnant consciousness. We have to take action and do what is ours to do to nourish and love ourselves, each other and the planet. It does not have to be a drastic thing. Simplicity can be profound. "Kindness is my religion," says the Dali Lama.

The challenge is to become living love right here and right now, no matter what the circumstances. Life often twirls and swirls around us, uprooting everything we think we want, everything we were so sure we knew. Life has a way of giving us a swift kick in the behind. We never can know what our next change or challenge may come from. A Japanese proverb reminds us that: "Even monkeys fall out of trees. "However, there is no experience that is so devastating or damaging that we cannot rebuild our lives. I may disagree with physicist Stephen Hawking's conclusion that the universe can be explained by science so there is no need for God. However, I greatly admire his strength to continue with his life and work in spite of drastic changes in his physical body. He just keeps on adapting.

Nothing need push us down, hold us there, and keep us immobile. It is possible to connect with a vast reservoir of strength that Barbara Marx Hubbard calls our evolutionary driver. I believe we can call that driver the Christ of us, the Divinity in us, the God in us. I've discovered that my evolutionary driver becomes divinely discontent whenever I lose my way or go unconscious. When we are wise enough to surrender to our evolutionary driver and then trust the guidance that comes, we experience a smoother journey.

My favorite Bible passage reminds me to keep my faith and focus in the midst of radical and scary changes: "Neither death, life, angels, principalities, nor things present, nor things to come, not powers, nor height, nor depth or anything else in all creation can separate us from the love of God." (Romans 38-39) The challenge is to absorb and live that truth so that we can stay centered in the midst of life's storms of radical change.

When we have the rock of faith to stand upon, we don't hesitate. We dare to dive wholeheartedly into life. We celebrate the fact that we are dynamic ever changing process; life is dynamic ever changing process; God is dynamic ever changing process. It takes courage to release the familiar and seemingly secure in order to embrace the new. I have found that there is no real security in what is no longer meaningful. There is more security in the adventurous and the exciting because in movement there is life.

Someone once said, "To remain tight in the bud is more painful than the risk it takes to bloom." I trust that the light of our own divinity, contacted and embraced, will give us the wisdom to navigate through any and all experiences of change and challenge. We will be guided when to walk, when to run, when to stand still; we will be shown the way.

I've lost track of how many times I've started over, and I never know ahead of time when that next challenge will come. After initial clinging to how I think things should be, I let go and realize that it's never too late. We are never too old to deal with change, and it is never too late to "pick ourselves up; dust ourselves off and start all over again!" There is wisdom in the following:

Start Over

When you've trusted God and walked His way
When you've felt his hand lead you day by day
But your steps now take you another way—start over.
When you've made your plans and they've gone awry
When you've tried your best and there's no more try
When you've failed yourself and you don't know why—start over.
When you've told your friends what you plan to do
And trusted them and they didn't come through
And you're all alone and it's up to you—start over.

When you've prayed to God so you'll know His will
When you've prayed and prayed and you don't know still
If you stop because you've had your fill—start over.
When you think you're finished and want to quit
When you've bottomed out in life's deepest pit
When you've tried and tried to get out of it—start over.
When the year has been too long and successes few
When December comes and you're feeling blue
God gives a January just for you
So don't just sit there—change the view—start over.
—unknown

It has certainly been my experience that no one I know or have known about is exempt from dealing with drastic changes. There is no way of avoiding unwanted events, but by the grace of God, there is a way of dealing with them and moving on to higher ground. If we can meet life with love and an open heart, we will learn and grow; we will make spiritual progress—and we will find the Peace of God that is our divine inheritance.

Is There a Crack in Your Foundation?

"Not taking responsibility for our own life is
the greatest stumbling block to progress."
—Barbara Mary Muhl

We know and understand the importance of foundations in our homes, our roads and bridges. If they are cracked and not mended, when the inevitable storms come, basements flood, roads disintegrate and bridges collapse. When you and I don't have a solid spiritual foundation, every storm in our life creates a crisis that destroys our peace and often threatens our physical and psychological well being.

We read in Matthew 7:24: *Everyone then who hears these words of mine and does them will be like a wise man who built his house upon the rock; and the rains fell, and the floods came, and the winds blew and beat upon that house, but it did not fall, because it had been founded on the rock.* If we build our foundation on the solid rock of our true spiritual identity, we will be given the grace to weather any and all storms in our lives. Our solid foundation is a connection with the deep peace of our true Christ nature. Our solid foundation is a love for one another that goes beyond appearances and circumstances.

When we can see beyond appearances, we can separate a person's unskillful actions from his essence. Course in Miracles teaches that everything is love or a cry for love. When we incorporate that as a foundation stone in our lives, we treat others as we would like to be treated, no matter what the circumstance. No matter what someone says or does, we stay centered in peace. We stop blaming other people and circumstances and accept responsibility for our own lives.

Infinite Way founder Joel Goldsmith reminded us that "unless we <u>live</u> our faith, our religion is a corpse." We cannot live our faith if we just intellectually *know about* spiritual principles without demonstrating them in our everyday lives. We must go deep enough to experience Spirit, listen to Spirit, and resonate with Spirit. We must activate the truth we know in our heads by laying the foundation of that same truth in our hearts. The longest spiritual journey we may ever take is the one between our head and our heart.

In Spirit we have an unlimited line of credit, but we must activate that credit, just like we have to activate our plastic credit cards before we can use them. We can have knowledge and know we have it, but it can't work for us unless and until we activate it, and take it out of our wallet and use it. We begin to activate the Christ consciousness in ourselves when our desire for Spirit is stronger than all else.

A spiritual student went to his teacher and asked how he could find God. The teacher took him to the river and had him kneel down in the shallow water. The teacher pushed the student's head under water and held it there a long time. Finally, the teacher pulled the student's head up and asked, "What did you want more than anything else? "To breathe air!" the student cried. And the teacher said: "When you want God as much as you wanted air to breathe, you will find God."

When we truly want to experience the truth of our being, which is the divinity in us, we make our spiritual life our priority. We don't do spiritual practices so that we can be prosperous, find our soul mate, or manifest the perfect job and home. We truly seek the kingdom First, and then trust that the things we need will be added.

When we go within and meditate and pray, we do it in order to experience God; we know that God is enough. We pray for Divine Order and Highest Good because we understand that on the human ego level we do not know our best interests. We sincerely look for God where God can be found. If we are continually looking 'out there' for guidance, satisfaction, and happiness, we fall into the ego's trap. Its goal for us is to "seek and never find."

It is so easy to talk the talk—to call attention to how spiritually advanced we are; how many workshops and woo-woo experiences we've had. It has been said, "A Saint is a Saint until he knows he is one." So often when storms come, we step right back into our attack and defend positions and forget the truth we know. That's the crack in our foundation—when we put God first on Sunday and allow the ego to rule the rest of the week. Then we make ourselves susceptible to collapse when the pressures and storms come.

You and I have the most precious spiritual gem right in the pocket of our own heart, in the spiritual core of us. But we look everywhere else but where the true treasure is—inside ourselves. To excavate that treasure, we must remove the murky and false ideas and actions that cover it up. We must learn to become the watcher of ourselves in each moment so that we may see what is in ourselves that needs healing or change. We don't want to be the judge or the critic, but the neutral watcher who sees how we are thinking and acting and the consequences of it.

The watcher is the higher part of us that observes the ego movie in progress and by the very act of watching, the movie script will rewrite itself and result in a more skillful outcome. We begin to plug into love and unplug from separation and fear. The truth that we are, the love that we are, wants to be found, acknowledged and lived. It even manages to shine forth at times in spite of our efforts to ignore it.

We are challenged to continually and with our whole heart to build a solid spiritual foundation. When we have that we know absolutely and with no doubt that when we go within to find truth, we will find it. Standing on a firm foundation we never give up trusting Spirit. Love, Peace, and Joy naturally unfold in and around us and we are blessed and a blessing.

Closing Prayer:

Dear Father-Mother God,

We would open our minds, our hearts, and our lives to you. We want to lay up for ourselves treasures in heaven, treasures of the Spirit that can never be taken from us. We want to claim your love and peace and joy which is your gift to us and ours by divine right. May we have the strength and wisdom to claim our inheritance, here and now, without delay. We pray in the name and through the power of Jesus our elder brother and way shower and in the name of the Christ divinity we all share. Thank you God and so it is. Amen.

Living the Answers to Our Prayers

"If you have only two cents left in the world,
Spend one on a loaf of bread and the other on a lily."
—Chinese Proverb

There was once an old sailor who fell asleep on the bar room table; his buddies decided to play a trick on him. They rubbed some limburger cheese into his beard. When the guy woke up, he ran outside to get some fresh air then came back in and said: "It's no use—the whole world stinks!" Whether the world stinks or not depends on what we believe—what we think and feel about it. All too often other people put the stinky stuff under our nose; the solution is to see it for what is.

The *Candid Camera* show once played a trick on drivers seeking to enter the state of Delaware. As cars approached the toll booth after driving over a bridge, actors dressed as policemen informed drivers that they would not be able to enter the state today because "Delaware is closed for repairs." The reactions of the drivers were quite telling. Some just turned around and went back to New Jersey. Others became angry and argued with the fake cops. One woman asked, "Is Pennsylvania open?" The gag was funny, but the drivers' predicament is not very different from the limits you and I may have accepted from other people telling us what we could or could not do.

Great teachers have told us that *all* limits are illusory, and anytime we run into a wall or a closed door, the first place to try to open it is in our own mind. In the year 1900, for example, the director of the U.S. Patent Office sent a letter to President William McKinley recommending that "since everything that could possibly be invented has already been invented, I propose that the patent office be closed."

Eighteen publishers turned down Richard Bach's *Jonathan Livingston Seagull* before Macmillan finally published it and sold seven million copies in the U.S. alone during the next five years. Walt Disney was fired by a newspaper editor for lack of ideas. Fred Astaire was rejected at his first movie audition because he was slightly balding.

Then there was George Danzig, the college student who came in late to a math class and found two math problems on the board. He copied the problems, took them back to his dorm room for homework, solved, and turned in his answers at the next class. The following night his professor pounded on his door and asked George how he had solved the problems. "What's the big deal?" asked Danzig. "They were just homework." "The big deal is that they were *not* just homework," the professor explained. "These were classically unsolvable problems, and you have solved them."

So the next time someone tells you that Delaware is closed, or your ideals are harebrained or won't work or are impossible, know you don't have to buy into it. Consider that the "limit cops" who stop you have been dressed by candid camera, and you don't need to turn back to New Jersey or try to get into Pennsylvania as an alternative.

What we believe about what we can do, determines whether or not we even take the first step toward it. What does the Bible, what does Jesus have to say about it? Mark 11:24 states: "Whatever you ask in prayer, believe that you have already received it, and it will be yours." Faith is the substance of things hoped for, the evidence of things not seen. The science of quantum physics tells us that we change the very nature of particles and how they behave by observing them, focusing upon them.

Greg Braden, a genius computer scientist and now a world traveled teacher and author spells this out clearly in his book: <u>The Spontaneous Healing of Belief:</u> subtitled Shattering the Paradigm of False Limits. As a result of extensive research into many religions and philosophies, he wants to get the word out that actually believing the prayer, feeling the prayer, knowing you already have what you ask for and being grateful for it now, is the answer. He believes that we must transcend the doubt that too often accompanies our desire. There is a difference between working <u>toward</u> a result and thinking and feeling <u>from</u> it.

A philosopher known in his lifetime only as Neville shared many case histories that describe the 'miracle' of living from the outcome. Here's one that is simple, clear and innocent. A businesswoman came to Neville for advice and he told her about living from the answer and gave her instructions about how to do that. The woman's nine year old grandson was visiting from out of state and had been with her during the meeting. As they were leaving, the boy turned to Neville and stated excitedly, "I know what I want and now I know how to get it!" I want a puppy and every night just as I'm going off to sleep I'm going to pretend that I have a dog and we are going for a walk."

Adamant about all of the reason why he could not have a dog, the woman explained to her grandson, once again, that his parents would not allow it; his father did not like dogs and the boy was too young to care for one. There would be no dog—and that was it! That is, until six weeks later when the woman called Neville in amazement.

Following the day in the office, the boy practiced everything he'd heard. While he was playing with his toys, he listened and absorbed the details of their talk. He applied them, and he imagined his new dog lying in bed with him. He believed and acted as if the dog were already with him. In his beliefs, he lived his experience as though it were real. In his imagination, he petted the dog and actually felt its fur. Not long afterward, the boy's school had a special contest in support of Kindness to Animals Week. Everyone in his class wrote an essay titled "Why I would like to own a dog."

After the entries were judged, the boy's won and he was awarded a young Collie pup. The boy's parents had a change of heart and the Collie pup was welcomed into their home. The interesting thing is that the boy always wanted a Collie and that was the kind of dog he was visualizing and feeling that he already had it. Wayne dyer keeps telling us, "Don't say: I'll believe it when I see it; know that you will see it when you believe it.

We must believe in our heart and emotionally accept and feel the vision, or the prayer, right now—not in the future, but right now. I'm sure the boy in this story felt love for this animal as he slept with it, petted it and felt its fur. He was not thinking about it as a future event but as happening right then. That's living from the answer. That's asking in faith believing. That's giving thanks in advance. That's trusting.

The problem we too often have is that we allow fear and doubt to chase our good away. We want something, but we think it's too good to be true or we don't deserve it, or that could never happen for us. Those thoughts and feelings rob us of our power. They are the limburger cheese under our nose causing us to think the world stinks—at least for us. The Bible tells us: pray without ceasing. The truth is that we are always, with every thought, feeling, emotion, praying. We are either praying positively or negatively thereby making our own experience of the world.

Hafiz, a mystic poet who lived 1320-1389, left behind some marvelous and often outrageous poetry. Here's some advice from his poem To Build a Swing:

> You carry all the ingredients
> To turn your life into a nightmare—don't mix them!
> You have all the genius
> to build a swing in your backyard for God.
> That sounds like a hell of a lot more fun.
> Let's start laughing, drawing blueprints,
> gathering our talented friends.
> I will help you with my lyre and drum.
> You carry all the ingredients to turn your existence into joy.
> Mix them! Mix them!

The Gold in Change and Challenge

"To deny change is to be an accomplice
In one's own unnecessary vegetation,"
—Gail Sheehy

To be human is to be challenged by changes, but there is gold to be mined in each experience. Challenges come in all sizes and shapes. Some seem horrendous such as those that are experienced in war, painful illnesses or when we lose a loved one. Some are relatively minor bumps in the road of life, but as long as we are here in Earth School, we will experience changes, challenges and transitions.

Sometimes we are jerked every which way but loose by both major and minor challenges; sometimes we handle them wisely, oftentimes not so well. The question becomes WHAT can we do to come to the point where we more often than not handle our changes, challenges and transitions with clarity, focus, ease and grace?

It is important to develop a spiritual immune system, a spiritual strategy, a spiritual work ethic that will build within us a solid sanctuary from which our Higher Christ Self can guide, direct and sustain us. Otherwise our human level ego will lead us down the path of fear, anger, resentment, anxiety and self-pity. Such frames of mind take us into a place where we feel helpless against the circumstances and events of life. We become puppets of happenstance—pulled up when we like what's happening and pushed down into depression and despair when we don't like what's happening.

I dare to state that virtually everyone here in Earth School comes up against changes they don't want or like. Before I began to build a spiritual life, I lived a yo-yo existence, a Soap Opera existence, which I wrote about in <u>From Soap Opera to Symphony</u>. This spiritual autobiography dramatically documents my climb out of Hell. But the truth is that I am not done learning yet, and if I'm not careful, I can get myself right back down into a pit. That's life in Earth School. That's why Jesus taught: be IN the world but not OF it. That's what we must do if we want to build our spiritual immune system, which creates a base for advancement to the next level of existence.

Many wise writers such as Edith Wharton remind us to be unafraid of change: "One can remain alive long past the usual date of disintegration if one is unafraid of change, insatiable in curiosity, interested in big things, and happy in small ways." We can learn to transcend our problems by taking a higher view of them by using them as catalysts for spiritual growth. It is possible to let whatever happens be our teacher, not our enemy. When we make change our enemy, we become slaves to outer events and happenings and live a mechanical life of ups and downs. Spiritual progress is then a foreign idea seemingly beyond our reach.

We must use ALL events and not be lulled into believing that those small daily irritations don't count. They do, and dealing with daily irritations is a good place to begin working with ourselves. We can observe what we are thinking and feeling and make choices not to go down negative paths where we allow our ego judgments, dislikes and irritations to rule us. Whenever we put our ego in charge, we set ourselves up for the experience of Hell. Fortunately, it is possible to learn to choose again, to choose a higher way.

Heart Prints

Why should we bother to do this besides the fact that we will be happier? We need to understand the purpose our Earth School incarnations, which is to experience the Peace of God rather than to merely intellectually "know about" our Oneness with God and with each other. It means moving up into a higher vibration. It means becoming sealed into a space of light and love where darkness and hate cannot penetrate. Uproar cannot penetrate it. The goal of our journey is to become a radiating center of Divine Love and Light. By the grace of God, everyone gets as many chances as needed to reach that goal.

If we are NOT ready for the spiritual effort it takes to progress, we just go ahead and suffer until we get tired of our own misery. This is exactly what the Prodigal Son did. He wanted to spend his inheritance in riotous living and ended up being miserable and eating with the pigs. Then he realized he needed to go home to the Father. Most of us have done a lot of dining with the pigs. Hopefully, most of us here are tired of it and look for a better way, a higher way.

I wish the spiritual path did not have so many seemingly inviting side paths, so many temptations to say "To hell with it. I want what I want when I want it. If things don't go my way, I'll just get the satisfaction of indulging in my negativity." I've certainly been down many of those side paths, and found out the hard way that while they may temporarily satisfy, they inevitably lead to the experience of hell on earth.

So what is the most practical, useful, wise way of dealing with all the changes, challenges, transitions and irritations in life? Exactly how can we keep from being jerked around and led astray by them? We can gain valuable wisdom from the story of The Donkey in a Farmer's Well: One day a farmer's donkey fell down into a well. The animal cried piteously for hours while the farmer tried to figure out what to do. Finally he decided the animal was old and the well needed to be covered up anyway. It just wasn't worth it to retrieve the donkey. He invited all his neighbors to come over and help him. They all grabbed a shovel and began to shovel dirt into the well. At first, the donkey realized what was happening and cried horribly.

Then, to everyone's amazement, he quieted down. A few shovel loads later, the farmer looked down the well and was astonished at what he saw. With every shovelful of dirt that hit his back, the donkey was doing something amazing. He would shake the dirt off and take a step up. As the farmer's neighbors continued to shovel dirt on top of the animal, he would shake it off and take a step up. Pretty soon, everyone was amazed as the donkey stepped up over the edge of the well and trotted off. The Point: Life is going to shovel dirt on us; all kinds of dirt. The trick to getting out of the holes we find ourselves in is to shake it off—release it—and take a step up into Spiritual consciousness.

Here is my strategy, my plan of action for "stepping up."

1. Meditation every day. This is training in coming back to center every time our thoughts pull us away. When we can release thoughts and move behind them, we get closer to the pure Divine Hum that is God. It is like unto building a path and a platform on stilts above a swamp full of quicksand. Meditation helps us gain a wider perspective and tunes us into our Higher Self. It helps us rise above events so that we can transform them into lessons learning and growth instead of living as slaves of happenstance.

2. Read inspirational and helpful books listen to uplifting material; leave behind the negative films and unwholesome ideas. We cannot begin to separate ourselves from a negative life and negative emotions until we stop feeding on them. If we eat them for breakfast, lunch and dinner, what else can we expect? We become hypnotized by them and allow them to eat us. Has anyone ever said to you, "What's eating you?" If we don't want to become consumed by the darker side of life, it behooves us to feed on healthy, inspirational and light filled material.

3. Become involved with a spiritual support community. It is very helpful to pray with and encourage others on the path and to allow them to pray with us and encourage us. We are all capable of "losing it." In those times I'm in the middle of a change and challenge I have certainly had moments of "losing it." I am so grateful for my network of spiritual friends and supporters. I do practice what I preach (most of the time), and by the grace of God, I manage to get back on track more quickly than I used to. My Unity minister in Grand Rapids Michigan was fond of saying to us "Yep folks, this stuff works!" And indeed it does. Although we still have to deal with the changes, challenges, and irritations of life, we do have the tools to use if we are willing to use them. I encourage you to prove to yourself that "this stuff works!"

Play the Ball Where the Monkey Drops It

"Let life happen to you.
Life is in the Right, Always."
—Rainer Maria Rilke
"Trust would settle every problem now."
—Course in Miracles

When the British ruled India, they built a golf course in Calcutta. But this wasn't quite like England. Monkeys abound in India and they didn't understand that they needed to stay off the golf course. The British built a fence which the monkeys easily climbed over. They tried capturing the monkeys and taking them away, but more came back. Finally, they surrendered and made a new rule: Play the ball where the monkey drops it. Sometimes a ball would land in the middle of the fairway but a monkey would carry it off and drop it into rough. Sometimes a ball would land in the rough and be carried back and dropped onto the fairway or green. The new rule became play the ball where the monkey drops it!

What a wonderful metaphor for life! While making our plans, we try to organize everything nice and tidy and then something comes along and changes it all up. It can be frustrating, disappointing, aggravating! We do what we can to straighten it out; sometimes that works; sometimes is does not work. What to do? If everything we know to do isn't working, we have no choice but to "play the ball where the monkey (life) drops it. We always prefer the ball to be on the fairway, but often it ends up in the rough, a sand trap, or at the bottom of a water hazard.

The monkey of life often seems cruel as we go through divorces, loss of loved ones, job loss, maybe even losing our home. There is no denying that there is pain and suffering and outrageous injustice out there. When I've gone through some rough times, it felt like a madman ripped off one of my limbs and ran off with it. There was nothing to be done but endure and try to make sense of it all. The temptation is to give up on life. Some turn to alcohol or drugs or insanity. However, there is a way to prevail, to survive and ultimately to thrive.

It often starts with the realization that there has to be a better way and we are ready to find it. Jesus said, "Seek and ye shall find." And so we do. The grace of God kicks in and what we are ready for appears. Perhaps it is a teacher, a book, a movie or words of a friend. Something opens up. The monkey drops the ball back onto the fairway and we're ready to go from there without cussing out the monkey. We are ready to make a decision to leave our bitterness behind and to search for a way to move forward in the game of life. If on the next play the monkey takes the ball into a hazard again, we play it from there and know "that's just the way it is."

Enlightened teacher Byron Katie's teaching is that we must learn to accept, and yes even love, "what is." We can make decisions about where and how to get on with it at any given point, but right here and right now, we embrace what is. We bless the monkey and the ball and we bless wherever the monkey has dropped it. And we acknowledge that the monkey seems to drop it in some very strange and difficult places! I'm thinking about the case of J.C. Dugard who was kidnapped by a very mentally ill man and kept captive for years—even bearing his two children before she was finally rescued. She was just 13 when captured and bore her first child when she was only 14; at the time, there was no one around to help her through the labor.

In cases like this, we would expect the person to be seriously psychologically damaged. I happened to see the first part of J.C.'s interview with Dianne Sawyer. I was amazed at her obvious strength and wisdom. She had managed to find ways to stay sane, to educate herself and her children the best she could with what she had to work with. She has actually written a book about her experiences in hopes that it will help keep these kinds of outrageous events from happening to others. She has been reunited with her Mother and sister, has responded well to therapy and is about the business of moving forward with her life.

Is what happened to J.C. right, fair, just, or in any way reasonable? Absolutely not! But the ball was dropped and she had no choice but to do the best she could right where she was. You and I have to make those same kinds of choices concerning how we're going to conduct our lives. Are we going to become bitter and whine and complain or are we going to continue to play the game of life best we can? I'm not talking about becoming a martyr. I tried that for awhile before I knew better. Perhaps being a martyr is a step above being bitter, but that's not so healthy either. To be a martyr, we need to accept the role of victim.

One of the best understandings I've received on this spiritual journey is to stop being a victim of anything—whether child abuse or neglect, marital neglect or cruelty, death of my son, handicap of another. There are no victims, just learners on the path, just people living out the issues in their Karmic Bank. The whole point of our existence here is to "wake up" to the truth that we are spiritual beings, beloved of God.

We wake up by forgiving, loving, helping, feeling joy and gratitude no matter where the monkey of life drops the ball. I've also discovered that the more we learn, grow, meditate and feed on higher truths, the more we are graced with love, peace, and harmony beyond what we might have imagined in the midst of our earlier challenges. The more we stop fighting life's monkeys and learn to laugh at ourselves instead, the more joy we experience. I have learned that sometimes out of the worst situations come the best outcomes. It all depends upon how we see it and how we handle it—whether we curse or bless it or understand that ultimately it is for good because in the end the Universe is on our side!

I love the Bible story of Joseph whose jealous brothers threw him in a pit and left him to die. He was rescued and ultimately became an advisor to the Egyptian Pharaoh. Famine fell over the land of Israel and Joseph's family was starving. Egypt had lots of grain thanks to Joseph's correct interpretation of the Pharaohs' dreams. The brothers came to Egypt asking for help and saw that Joseph was in a leadership role. They were fearful and ashamed at what they had done. Joseph replied: "You meant it for harm, but God meant it for good." Our job is to see the good in all things, no matter what the appearance.

In the end, we experience life the way we perceive it. The Course in Miracles is all about teaching us to see with "true perception," which means to see with eyes of love and forgiveness with Holy Spirit as our guide. We misperceive when our ego, our sense of separation from God, is in charge. Our ego is always going to cuss and complain and feel victimized when the monkey does not drop the ball where we want it. So we have the choice of listening to the Holy Spirit, which is the Voice for God, or listening to our ego. The spiritual journey is simple and very profound at the same time. The simple instructions are not always so easy and simple to follow. Fortunately, we have our resources: meditation, prayer, spiritual reading, and spiritual community. We are never alone.

St John of the Cross lived between 1542 1591. He was imprisoned, starved and tortured for his beliefs. When his imprisonment was over, he began to write poetry. The theme of the following poem is congruent with the idea that we must "play the ball where the monkey drops it." And just maybe, God is telling the monkey where to drop it?

Development

Once I said to God, "How do you teach us?"
And he replied, "If you were playing chess with
Someone who had infinite knowledge and
Wanted to make you a master of the game,
Where would all the chess pieces be at every moment?
Indeed, not only where he wanted them, but placed where all were
Best for your development; and that is every situation in one's life."

Soul Searching

"If you think you know already,
how can you take in new knowing?"
—Maurice Nicoll

If we are to continue to learn and grow spiritually, we must ask ourselves such questions as: Where am I? What ideas am I interested in? Is my mind closed or open? Am I so busy with everyday life and appearances that I have no interest in exploring new ideas or expanding my consciousness? Is it all too airy fairy? Do I study and think about spirituality and expanding my consciousness, but then revert back to how I responded before I was exposed to higher ideas and ideals?

It is all too easy to become engaged in coping with the outer daily details and assaults of life. Without a higher center of truth, which comes from daily spiritual work, from studying and applying that work, we can become stuck in a limited perspective which leads to a limited life. Pema Chodrin Buddhist nun and author says: "A much more interesting, kind, adventurous and joyful approach to life is to begin to develop our curiosity. To lead a life that goes beyond pettiness and prejudice and always wanting to make sure that everything turns out on our own terms. To lead a more passionate, full, and delightful life than that, we must realize that we can endure a lot of pain and pleasure for the sake of finding out who we are and what this world is, how we tick and how our world ticks, how the whole thing just is."

As we become more conscious, we will realize that each day we have been handed exactly what it is we need to work on. If we can see that these experiences are necessary for us, we will stop complaining that life is not fair. Truth is, life is often not fair on the surface, but at a deeper level, it is always accurate. The universe is vast, and it is good to remember that this is so. The Universe contains billions of stars arranged in great masses called galaxies. Our sun is a star in our galaxy, the Milky Way. As we look up we see a thick band of stars overhead. There are about 100,000 million stars like suns in our galaxy. The telescope at Mt. Wilson in California has discovered that there are some 100,000,000 of these galaxies within the limits of its range, which penetrates to a distance of a trillion light years. In this universe, vast beyond belief, of incredible depths, the earth swims as a minute speck, and we are still more infinitely minute specks in terms of physical magnitude. (from volume v. Nicoll commentaries)

So, we must ask ourselves, does what we do matter? Where and how do we fit into all this? I have always been interested in exploring these questions, interested in going deeper into things, and because of that interest the universe has rewarded me with opportunity to look into the deeper issues of life. I'm a soul searcher and try to inspire others to search also. That's why I love philosophy and studied that in college along with Literature, which is full of philosophy.

However the trick is to glean what is Truth with a capital T from the plethora of ideas and philosophies. Here is where the work begins as we try out and work with the ideas and apply them to our lives. The New Testament and the teachings of Jesus are to the point and usable, if we will apply them. When asked what is most important, Jesus replied that to Love God and our neighbor as ourselves is the most important. Love covers it all because it includes forgiveness of self and others as well as the golden rule of do unto others as you would have them do unto you. Of course all other great spiritual teachings agree with these principles.

The soul searching comes in when we take the time to examine our thoughts and actions, to take an honest look at what is going on within ourselves and how we are relating to others. It comes in when we can see the experiences of each day as exactly what we need to learn from. I am reminded of a story:

An elderly carpenter was ready to retire. He told his employer/contractor of his plans to leave the home building business and live a more leisurely life with his wife enjoying his extended family. He would miss the paycheck, but he needed to retire. The contractor was sorry to see his good worker go, and asked him if he would build just one more home as a personal favor. The carpenter said yes, but in time it was easy to see that his heart was not in his work. His workmanship became shoddy, and he used inferior materials. It was an unfortunate way to end his career. After the carpenter finished his work and the builder came to inspect the house, the contractor handed the front door key to the carpenter and said, "This is your house; it's my gift to you."

What a shock! What a shame! If he had only known he was building his own house, he would have done it all so differently. Now he had to live in the home he had built none too well. So it is with us. Sometimes, we resort to building our lives in a distracted way, reacting rather than acting, willing to put out less than our best. When we don't give our best effort, we find that we live in the situation we have created. We need to think of ourselves as the carpenter of our own life, and to realize that it deserves to be built in integrity.

Life does have a way of presenting to us exactly what we need. It seems that the carpenter in this story was given the chance to see that it matters what he does and it matters how he lives his life. This is true for all of us. Let's try to do enough soul searching and applying spiritual growth principles to our life that we don't have to learn our lessons the hard way. Much of my own life has been about learning the hard way, but once I began to examine and apply spiritual principles, things changed. I certainly still had challenges, but instead of cursing them, I looked to see what it is that I was supposed to be learning from them. Now, I look at them as exactly what I need to experience in order to progress. That certainly takes away the sting and the tendency we all have to feel victimized by events.

Soul searching is not a waste of time. It is essential if we truly want to expand our consciousness. I believe that is what we are doing here in Earth School and that we will stay here lifetime after lifetime until we get the job done. Why not get started? It is a very rewarding journey!

Standing On Holy Ground

"Higher influences are playing on us
at this moment, but if we are glued
to our senses and completely identified
with all that we are doing, we cannot become
aware of these influences."
—Maurice Nicoll

"The quickest of us walk around well wadded
with spiritual density."
—adapted from George Eliot

God said to Moses: "Take the shoes from off your feet for the place you are standing is Holy Ground." Why did God tell Moses to take off his shoes? Symbolically and metaphysically, feet represent understanding, and shoes in this instance represent what covers up our understanding—which is our well wadded spiritual density. So if we are going to approach God, if we want to be open to higher influences, we must remove what blocks our understanding—those thick platform shoes of spiritual density.

Shoes represent our ignorance, resistance to truth and a higher way, our limitations, our history, our drama, our fears, our situation of being caught up in appearances out there so that we can't look for God where God can truly be found—within. We don't want to remove our shoes because we believe we can't get along without them; we are attached to them. We don't want God messing with our comfortable insulated shoes. Sometimes we need a good shaking up to wake up, but of course we resist that!

The Persian poet Hafiz precisely describes our predicament in the following poem:

Tired Of Speaking Sweetly

Love wants to reach out and manhandle us,
Break all our teacup talk of God.
If you had the courage and
Could give the beloved His choice, some nights,
He would just drag you around the room
By your hair,
Ripping from your grip all those toys in the world
That bring you no joy.
Love sometimes gets tired of speaking sweetly
And wants to rip to shreds
All your erroneous notions of truth
That make you fight within yourself, dear one,
And with others,
Causing the world to weep
On too many fine days.
God wants to manhandle us,
Lock us inside of a tiny room with Himself
And practice His dropkick.
The Beloved sometimes wants
To do us a great favor:
Hold us upside down
And shake all the nonsense out.
But when we hear
He is in such a 'playful drunken mood'
Most everyone I know
Quickly packs a bag and hightails it out of town.

Can you relate to that? I can. Before I knew better, I was well wadded with spiritual ignorance and clueless about the importance of an inner spiritual life. I kept my distance from the faraway God in the sky except when I desperately needed something that I thought would help me create a picture book life. Being lost in the outer world of appearances and attachments was my equivalent of "hightailing it out of town." I had no clue that I was one with God and that it was my destiny to know this oneness.

There is a story about a little boy in the Tennessee hills whose mother gave birth to him out of wedlock. This was back in the days when great shame was attached to this situation. People in his little town were cruel and were constantly asking him, "Who's your daddy?" He made a practice of staying away from people who asked the question. When he went to church, he scooted out the back early to avoid them. But one Sunday the new preacher ended early and unexpectedly, and the boy could not get out before the crowd. Just about the time he got to the door the preacher put his hand on his shoulder and asked, 'Son, who's your daddy?' He could feel the eyes of everyone looking at him. He was embarrassed and did not know what to say.

The new preacher sensed the situation around him and using discernment straight from the Holy Spirit said to the scared little boy "Wait a minute! I know who you are! I see the family resemblance now. You are a child of God!" With that he patted the boy on his shoulder and said, "Boy, you have a great inheritance. Go and claim it!" With that the boy smiled for the first time in a long time and walked out the door a changed person. Whenever anybody asked him, 'Who's your daddy?' he'd tell them, "I'm a child of God."

It just so happens that this is a true story that the former governor of Tennessee Ben Hooper told many times about himself. He began to stand on holy ground when he took off the shoes of shame and began to understand who he really was. I relate to this story because I too was a so called 'illegitimate' child, born to my mother when she was barely fifteen years old. I lived a rough and tumble life in and out of foster care for nine years before I was finally adopted into a stable family. During those years I was never taught about my worth or value, but indirectly taught that I was nothing and a nuisance.

When I was 18, I needed my original birth certificate for employment with Michigan Bell. It felt like a kick in the face when I read the question with a small block with the answer yes or no. Question: Legitimate? And the no block was checked. My main goal for many years after that was proving my worth & legitimacy with achievements, but I never really began to feel it inside myself until I found Unity and its wonderful teachings about the Christ of us, the divinity of us. I learned to know and to teach and say: "I'm a child of God, and God has no illegitimate children!"

I'll always be grateful for the Unity teachings that led me to take off my shoes of ignorance and to claim my divine inheritance. It has been my privilege and pleasure over the years to spread the word about the truth of us and about what we need to do to take off the shoes of ignorance and move ahead on the spiritual path. My goal is to remind myself and to teach others to not run out of town when God wants to deal with us. The poet Hafiz also said: "Look for God like a man with his head on fire looks for water." In other words we must take our spiritual life and our connection with God seriously and make it our number one priority. Otherwise we still run around with our feet covered because we can't bear to give up the shoes of the outer world; we think we might have to sacrifice too much.

We are standing on holy ground when we have the will to get on and stay on the spiritual path no matter what. We can and must develop a spiritual stronghold, an inner fortress in ourselves that merges with our divinity and live from that. We must stop being tossed around by appearances. We won't realize we always stand on Holy Ground when our shoes of ignorance are still on our feet covering our true understanding.

I have discovered the hard way that unless I stay awake and willing on my spiritual path, it is all too easy to slip back. The human level ego loves it when we do regress because it feeds upon the negative energy that comes with the regression. Therefore, we need all the help we can get. We need to be open and receptive to higher teachings. Ekhard Tolle reminds us in his book A New Earth: "Our ego attempts to convince us that we <u>are</u> our body, emotions, thoughts, roles and circumstances. Our ego would have us sacrifice our true identity to find a little treasure of its own." Whenever we make that ego choice, we are running out of town and away from God. A sense of isolation, loss and loneliness inevitably follows that choice. Yet, we deprive ourselves unnecessarily and live in spiritual poverty all the while we have a spiritual bank of treasure untold right where we are standing.

Brother Lawrence was a true mystic who removed his shoes and consistently stood on holy ground; our challenge is to make spiritual progress toward the same goal:

"I began to live as if there was none but God and I in the world. I make it my business only to persevere in his holy Presence, where I keep myself in a simple attention and a general fond regard to God, which I refer to as an actual presence of God, an habitual, silent, and secret conversation of the soul with God. This often causes me to have feelings of inward rapture and sometimes outward ones! They are so great that I am forced to have to moderate them and conceal them from others."

Our goal is to have our own secret conversations with God. Why not? We can choose to remind ourselves that God is nearer than our breathing and closer than our hands and feet. Let us dare to know that we are indeed standing on holy ground.

Sweet Peace

"I will be still and let the earth be still along with me.
And in that stillness we will find the peace of God.
It is within my heart, which witnesses to God Himself.
—A Course in Miracles

Do you find it challenging to find peace in your life? Is there too much to do, too many pressures, too many demands? Have you been hit over the head with job loss or a physical malady? As actress Gildna Radner said when she was challenged with cancer and eventually lost the battle: "There's always something." And she was so right!

I'd like to share the following story with you:

There was once a great kingdom where the king held court seated upon his throne. Lords and ladies came and went: diplomats, generals, and merchants by day, parties and balls in the evening—endless intrigue and romance. The court was a whirlwind of activity night and day.

Then one day the king died, but no one seemed to notice. The frantic activity continued unabated, with people rushing about as usual, hardly aware that the central power and authority of the kingdom was missing. Yet in their hearts the people felt a strange emptiness.

One day an old friend of the king came to visit, unaware that the king had died. The court was still bustling and the friend asked, "Where is the king?" People looked at each other with puzzled expressions and finally, laughing hollowly, someone said, "Why, whirl is king!" And they resumed their meaningless activity. Does this sound a bit like our modern world? There is so much activity, but at the same time so many people's lives are empty and meaningless right in the midst of too much to do and addictive distractions of all kinds. No wonder it is such a challenge to find peace!

The first step to finding peace and making it a foundation rock in our lives is to get off the battlefield. How do we make our lives a battlefield? Too often we listen to the voice of our ego which is like a scavenger dog, ever on the lookout for the slightest bit of evidence that someone has made a mistake or wronged us in some way. It is a mental attack machine and its ammunition is judgment, blame and guilt aimed at others as well as ourselves.

Our egos love to cheer us on in our peace stealing aggravations. We don't mind sharing our pet peeves and irritations: traffic, high prices, other people's habits and mannerisms, and we can always find something in the news of the day to be upset about. Many people were upset awhile back when a Libyan prisoner in Scotland was given a compassionate release because he was dying of cancer. He was serving a life sentence for being involved in the plot to blow up a plane over Lockerby, Scotland. No doubt we need to stop such acts of violence and we need to keep dangerous people locked up in prisons.

But the issue in this case is, do we want vengeance for its own sake, or do we want to show mercy? If we keep feeding into the cycle of violence and vengeance, more and more is created. We see this in many places in the world, especially the Middle East. The best way to defeat an enemy is to make him our friend, and Jesus advised us to love our enemies.

If we must watch the news, let's do it in a way that we just might be able to find some peace in the process: Perhaps make a prayer project out of it. Don't buy into the hate and fear. Send light and peace to the area. Pray for all those who made their transition that they may have a smooth passage into the light. Pray for survivors by sending prayers of love and light. If you are guided to do something positive and loving, do it.

We need to remember that there is always a higher way to see things. Earth suits come and go; bodies are temporary; souls have the opportunity to learn and grow through every experience. Our job is to send love and peace out into the world. The following excerpt of a piece from Gregory Flood gives perfect advice in this area:

> The Infinite is never in conflict with Itself.
> There is no war in the mind of God.
> That's where all of us are.
> It's the only place anyone can be.
> I choose to live a life of peace,
> no matter what life the world around me lives.
> There is nothing for me to do.
> There is only something for me to be.
> I choose to be at peace.

Spiritual teachers through the ages have pointed the way to peace, but too often we get caught up in the whirl of life and caught up with the ego's advice to keep searching outside of ourselves so that we seek but never find. What to do? I can speak with some authority about this one. For years, I was anything but centered in peace. I engaged in frantic searches for fulfillment through relationships and accomplishments. Nothing wrong with relationships and accomplishments unless we use them as a means to plaster ourselves together so we won't fall apart.

I came to a point where I realized that I would not find peace in the whirl of the world's ideas. I would never be able to tap dance fast enough to bring about my notion of what I thought I had to have in life to be happy. I became driven to find a better way. When we sincerely do that, the grace of God kicks in and what we need comes to us. I learned to meditate. I learned to just stop and rest my mind. I could not find peace and God out there in the whirl. The Bible tells us: Be still and know that I am God. That's the only way. Be still. Stop. Out of the stillness comes clarity and direction.

Have you noticed that when you are upset and on your horse riding off in all directions, that you are exhausted as a result? Meditation is a great conserver of energy. I learned that early on. Those who meditate can do less and accomplish more. When we are in whirl mode, we do more and accomplish less. This is true because, in meditation, we are tapping into the universal source of energy, peace, and wisdom instead of the whirl of busyness in the world.

People resist taking the time to meditate because of the lure of the whirl; the lure of the voice of the ego is very strong. So strong that we live countless lifetimes caught up in it. The question is, are you ready to stop? Are you ready to make peace your one goal? Are you ready to find the sacred place of the Most High deep in the silence of your own heart and mind?

That process has always been a foundation stone of Unity. Unity teaches us that God is to be found within ourselves, not in searching for an old man with a white beard who lives up in the sky. Who and what we are IS

Spirit. We are Spirit dreaming we live a separated human existence. Are you ready to wake up and end the dream? It's time to start—the truth is right there in your heart.

The Unity movement itself is based on what our founders Charles and Myrtle Fillmore gained from sitting in silence each day. They tapped into the universal source in their own hearts and found instruction and guidance. The legacy they left the world has been an incredible blessing in many lives, including mine. Perhaps the greatest legacy they left is also the one that Jesus the Christ also left: The Kingdom of God is within you. Look there.

I'll leave you with the affirmative statement that Charles and Myrtle used to attune themselves, to settle down and to enter the silence:

I am now in the Presence of Pure Being,
Immersed in the Holy Spirit of life, love and wisdom.
I acknowledge Thy presence and Thy power, O blessed Spirit.
In thy Divine Wisdom I now erase my mortal limitations
And from Thy pure substance of love,
Bring into manifestation my world,
According to Thy perfect law.

Taming The Monkey Mind

"The memory of God comes to the quiet mind."
Course in Miracles

What is the monkey mind? It is our anxious, jumpy, scattered, fearful, angry mind which thrives on uproar and conflict. It looks upon peace and quiet as boring and wants no part of it. The monkey mind believes in separation. To the monkey mind, life is a battleground, and its mode of operation is attack and defend. How do I know all this? Because my monkey mind ran my life for many years until by the grace of God, I found a better way and was given a spiritual tool kit that I could use to wake up from my insanity.

The first and most important tool for taming the monkey mind, also known as the ego mind, is meditation. The purpose of meditation is to assist us in placing our attention, our awareness, past, above, and beyond the churning of the monkey mind. We cannot prevent those thoughts and emotions from occurring, but we can choose to allow them to pass by, just as the wind moves the clouds away and we see the clear blue sky. There is a peaceful clear blue sky within us that is pure spirit and our true identity. Meditation connects our minds with our true identity. In this serene and quiet space, the monkey mind fades into the background, and as we meditate regularly, our life experience becomes more peaceful, loving, and serene.

The monkey mind wants its own way, but in this world it is not possible to always have our own way. How can we handle that dilemma? A great solution was put forth a few years back by spiritual teacher Ken Keys: "Upgrade your ego-backed demands to preferences." And we can even go beyond preferences by trusting that all is unfolding just exactly as it should be. We can begin to learn to "love what is" and go from there to take appropriate action.

We cannot demand that people or circumstances be fair. Much of the time life simply is not fair. However, we can use every unfair experience as a catalyst to teach us love and forgiveness, which is how we can find peace. It's a good idea to memorize the Serentiy Prayer and say it back to ourselves whenever we are upset:

> God grant me the serenity to accept the things I cannot change;
> the courage to change the things I can
> and the wisdom to know the difference.

When caught up in circumstances of everyday life, it's easy to allow our monkey mind to get caught in the drama, the fight, the battle with the motivation to win at all costs. I have been engaged in that activity myself and all I ever got out of it was misery and frustration. There is a better way. What Jesus taught is extremely practical. He lived in a time when life under Roman rule was not gentle or fair. He gave practical and helpful advice about how to deal with it all. Roman soldiers could demand that Jews carry their loads for a mile. Jesus told them to carry the load an extra mile. What sense does that advice make?

Whenever we're forced to do anything, we usually resent it. But if we can decide to go ahead on our own and do something extra, helpful, and kind,—not asked for—a positive peaceful attitude rises in us. At the same time it often changes the attitude of the person who is demanding of us. Jesus also advised us to "turn the other cheek," which means turn our mind in another direction, stop taking offense. When anyone "does us wrong" so to speak, it is not easy to get the monkey mind to quiet down. It celebrates grudges and injustices and likes to keep them active for years. However, we don't have to allow it—we can turn our minds in a better direction.

I've found it helpful to see that people who treat us badly or unfairly are unhealed people. If we can come up higher in consciousness and turn the other cheek and bless them and pray for their healing, we have set ourselves upon a path of peace. The Course in Miracles tells us "everything is love or a cry for love." Much of our world is crying for love. What are you and I to do about it all? Our job and the only sane action we can take is to first and foremost find peace in our own minds and hearts and pray and send blessings to the rest of the world. It is appropriate to remove ourselves from the presence of unhealed people acting out, but we don't need to throw them out of our heart. We can bless and pray for them, and if something specific needs to happen in the outer, we listen for guidance from the spirit of truth within us and follow that guidance.

An understanding loving heart is also a peaceful heart. When we cultivate peace within ourselves, when it flows through us like a river, it affects and transforms our lives. When our life is transformed by peace, it affects and heals those around us. As we upgrade our scattered consciousness into one of peace and serenity, we automatically become less judgmental. We surrender our judgments to the higher Christ Mind that does not judge; it only loves.

An amazing woman named Mildred Norman who became Peace Pilgrim took the principle of peace to heart and merged with it. At the age of 44 she began walking; she crossed the United States six times, and walked for the rest of her life. She wore navy blue slacks and shirt, tennis shoes and a self-designed blue tunic with pockets around the bottom where she carried her only possessions,—a comb, a folding toothbrush, a pen and small blue leaflets to pass out on the way. On the front of the tunic were the letters PEACE PILGRIM, and on the back was—WALKING COAST TO COAST FOR PEACE—and later, 25,000 MILES ON FOOT FOR PEACE. This was her outfit for the rest of her life, with new clothes being bought for her and new letters sewn on by friends as the old ones wore out.

She moved north in the summer and south in the winter, and after the first 25,000 miles, she stopped counting. She went without food until it was offered to her or she found it in the wild. If no one offered her a place to sleep, she slept wherever she could, such as a bus station or a corn field. To audiences large and small she talked about peace in the world and peace within. Peace Pilgrim touched the lives and hearts of thousands of Americans. They were charmed by her simple but cheerful presence and profoundly inspired by her message and her remarkable lifestyle. The following is a sampling of her wisdom:

We must walk according to the highest light we have, encountering lovingly those who are out of harmony, and trying to inspire them to a better way. Whenever you bring harmony into any unpeaceful situation, you contribute to the cause of peace. When you do something for world peace, peace among groups, peace among individuals, or your own inner peace, you improve the total peace picture.

There is within the hearts of people deep desire for peace on earth, and they would speak for peace if they were not bound by apathy, by ignorance, by fear. It is the job of peacemakers to inspire them from their apathy, to dispel their ignorance with truth, to allay their fear with faith that God's laws work—and work for good. A few really dedicated people can offset the ill effects of masses of out of-harmony people, so we who work for peace must not falter.

Good will win in the world. The darkness that we see in the world today is due to the disintegration of things that are not good. Only the things that are good can endure. Yes, love will win in this world. Those who are filled with hatred are desperately unhappy and desperately—even though unconsciously—seeking a better way. Only those who are filled with love are serene and at peace. (from Peace Pilgrim web site.)

The evening before Peace Pilgrim died in 1981, she spoke to a large audience in Indiana. The next day, she left her 73 year old earth suit behind at the side of the road where she had been walking. Her spirit lives on, still inspiring us to find the peace of God within ourselves and to share it. The Christ of us is our center of peace, love and joy. Our task is to quiet the monkey mind so that we may fully experience the truth of our being. In doing so we become blessed and we become a blessing to our world.

I leave you with a peace prayer from the Course in Miracles: Dear Holy Spirit, we come to you today to seek the peace that only you can give. In the quiet of our hearts and the deep recesses of our minds, we listen for Your Voice. Today we let Christ's vision look upon all things for us and judge them not. The peace of God is everything we want. The peace of God is our one goal; the aim of all our living here, the end we seek, our purpose and our function and our life while we abide where we are not at home. We would give your peace to those who suffer pain, or grief or loss, or think they are bereft of hope and happiness. We send light and peace into the world with faith that the light we send makes a difference. Amen.

The Bugaboo of Mood Swings

"Even in the deepest sinking there is the
hidden purpose of an ultimate rising.
The source of light is not withheld from us
unless we ourselves withdraw from it."
—Hasidic saying

Our moods provide the lens through which we experience life unless we can find a way to observe them and not become so identified with negative moods that we become a victim of the tyrant of moods. That was my experience for many years. I certainly still have moods, but now that I can see negative moods for what they are—coming from the ego tyrant having a tantrum—I can more often put dark moods in perspective and thus return to a peaceful center instead of being completely taken over

What does the mood tyrant in us want? Everything to fall into place exactly as we think it should! But life does not unfold like that. If we believe we must have all the material things, relationships, and circumstances that we want, when will enough be enough? When will we be satisfied? Probably never. There is always more to desire, more to do, more to have, more success to achieve. Until we catch on to the tricks of the restless and insatiable monkey mind, we live on an emotional roller coaster: When we like what's happening, we're excited about it and on an emotional high. When things are not going our way, we can get caught in a sad and dark mood.

I'm not talking about denying or burying emotions—we need to feel what we feel—but instead of clinging and making a story of them, we can let them pass through and return to center. "Moods are not so much overcome as transcended," David Hawkins points out. We transcend them by going over and beyond them to our center. It's not so easy to explain exactly what "center" is, but I'll try. It certainly helps to be a meditator because that is practice in accepting and releasing thoughts and emotions. Being centered is being able to witness the passing show of thoughts and emotions without being caught up in them.

Moving through life in a centered state is moving through life in a state of "walking with eyes open meditation." The witness sits in the center of peace, love and joy knowing that is the Reality and experiencing it—not just knowing about it. The witness, the higher Self, is aware of the big picture and experiences the peace of God in the midst of any and all circumstances that the ego is quick to label either wonderful or terrible. From the highest viewpoint, it just IS. God IS and all is well, we say in our prayer of protection.

A wonderful enlightened woman, author and teacher Byron Katie is all about teaching us to Love What Is. She asks, "Should this be happening?" and the answer—IS it happening?" (If it is, then it SHOULD be.) It is what it is. When we can accept that and go from there, we can move onward and upward. We can decide what action might be appropriate and take it, or it may be appropriate to just let it go. We don't have to tear ourselves apart with our own miserable moods. I am so grateful that through spiritual practices I finally found a way to "manage my moods" so that even when a dark mood threatens to overtake me, I have a means to deal with it.

Course in Miracles is a wonderful teaching tool for this with such lessons as, "I can choose to see this differently," and "I can choose peace instead of this." I have used Course in Miracles nearly every day for many years in order to keep myself straight. The ego makes it easy for us to slide backwards, and the purpose of spiritual disciplines is to build our spiritual strength and wisdom.

A section in the Course in Miracles really "nails" the ego tendency to get caught up in moods. It's called This Need Not Be (text Chapter 4 section IV). I'll share just a few thoughts: "When your mood tells you that you have chosen wrongly, and this is so whenever you are not joyous, then *know this need not be.* When you are sad know *this need not be.* Depression comes from a sense of being deprived of something you want and do not have. Remember you are deprived of nothing. Your mind and mine (Jesus) can unite in shining your ego away, releasing the strength of God into everything you think and do."

Even Jesus had to retreat and pray; even Jesus was tempted by his ego, which the Bible calls the devil. As long as we are here in the vibration of Earth, we have work to do and lessons to learn. In order not to get caught and dragged down by moods, we must do our meditation and spiritual work in order to keep from falling into that black hole of despair and depression. The following is a simple and clear way of explaining how we make progress:

An Autobiography in Five Chapters

Chapter 1

I walk down the street.

There is a deep hole in the sidewalk.

I fall in.

I am lost . . . I am helpless.

It isn't my fault.

It takes forever to find a way out.

Chapter 2

I walk down the same street.

There is a deep hole in the sidewalk.

I pretend I don't see it.

I fall in, again.

I can't believe I am in this same place.

But it isn't my fault.

It still takes a long time to get out.

Chapter 3

I walk down the same street.

There is a deep hole in the sidewalk.

I see it is there.

I fall in . . . it's a habit . . . but, my

Eyes are open.

I know where I am.

It is my fault.

I get out immediately.

Chapter 4

I walk down the same street.

There is a deep hole in the sidewalk.

I walk around it.

Chapter 5

I walk down a different street.

—anonymous

We all need to ultimately walk down a different street. But we start from where we are and keep our eyes on the goal of emotional freedom in Spirit. When I was caught up in the high highs and the low lows, I thought that was what Thoreau meant when he said he wanted to "suck the marrow from the bones of life." I was afraid that there might be such a thing as "too much tranquility." I was living my soap opera to the hilt because I didn't know a better way. I did that until I was so miserable I knew there HAD to be another way! That's when the grace of God stepped in and showed it to me.

That's when I found peace and joy in meditation and in the teachings of Ram Dass, Course in Miracles, Unity and others. That's when I began to realize that my history is not my identity. No matter what roads we've traveled or what we have chosen and experienced, our true identity in God is untouched and pure. The journey of awakening is one of understanding and experiencing who we truly are: sons and daughter of the living loving God. Our Christ identity is our true identity. All the ego identities we have assumed since we left the Garden of Eden in consciousness are not our Reality. Our Reality is not our body, our emotions, our status in life—our true identity is Pure Spirit. Being centered beyond moods, appearances, and our stories is the key to a life of peace and joy.

I share my Soap Opera story because by the grace of God I have moved past it; I put it out there to be what I hope is an inspiration for others to realize they can overcome any kind of experience through Spirit. St. Paul said, "I can do all things through Christ who strengthens me." And yes, we can, if we have the willingness to do so. And I believe you do have the willingness or you would not be reading this. Learning to manage our moods and to move past them is a big step forward in our psychological and spiritual growth, and I'm here to say that although it is not always easy, with Spirit it can be done.

One of my favorite enlightened teachers, David Hawkins advises us to "Choose to be easygoing, benign, forgiving, compassionate and unconditionally loving towards all life in all its expressions, without exception, including oneself. Trust in the love, mercy, infinite wisdom, and compassion of Divinity that sees through all human error, limitation, and frailty. Transcend the negative by merely choosing the opposite. With the internal discipline that stems from passionate commitment, the negative choices are no longer seen as options."

The Elephant and the Bamboo Stick

"Lots of people like to be seeking God,
but not too many actually want to get there."
—Ram Dass

One of the first things I heard on my spiritual quest after I had started meditating was: "Do less and accomplish more." In the years since I first heard that wisdom, I have fallen short of the ideal. Yet, I do much better than before this long spiritual growth process started. It's been said that we must not beat on ourselves if we have not as yet achieved spiritual perfection; if we are making spiritual progress that is all we can reasonably ask of ourselves.

I realize more deeply every day the importance of calling a halt to our mind's tendency to run around in circles and go nowhere. Our minds prod us into a frenzy of hurry and scurry, where we run full steam ahead and wear ourselves out, but still don't accomplish what we want. I have a loop in my brain that keeps saying, "you can do one more thing," and when that one more thing is done, the mind keeps telling me, "you can do one more thing," until I exhaust myself physically and mentally.

Certainly, at those times I am far from being "poised and centered in Christ Mind." I'm running around with ego mind trying to get things done on the human level. Ultimately there is no way to satisfactorily accomplish that. The solution is to Stop! Be in the moment! One thing at a time!

I love the story of the elephant and the bamboo. In India, when the trainer takes the elephant through the village and the marketplace, its trunk is very busy. It wants to pick up a banana here and an orange there and see what is over there in another merchant's stall. So the trainer gives the elephant a bamboo stick to hold in its trunk. Then, the elephant holds its trunk steady and looks straight ahead because it has something to hold onto. We can compare our minds to the elephant's trunk, always wandering and making mischief. But we can give our minds the equivalent of the bamboo to hold unto.

Actually we are given many helpful things for our minds that are equivalent to the bamboo, but we have to be willing to pick them up and use them in our lives. They do us absolutely no good if we merely know about them and don't use them. When furniture gets dusty, just knowing about the dust cloth does not help. We have to pick up the cloth and wipe the dust off the furniture. Just so with our spiritual tools. Unless we pick them up and use them, they can't help us.

We talked recently about the mantram we can use in the midst of our busy day. We can choose a word or short phrase to repeat to ourselves whenever we feel upset or stressed. Also, we can repeat it while waiting in line or in traffic to keep ourselves calm. The mantram is the stick of bamboo for our frantic brain. It slows us down and makes it easier to focus on the task at hand in the present moment. Time does not hurry us, we hurry ourselves. When we can just stop and see there is always only the present moment and do the best we can in this present moment, we automatically relax. That's when we can "do less and accomplish more."

It is all too easy to dump our vitality into a black hole of worry and scurry. When we worry or become stuck in past pain and anxiety about the future, we are training the mind to escape from the present moment and become tangled in its own web of dysfunction. Course in Miracles tells us that when we heal the past in the Present, we clear the future. It's very difficult to stay in present moment awareness when we are carrying a basket of unhealed issues. They are bound to interfere with our peace.

How do we deal with unhealed issues so that we may free ourselves to live in the now moment? The first step is the willingness to look honestly into our past without condemnation of ourselves or others. The purpose is to clear the debris, not to attack, blame, or make ourselves victims. In the final analysis, we are not our history, but <u>we will be at the mercy of our history</u> until we see it for what it is—experiences, lessons, opportunity for growth, opportunity for our soul to learn forgiveness. Once we see all that, we can then go about the inner soul work of healing and forgiving. It's good to have a counselor or spiritual advisor to help us through the process in the beginning. The purpose is to free ourselves to be able to move on with an uncluttered mind and heart and thus make wiser choices that are not the result of our early pain and dysfunction.

The mantram is an invaluable tool to use in the midst of any pressures or difficult experiences of earth school. We are sometimes given a lot to deal with, but we are also given the tools we need to cope with human events. Whenever we are pulled back into the pain, we can choose to keep repeating the mantram. The mantram is a holy name or phrase that has a long tradition. It might be something like Shalom (peace) or a name for God in any language, such as Elohim, Adonai, ElShaddai (Hebrew). Jesus, Jesu Christu, Jeshua (Christian). It might be a phrase such as Peace Be Still, or I Am the Beloved. Find one that fits your heart and mind and stick with it.

Using the mantram during the day and to fall asleep does not substitute for several minutes of closed eyes seated daily meditation. These tools work together to move us forward on our spiritual path. They are both mind training in release and help us to at least briefly experience the ISness of Pure Being. Instead of our thoughts, issues, and problems.

It's been said that inertia is the culprit, and that is very true. We get caught up in daily routines and wear ourselves out in coping to the point we are overwhelmed and have very little energy left over to devote to our spiritual progress. This is the human ego's plan to keep us stuck in the rut of our misery and ignorance. The ego loves our inertia and procrastination when it comes to dedicating some time and effort to advance spiritually. It just seems like too much effort when it's all we can do to cope with what's in front of us on the human level each day.

My suggestion is to start with a mantram, and when you discover how helpful that is, move on to five minutes morning and evening before sleep to sit in regular meditation and gradually increase the time. When you see how this helps you deal with your life in a more peaceful and effective way, you will have overcome your inertia. Here are the spiritual tools that I have used and that I teach for us to survive and thrive in this world of lessons and challenges.

First and formost: Meditation and Use of the Mantram and in-depth study of high spiritual material, spiritual food for the mind and soul . . . (Course in Miracles, Goldsmith, David Hawkins, Ekhart Tolle, Byron Katie, Ram Dass & many others)

Second: Forgive yourself and everyone else—no exceptions

Third: Learn from your challenges and experiences. We each have specific earth school lessons that will repeat until we learn from them.

Fourth: Bless everything—every person, every lesson, every experience. Bless everything and then release it to Spirit. Feel your oneness with all life,—everyone and everything.

Fifth: Use your experiences and the wisdom and compassion you have gained by being willing to allow Spirit to heal and bless you. Our assignment is then to allow the love of God to move through us to love and serve one another.

Each one of those steps must be taken when we are focused in present moment consciousness, focused on right here and right now. That's why meditation and the use of the mantram can transform us. Both practices pull the mind back to "here and now." When we bring the rushing process of the mind to a healing stillness, we rest completely in each moment. We learn to live life "first-hand" here and now in the moment. When we live in the past or future, we remove ourselves from the River of Life that is constantly streaming itself into us.

We love to talk and philosophize about God and Truth and How it All Is. There is nothing wrong with that, but if we focus on that and neglect our private individual daily spiritual work—which includes the five steps I just gave you—we are stuck on the surface, stuck in "knowing about" when the goal is to experience at depth the love of God moving through our being and out into the world to bless it. Let us not be one of those people who talk about seeking God, but delay the serious spiritual work it takes to get into higher consciousness, to Know God. Please don't be afraid to take the plunge into deeper spiritual waters!

Come to the edge! We might fall.
Come to the edge! It's too high!
Come to the edge! So they came—

And He pushed

—and they flew!

(—Appollinaire)

It's our spiritual destiny for our spirit to fly free. Coming to the edge of our human resources and pushing beyond with spiritual tools is threatening to the human ego. However if we are willing to come to the edge with surrender and trust—we will fly!

The Task of Balancing Life

"We take delight in things; we take delight in being
loosed from things. Between these two delights,
We must dance our lives."
—Rinpoche

One of the most important secrets to keeping our lives balanced is to laugh a lot. Therefore, to make it possible for you to attend church regularly, ask your minister to make the following announcement of changes you think might help:-Cots will be placed in the foyer for those who say, "Sunday is my only day to sleep in.—There will be a special section with lounge chairs for those who feel that the pews are too hard.—Eye drops will be available for those with tired eyes from watching TV late on Saturday night.—Steel helmets will be available for those who say, "The roof would cave in if I ever came to church."—The sanctuary will be decorated with both Christmas poinsettias and Easter lilies for those who never have seen the church without them.—Doctors and nurses will be in attendance for those who plan to be sick on Sunday.

Laughter is healing and a person with a great sense of humor is more than likely a well balanced person. Balance is important in every area of life on earth, especially our environment, which our human population struggles to value and protect. Sometimes with an intention to do a good thing, mistakes are made:

Kudzu was introduced to the US in 1876 at the Centennial Exposition in Philadelphia. Countries were invited to build exhibits to celebrate the 100th birthday of the US. The Japanese government constructed a beautiful garden filled with plants from their country. The large leaves and sweet smelling blooms of kudzu captured the imagination of American gardeners who used the plant for ornamental purposes.

Florida nursery operators discovered that animals would eat the plant and promoted its use for forage in the 1920's. During the 30's the Soil Conservation Service promoted kudzu for erosion control. Hundreds of young men were given work planting kudzu. Farmers were paid as much as eight dollars an acre as an incentive to plant fields of the vines in the 40's.

The vines were successful food for animals and certainly were great at preventing erosion, but they have also killed many trees. In the southern US, many trees, buildings, and fences are covered with kudzu. It grows at the rate of one foot per day during the summer and is extremely hardy. Kudzu is killing many trees as it quickly wraps itself around the trunk and branches and suffocates the trees. What was once thought to be a wonderful plant is now considered a nightmare by many.

Sometimes we can just have too much of a good thing. Factors in our own lives can be compared to the kudzu. We thought food buffets and fast food was such a great thing, but not monitored and balanced, they lead to overeating and obesity.

Kudzu can also be compared to the ever growing demands we put on ourselves and each other. We allow busyness to take over our lives and suffocate us, just like the kudzu covers trees preventing them from getting needed sunshine. We get zapped and squeezed in by too many demands. Buffets, fast food, and activities and responsibilities are all here and are useful when in balance and moderation—the danger is in letting them consume us to the point of harm.

Balance in our life is the secret to success and happiness. We have often heard the admonition: "All work and no play make Jack a dull boy." Other things we need to balance: exercise and rest, quiet time alone and interaction with others, study and applying what is studied, being serious with being goofy. Sometime the best help I can give someone is to join them in a session of "silly therapy." It can help put things in a proper perspective.

Our elder brother and wise teacher Jesus set a great example for us. His life was wonderfully balanced. He spent time in the world, often with crowds, teaching and interacting with them. He also withdrew often for rest, renewal and prayer. He demonstrated the perfect way to prevent burnout. We need to remove ourselves from our mad whirl of life. We will come to balance as we take time to be still and commune with the Spirit of God in us

The Bible tells us in Ecclesiastes that there is a time for everything under the sun. This is illustrated beautifully in the following story. A busy and successful and tired man who did not want to be bothered was waiting in a parking lot for his wife to get off work. A homeless man came across the parking lot and began to wipe off his car. "I hope he doesn't ask for money, the man thought. He didn't. He came and sat on the curb in front of the bus stop. After a few minutes he spoke, "That's a very pretty car," he said.

When he didn't receive an answer, he just sat there quietly. The expected plea for money never came. As the silence between the men widened, something inside the man in the car told him to ask the man on the curb if he needed help—and he expected that man to ask for money. So he reluctantly asked, "Do you need any help?" The man on the curb answered in three simple profound words that the man never forgot: "Don't we all?"

The man in the car was feeling high and mighty, successful and important, above a bum in the street until those words hit him in his heart. "Don't we all?' The man in the car realized that he did need help, maybe not for bus fare or food or a place to sleep, but he needed help. He reached into his pocket and gave the man on the curb not only enough for bus fare, but enough to get a warm meal and shelter for the day.

The three words, "Don't we all," ring true in so many ways for all of us. No matter how much we have, no matter how much we may have accomplished, we all need help too. And the balance of that is that no matter how little we have, or how loaded we are with problems, we can give help. A great way to give help is to see someone surrounded with love and light.

We can never know when we see someone who appears to have it all that they may need our help, waiting for us to give them something they don't have. Perhaps it is a different perspective on life, a glimpse at something beautiful, or a respite from daily chaos. Maybe the man on the curb was more than a homeless stranger wandering the streets. Maybe he was sent by a power great and wise, to minister to a soul too comfortable in himself. Maybe God looked down, called an Angel, dressed him like a bum, then said, "Go minister to that man sitting in his car; he needs help." Don't we all? The balance of giving and receiving is presented to us in many ways.

I recently spent some time with my dear friend Jean. We have been friends since high school. We've stayed in contact because she lives in Houston and actually took care of my granddaughter for her first two years so she would not have to go to day care. Jean is challenged to keep her life in balance because her husband has Alzheimer's and needs to be in a home. He does not recognize her or any of their children, but she still goes to the home every day and helps him with his lunch.

Jeam also does yoga, goes to a quilting class and other activities at her local Senior Center, is active in her church and has a circle of loving friends and family. When she needs cheering up, she listens to gospel music. She smiles and laughs frequently and when asked how she manages to be so strong, she answers: "My faith and my church." I love and appreciate my dear friend as she courageously leads a balanced life in spite of all obstacles.

Jean reminds me very much of the man in the following story—which I have sent to her. It's told by a nurse: It was a busy morning, approximately 8:30 am when an elderly gentleman, in his 80's, arrived to have sutures removed from his thumb. He was in a hurry because he had an appointment at 9am. I took his vital signs and had him take a seat. While taking care of his wound, we began to chat. I asked him if he had a doctor's appointment since he was in such a hurry. The gentleman told me no, that he needed to go to the nursing home to eat breakfast with his wife. I then enquired as to her health. He told me she'd been there awhile and that she had Alzheimer's.

As we talked and I finished dressing his wound, I asked if she would be worried if he was a bit late. He replied that she no longer knew who he was, that she had not recognized him for five years now. I was surprised and asked him, "And you are still going every morning, even though she doesn't know who you are?" He smiled as he patted my hand and said, "She doesn't know me, but I still know who she is." Love shows up in many different ways. And we all have opportunities to give and to receive no matter what situation we find ourselves in

True balance is being poised and centered in Christ Mind—that secret place of the most high where nothing can disturb the calm peace of our soul. True balance is giving and receiving love and blessings. True balance is continually replacing our fears with love. The following poem is a beautiful statement of what a balanced life might look like:

> I will not live in fear of falling or catching fire;
> I choose to inhabit my days,
> To allow my living to open me
> To make me less afraid, more accessible,
> To loosen my heart
> until it becomes a wing, a torch, a promise
> I choose to risk my significance,
> To live so that which came to me as seed
> Goes to the next as blossom,
> And that which came to me as blossom
> Goes on as fruit.
> —Dawna Maikiva

SECTION FOUR
Justice, Mercy, Forgiveness

"Out beyond ideas of right doing and wrong doing
There is a field. I'll meet you there."
—Rumi

Divine Restoration

"The spiritual world is like a bird of Paradise
longing to be seen. It flies so close to our eyes
that its lovely feathers brush our pupils."
—Swedenborg

Sometimes it's difficult to trust in Divine Restoration when the world out there looks like we are not being treated kindly or fairly. Yet from a higher spiritual perspective there is divine order. We are assured by Joel in the Bible that "The Lord will restore the years the locust has eaten." Yet, we need to make room in our own consciousness to recognize the restoration. Enlightened teacher David Hawkins reminds us, "When one's attitude toward everything becomes a devotion, Divinity reveals Itself."

However, until we know and trust the Christ of us to make all things new and trust in ultimate divine justice and divine restoration, we judge by appearances and block our good. A story illustrates the point: Once upon a time there was a king in a tropical land who had an advisor who was positive and enthusiastic. The man was so optimistic, in fact, that the king began to feel irritated by his aide's relentless willingness to look on the bright side of things. While the king and his advisor were on a trip through the jungle, the king was chopping with a machete, and he inadvertently cut off one of his toes.

The advisor's response shocked the king: "All is well! Somehow there is a blessing in this!" That was the last straw. The king, who could not see any good in losing his toe, picked up the lieutenant and threw him in a pit and left him there. On his way out of the jungle, the king was seized by a band of headhunters who decided that the king would make an excellent sacrifice. The natives took him to their priest to be readied for the ceremony. When the priest saw that the king's toe was missing, he told him, "We must have a perfect specimen for the sacrifice, and you are flawed. You are free to go."

Elated to be released, the king returned to the pit to rescue his aide. He found him sitting in the pit whistling peacefully. "I must apologize to you!" the king shouted as he helped his advisor out of the pit. "You gave me the best advice, and my response was to try to do away with you. Can you ever forgive me?" "No apology necessary," answered the aide. "There was a great blessing in your throwing me in the pit. You see, if I had still been traveling with you, the headhunters would have taken me for the sacrifice!"

It is difficult for us to realize that good can come from difficult times and difficult events. The problem is our focus. If we focus upon what is wrong and bad, making ourselves a victim, kicking and screaming in protest, we will suffer. That doesn't mean we won't grieve our losses; it does mean that we won't stay stuck in grieving our losses and stuck in the habit pattern of seeing only the dark side of things. I have discovered for myself the truth of this because at one time I was a screaming, kicking victim living in a cruel world—and I suffered mightily.

Like the king in the story, I used to be irritated by people who would proclaim, "Well, it's probably for the best." Like many people, I had to live in the dark ignorance of my own mind for quite some time before I realized there had to be a better way and became determined to find that better way. Let's examine Joel's statement about the restoration of the years the locust has eaten. To restore means to make beautiful again.

The years the locust has eaten can be seen as those despairing periods in our lives that seem empty of good and full of pain and problems. Believe it or not, through realization of spiritual truth, it is possible to see our painful past in a new light, and it will be restored by spiritual truth from painful to perfect.

The secret is to heal and release the loss and go for the gain. How can we do this? The first step in Alcoholics Anonymous is a good first step for all of us: "On the human level, my life is unmanageable and I need help!" What kind of help do we need? First and foremost—spiritual help—the easiest route to this is a positive all inclusive cosmic view and regular meditation. This puts us into direct contact with Spirit where we can learn to listen for instruction and guidance instead of operating at the human level of outside appearances

The following story is a great example of what can happen to us when we don't stop to ask for Holy Spirit's instruction and guidance. A hiker was on his way back down a mountain when he encountered a poisonous snake across the path. "Please help me!" the snake implored. "I need to get down the mountain and I could ride in your pocket." "Are you crazy? The hiker answered. "You are a poisonous snake."

The snake said, 'but I promise I won't bite you!" The snake continued to plead until the hiker relented, "Well, all right, if you promise." And he picked up the snake and took him to the bottom. The snake immediately bit him. As the snake was crawling away the hiker whined, "But you promised!" The snake replied, "You know what I was when you picked me up," and went on its way.

What can we learn from this story? What if the hiker had said, "Wait a minute here; I need to get guidance about this!" If he had done so, he might have heard, "better not do that because it is the nature of snakes to bite." He could have said to the snake, "I bless you on your journey, but you will have to find your own way down the mountain." Since he made a mistake and suffered the consequence, what's the next step?

We need to forgive everyone and every circumstance that we believe has wronged us in any way. This might even be life itself, the universe, even God. I discovered that I needed to do a blanket forgiveness of my total life. I came to realize that it is important to learn and grow from every mistake. I learned that blaming and judging others never brings peace. I learned to trust in ultimate divine justice and divine restoration. This is the key to waking up spiritually.

Peter asked Jesus how many times should we forgive. Seven? And Jesus answered, "seventy times seven,"—in other words as many times as it takes. It's been said that not to forgive is like swallowing poison and expecting someone else to die. Of course, we are only swallowing our own poison when we refuse to give up our anger, hatred and resentments. True and ultimate forgiveness takes place when we realize that no one has or could possibly harm our soul, the truth, the divinity of us. We know we have completed the forgiveness process when we can say to anyone we believe has harmed us and mean it, "I love you, bless you and release you to your Highest Good."

Divine restoration comes when we cleanse, heal forgive and release all the human level mistakes of ourselves and others. I recently visited the Brogan Museum in Tallahassee and was impressed by the beautifully restored Baroque paintings from the 15th and 16th century. Restoration reveals their brightness, beauty and artistry. Centuries of dust was removed and other damages repaired. These paintings look like they were finished in modern times. Restoration takes place in us when we allow God to restore our consciousness so that our attitude toward everything becomes a devotion. The dust and damage of our mistakes is cleansed, and then Divinity reveals Itself to us.

It is important to remember that what is truly ours is ours by Divine Right. As we tune into the love of God and realize our true identity, restoration comes by grace and we begin to live in the love, peace, and joy of God. The world opens and says "yes" to us in new and miraculous ways. We begin to trust as never before and see our life being filled with blessings.

That bird of paradise that Swedenborg talks about is seen and felt by us as its lovely feathers brush our pupils. We know that we are home in the mind and heart of God and we are grateful. Our Divine identity is established and can never be taken from us no matter how many snake bite incidents we may have ignorantly invited into our lives. God blesses all of us now and always, whether we are consciously aware of it or not. The Bible tells us that God's mercy shines equally upon the just and unjust. However, we won't experience that benevolence until we consciously open our hearts and minds to that Presence.

Dear Father-Mother God: May our hearts open and remain open to your loving and forgiving Presence. May we trust in the Grace of Divine Restoration. We give thanks that You bless us now and forever. Amen.

How to Deal With Failure

"There are no mistakes, no coincidences
All things are blessings to be learned from.
—Elizabeth Kubler-Ross

"If you're not prepared to be wrong,
you can't come up with anything original."
—Sir Ken Robinson

Why do we fear our failures and too often surround them with shame? We live in a "succeed and win" and a "lose and fail" society. Eskimos have dozens of words for snow: We have dozens of words for failure: setback, snafu, glitch, reversal, gaffe, goof, screw-up; the 'f' word seems to be "failure". Green Bay Packers long time coach Vince Lombardi said: "Winning isn't everything, it is the only thing!" He could have been coaching American life. If you have been buying into this approach to living, I hope you are willing to redefine the concept of failure. We need to realize that it is not a permanent condition, a fatal flaw or a contagious social disease.

In truth, the way we cope with so-called failure is what shapes our lives, not the situation or event that we label a failure. In fact success and failure are two sides of the same coin. If we are not willing to risk failure, we can't achieve success. For example heavy hitters, the ones who hit the most home runs, also strike out the most. Babe Ruth struck out 1,330 times, but also hit 714 home runs. B.H. Macy failed seven times before his store in New York caught on. We need to know that defeat can be a powerful growing experience. Our real strength comes from working through our defeats and finding out we can learn; then we are able to survive and even thrive. "A good education is not so much one which prepares a man to succeed in the world, as one which enables him to sustain a failure." (Bernard Bell, Chaplain, University of Chicago).

Why not gift ourselves with freedom from conventional ideas of success and failure? We too often believe that if we make any mistakes, we've failed. But life is just naturally full of mistakes and trial and error. Relax. Exhale. Embrace 'Oh Well,' and go on from there. I love the following advice: "When in doubt, go ahead and make a fool of yourself. There is a microscopically thin line between being brilliantly creative and acting like the most gigantic idiot on earth. So, what the hell, leap!" (Cynthia Heimel) So remember the advice: "If you're not prepared to be wrong, you can't come up with anything original."

We label as failures such things as a lost job, a business going under, a denied promotion, low sales, negative reviews, divorces, break-ups and disappointments in our children. Too often we feel betrayed, violated, destroyed, pummeled, terrified, angry, guilty, depressed, shattered—it can be a time of great confusion. Some psychiatrists say that during such times, we can lose our very sense of self. The more closely we identify with the job, endeavor, or situation, the greater the sense of loss and failure. I confess that early in my ministerial career, I experienced some so called failures that pulled the rug out from under my feet. Yet, they precipitated a needed deeper healing and understanding that have helped me to quickly and successfully weather heavy storms that came along later.

Our task is to totally re-interpret our story. But how do we do this? The very first thing is to move away from our victim role. This can happen when we realize that this problem or predicament is a lesson we consciously or unconsciously chose to learn. We may be pushed by events into seeking needed inner healing. As a result of these experiences, it is possible to become stronger, wiser, more loving, open, compassionate and understanding.

We can begin to understand that the word failure is our thoughts about the event, our judgment and interpretation. It's not so much the failure that is the problem but the emotion around it. So we need not worry so much about failure. It is a good idea to be more concerned about the chances we miss when we give up on life and don't even try. Winston Churchill said, "Success is not final; failure is not fatal: It is the courage to continue that counts."

Ted Koppel once said that he could have wallpapered his walls with the rejections he received in his pursuit of a job as foreign correspondent. At one point, he was so desperate for a job that he interviewed with advertising firms because he knew he could at least write. Even the advertising firms turned him down. But Ted did not give up and eventually became the host of *Nightline*.

Norman Vincent Peale was counseling a depressed man who thought of himself as a failure because of all the problems in his life. "I just want them to go away," he said. Peale's answer: "I know a place where there are 100,000 people and not one has a problem." "Great! I want to go there," the man answered. Norman Vincent Peale replied, "Okay, I'll give you directions to Woodlawn cemetery!" Problems and failures are an inevitable part of our life in earth school. They are not our enemy; they provide us with opportunities for soul growth.

Whenever we choose to handle life from the spiritual perspective, our life becomes a whole new ball game. Although our fears, insecurities, and thoughts of self-defeat are always waiting in the wings to pounce, we can call upon Spirit to guide and direct us. Even Jesus was tempted to resort to his human ego, but he said "get thee behind me Satan."

We need to say the same thing in whatever words we can relate to such as, "Get thee behind me negative ego saboteur. Get thee behind me Anti-Christ. Get thee behind me old ways of thinking and doing. Through the God power within me I choose to bless every lesson, every so-called failure and move forward in spirit. I am here in earth school to learn spiritual lessons—the greatest of these is unconditional love for myself and for others; I am here to learn to recognize my true identity as spirit—and to recognize the Christ in all!"

We look up to heroes who have faced and overcome tremendous challenges and so called failures. What is going on? Could it be that our soul sets up unique sets of lessons, problems and so-called failures in order to progress? What a liberating idea! Each person reading this has taken birth for healing and growth, and we need to see events in life as a means of accomplishing this. We need to see that the bigger the challenge, the more opportunity for advancement. Norman Vincent Peale said, "Although we need to comfort the afflicted; we occasionally need to afflict the comfortable!"

So let us remind ourselves that life is about choosing the peace of God and the love of God every day of our lives,—the down days, the up days, the days when we win, the days when we lose, the days when we fail, and the days when we succeed. It's about being open and receptive to the guidance, instruction, and inspiration of spirit—no matter what the outer appearance may be. We can learn something from the following story entitled: Cracked Pots.

A water bearer in India had two large pots, each hung on the ends of a pole, which he carried across his neck. One of the pots had a crack in it, while the other pot was perfect and always delivered a full portion of water. At the end of the long walk from the stream to the house, the cracked pot arrived only half full. This went on every day.

Of course the perfect pot was proud of its accomplishments. But the poor cracked pot was ashamed of its own imperfection, and miserable that it was able to accomplish only half of what it had been made to do. After two years of what it perceived to be a bitter failure, it spoke to the water bearer one day by the stream. "I am ashamed of myself, and I want to apologize to you. I deliver only half my load because of this crack in my side. The water leaks out all the way to your house. Because of my flaws, you have to do more work."

The bearer said to the pot, "Did you notice that there are flowers only on your side of the path, but not on the other pot's side? That's because I have always known about your flaw, and I planted flower seeds on your side of the path, and every day while we walk back, you water them. For two years I have picked these flowers to decorate my table. Without you being just the way you are, there would not be this beauty to grace the house."

Each of has our own unique flaws. We're all cracked pots. But our cracks and flaws make our lives together interesting and rewarding. We learn to be more accepting of ourselves and of others,—flaws, mistakes, and so called failures included! They are all part of the learning and growing process here in Earth School.

Living Outside the Box

"You didn't come here to nail
A bird to the ground. Things move. Life flies."
—Tama Kieves
"Little boxes on the hillside,
Little boxes made of ticky-tacky
Little Boxes, little boxes
And they all look just the same.
—Malvina Reynolds

The Little Boxes lyric is all about the confining boxes we too often accept living in because we want to feel secure. We're talking about inner boxes as well as outer boxes. We may live in a house just like the others on our street and still lead an expansive life. We could be confined to a wheelchair and still live free. The questions are, "Do we dare to go beyond what society and other people think is right for us?" "Are we willing to refuse to be nailed to the ground?" I have found that whenever I get stuck in psychological boxes, when the bird inside me feels nailed to the ground, it's not long before I get a serious case of Divine Discontent. That's when I think, "There has got to be more to life than this, and I must find it!"

It's important to take inventory of our lives by regularly looking clearly into what we're doing and why we're doing it. Too often we simply go through the routine because that's what we have always done, and before long we find ourselves in a hole. Will Rogers said, "When you find yourself in a hole, stop digging!"

We are challenged to shake off our consensual illusions of everyday life and to question what the larger society may call success. Is it having all the stuff we want? I used to want a nice home with white criss-cross curtains, a well behaved husband, and perfect children. I used to be angry at God because that did not happen. Now I know my spirit chose another path. Giving up my fairy tale illusions has been the bedrock of my learning and growth.

But let's be clear. What is a little box for one person may be just the right boundary for someone else. It's not a good idea to go around judging how other people live their lives. All we can do is make sure we're straight with ourselves and pushing out the walls of our own little boxes. Emerson tells us to, "Live with the license of a higher order of being." Why not bless the obstacles we are challenged to overcome because they are what push us into a higher order of being?"

Helen Keller is a great example of someone who refused to remain in her dark box and was shown the pathway into a higher order of being and who inspired so many with her overcoming. She proclaimed that "Life is either a daring adventure or it is nothing at all." You and I may not have such extreme challenges, but we can choose to live with a focus upon a higher order of being.

It all has to begin inside our own consciousness. St. Paul gave great instructions in his letter to the Philippians: "Whatever is true, whatever is honorable, whatever is just, whatever is pure, whatever is lovely, whatever is gracious, if there is any excellence, if there is anything worthy of praise, think about these things."

Each of our days can be an adventure in living even if it consists of sitting in our chair and exposing ourselves to higher more noble truths and meditating upon them. We can sit in our chair and meditate and send love and light out into the world. We can listen for the instruction and guidance of Holy Spirit who will tell us where to go, what to do, and what to say. It is possible to physically stay in the same place while experiencing an endlessly expanding horizon. On the human level we can't always know what is best, but the spirit of truth will blow the sides out of our confining boxes and then open up new paths for us when our soul is ready.

As for me, I have been quite a gypsy and I bless it. However, for most of my early years, my ideal was to live in a ticky-tacky house and lead a ticky-tacky life. My previous ideal is spelled out in another of the song's verses: "And the people in the houses all go to the university, and they all get put in boxes, little boxes all the same. And there's doctors, and there's lawyers and business executives, and they're all made out of ticky-tacky, and they all look just the same."

Now all that sounded like a great life plan to me! I'd had enough of being different, of growing up with an alcoholic father and being married to alcoholic husbands. I yearned for the regular ticky-tacky life all the while I was unconsciously creating the drama and trauma. According to my spiritual teachers, I set the whole thing up for myself in order to progress on my journey home to God. Eventually, I learned to bless every drama, trauma and obstacle because in healing and forgiveness can be found the peace of God.

Joseph Campbell said: "People look for the meaning of life. I don't' think that's it at all. I think what we're seeking is an experience of being alive, so that our life experiences will have resonance within our innermost being, so that we can actually feel the rapture of being alive."

If we are wise, we will pay attention to what facilitates aliveness. We will notice and go the other way from what diminishes us, deadens us, or numbs us so that we only skim the surface of life. We will stop hunkering down in our limiting boxes and dare to say yes to a higher order of being. The rewards of this consciousness expanding are great. We become quickened, energized, joyous and grateful to be alive.

Itzhak Perlman is a violinist who says yes to a higher order of being. He deals with the limitations of a handicapped body while embracing the fullness of his life. The following story by Jack Reimer appeared in the Houston Chronicle: "Itzhak Perlman came on stage to give a concert at Avery Fisher Hall in New York City. If you have ever been to a Perlman concert, you know that getting on stage is no small achievement for him. He was stricken with polio as a child, and so he has braces on both legs and walks with the aid of two crutches. To see him walking across the stage on step at a time, painfully and slowly, is an unforgettable sight.

He walks painfully, yet majestically, until he reaches his chair. Then he sits down slowly, puts his crutches on the floor, undoes the clasps on his legs, tucks one foot back and extends the other foot forward. Then he bends down and picks up the violin, puts it under his chin, nods to the conductor and proceeds to play. By now the audience is used to this ritual. They sit quietly while he makes his way across the stage to his chair. They remain reverently silent while he undoes the clasps on his legs. They wait until he is ready to play.

But this time, something went wrong. Just as he finished the first few bars, one of the strings on his violin broke. You could hear it snap—it went off like gunfire across the room. There was no mistaking what that sound meant. There was no mistaking what he had to do. People who were there that night thought that he would have to get up, put on the clasps again, pick up the crutches and make his way off stage to either find another violin or find another string for this one. But he didn't.

Instead, he waited a moment, closed his eyes and then signaled the conductor to begin again. The orchestra began, and he played from where he had left off. And he played with such passion and such power and such purity as they had never heard before. Of course, anyone knows that it is impossible to play a symphonic work with just three strings. I know that; you know that, but that night Itzhak Perlman refused to know that. You could see him modulating, changing, and recomposing the piece in his head. At one point it sounded like he was re-tuning the strings to get new sounds that they had never made before. When he finished, there was an awesome silence in the room.

And then people rose and cheered. There was an extraordinary outburst of applause from every corner of the auditorium. We were all on our feet, screaming and cheering; doing everything we could to show how much we appreciated what he had done. He smiled, wiped the sweat from his brow, raised his bow to quiet us, and then he said, not boastfully, but in a quiet, pensive reverent tone, "You know, sometimes it is the artist's task to find out how much music you can still make with what you have left."

We have every reason to burst forth from our ticky-tacky consciousness and to celebrate our freedom by living outside any and all boxes that might confine us! Let us find the wisdom and the courage to choose a higher order of being and then make music with whatever life presents to us. Remember, God is always with us, always cheering us onward and upward as we find the courage to break free of our boxes and live in the freedom of spirit.

Man Was Not Born To Cry

"A hero is an ordinary individual
who finds strength to persevere and endure
in spite of overwhelming obstacles."
—Christopher Reeves

We do a lot of crying here in Earth School. The singer Johnnie Ray was famous for his song, Cry: "If your sweetheart sends a letter of good-bye, you'll feel better if you go ahead and cry." And then there's always lots of crying going on in country music songs. I love this parody: "I've got tears in my ears from lying on my back in my bed crying over you."

On the human level, we cry over our losses; we cry because we don't get what we want; we cry because the world is in such a mess. The only way out is to rise above the human despairing level to the spiritual level, the cosmic level, the level of the big picture. Only then can we see our situation clearly. We can't see and understand the problem on the same level as the problem.

Every God realized being, every spiritual Master, has taught us that our major problem is our sense of separation and that the only cure is the truth: We are not separate from God, never have been and never will be. Philosopher Herbert Spencer assures us, "The one absolute certainty is that we are in the presence of an Infinite Energy from which all things proceed."

Our pain and misery stems from being immersed and stuck in our separation consciousness. We become sucked into every circumstance around us. We see ourselves as victims of these circumstances, and lead ourselves into anger, frustration, fear, and sadness, despair and depression. Then we sing another country song: "Gloom, despair and agony on me; deep dark depression gloom and misery; if it weren't for bad luck I'd have no luck at all; gloom despair and misery on me." Unfortunately, I sang that song for quite a few years.

By the grace of God, we are all destined to wake up to Who and what we are. And by the grace of God, when we are ready, what we need comes to us—the teachers, the books, the methods. To the degree that we understand that there is nothing more important than our spiritual growth, nothing more important than a conscious realization of the presence of God in our lives, we progress. The misery and tears transform into the peace of God in direct proportion to our acceptance and realization of the Spirit of Truth within us. Realization means experiencing, not merely intellectually knowing about it.

Jesus the Christ told us: "You are the Light of the World." What are we supposed to do about it? We must desire to discover, experience and express that light with all our heart, our mind, our very soul. We must be willing to surrender ego mind, and reach deep into the secret place of the most high to find the treasures of Spirit. Joel Goldsmith said: "If we are not already conditioned to serving out the balance of our time on earth as vegetables, we begin to question the meaning of life."

How can we get started? We must look for the way, the truth and the life of Spirit where it is to be found. The Bible tells us—"Be still and Know that I AM God." Spiritual awareness is developed in silence, not in thinking, listening to outside voices, or reading. These things can and do inspire us to do the work—they are tools that point the way. But we must do the work of going to God in silence for ourselves.

Jesus is our elder brother and shows us the way as we follow His teaching, but we most go directly to the Spirit within ourselves. We are free with the freedom of spirit and free to go within and upward in consciousness to God, or focus outward and get drawn into the world of separation. Jesus said, "Yes you are living in the world, but you don't need to be OF it!" We choose. We decide where to direct our minds; we decide who we will serve this day—God or Mammon—God or our human ego.

The Bible story of the Prodigal Son is the story of all of us. We have decided to go out from the Father and create a separate world for ourselves. The Father does not stop us because we have free will. We wander into the far country of sense consciousness where we live on a material level and squander our inheritance. We become miserable, eat with the pigs, and cry a lot.

The son came to the conclusion that he would be better off as a servant in his father's house and decided to return home and beg for mercy. But when the father saw him coming, he rejoiced and restored his full inheritance to him. Just so with us. When we get tired of living in chaos and misery, we are ready to return to our father's house. The father has not cut us off because we made wrong choices. The father is always there for us—our job is to simply go home.

Here in Earth school you and I wander into the far country for years, months, days, hours and minutes—and even lifetimes. We experience fear, pain, lack, limitation and do a lot of crying. But when we had enough, we set out on the road back to home. I'd like to share a story with you about a man who was crying out in the depths of despair, full of hatred about the circumstances of his life and angry at God. He discovered the healing power of forgiveness and was graced with the peace of God. He shared his poignant story in Guideposts magazine several years ago. Bud Welch was living in Oklahoma City when Timothy McVeigh blew up the federal building where his daughter Julie was working. She was killed and Bud Welch began to live on hate.

In the middle of his despair and anger, something happened. One night several months after the bombing, he was watching a TV update on the investigation and fuming at the delays, when the screen showed a stocky, gray-haired man stooped over a flower bed. "Cameramen in Buffalo today," a reporter said, "caught a rare shot of Timothy McVeigh's father in his—." Bud sprang at the set, but before he could switch it off, the man looked up straight at the camera. It was only a glimpse of his face, but in that instant Bud saw a depth of pain like his own. "Oh dear God, Bud thought, "this man has lost so much too."

That was all, a momentary flash of recognition; yet that face, that pain, kept coming back to Bud as the months dragged on, his own pain unchanged, unending. He stood at the cyclone fence around the cleared site of the Murrah Building, as he had so often in the previous months and looked at the shattered elm tree under which Julie had often parked and saw that the stripped and broken branches had thrust out new leaves. The thought came to Bud that McVeigh's execution would not end his pain; it was there to stay. The only question was what would he allow it to do to himself.

Bud quit publicly agitating for McVeigh's execution. A reporter, interviewing victim's families on the first anniversary of the bombing, heard about his change of heart and mentioned it in a story that went out on the wire services. He began to get invitations to speak to various groups. One invitation, in the fall of 1998, three years after the bombing, came from a nun in Buffalo. Bud thought about seeing Tim McVeigh's father on the television.

Something inside him said, "reach out." Bud asked if there was some way he could meet Mr. McVeigh, and the nun contacted McVey's church and informed Bud that he would meet him at his home on Saturday. This is how Bud found himself ringing the doorbell of a small yellow frame house in upstate New York. The door opened and the man whose face had haunted him for three years looked out. "Mr. McVeigh? I'm Bud Welch."

"Let me get my shoes on," McVeigh said. He disappeared, and Bud was shaking. The man emerged with his shoes on and they stood there awkwardly. "I hear you have a garden," Bud said finally. "I grew up on a farm." They walked to the back of the house where neat rows of tomatoes and corn showed a caring hand and for half an hour talked weeds and mulch.—They were Bud and Bill now and then went inside and sat at the kitchen table, drinking ginger ale. Family photos covered a wall. Bill pointed out pictures of his older daughter, her husband, his baby granddaughter. He saw Bud staring at a photo of a good-looking boy in suit jacket and tie. "Tim's high school graduation," he said simply. "Gosh," Bud exclaimed, "what a handsome kid!"

The words were out before Bud could stop them, and Bill could stop the tears that filled his eyes. His younger daughter Jennifer, 24 years old, came in, her hair damp from the shower. Julie never got to be 24, but Bud thought right away that the two would have hit it off. Jennifer had just started teaching at an elementary school, her first job too. Some of the parents, she said, had threatened to take their kids out when they saw her last name.

Bill talked about his job on the night shift at a Gener.al Motors plant. Just Bud's age, he'd been there 36 years. They were two blue collar Joes, trying to do right by their kids. Bud stayed nearly two hours, and when he got up to leave Jennifer hugged him like Julie always had. They held each other tight, both crying. Bud wrote later that he'd gone to church all his life and had never felt as close to God as he did at that moment. "We're in this together," he told Jennifer and her dad, "for the rest of our lives. We can't change the past, but we have a choice about the future."

Bill and Bud keep in touch by telephone, two guys doing their best. The broken elm tree near the Murrah Building was scheduled to be bulldozed when they cleared away the debris, but Bud spearheaded a drive to save the tree, and now it will be a part of a memorial to the bomb victims." It may still die," Bud wrote, "damaged as it is. But we're harvested enough seeds and shoots from it that new life can one day take its place. This is like the seed of caring Julie left behind, one person reaching out to another. It's a seed that can be planted wherever a cycle of hate leaves an open wound in God's world."

Yes, you and I can choose to move beyond the role of victim. We can reach out to others in love and service and leave our tears and sorrow behind. Spirit will always be with us to show us the way of love and forgiveness, and let us give thanks that this is so. Dear God of Love, move us, teach us, lift us to the high places that our hearts may be healed and joined with one another. We surrender our sorrows and our tears that by your grace they be transformed into peace and joy. You know the thirst of our souls, and you give us the living water of your Spirit and we are grateful. Amen.

Reincarnation Explored and Explained

"There is always some good in any thought which
strengthens the idea that life and the body are not
the same. Birth is not the beginning, and death
is not the end. All beliefs that lead to progress
should be honored."
—A Course in Miracles, Manual for Teachers

It seems that one of the biggest concerns about reincarnation is the issue of whether or not it is a Christian concept. At first, I thought it was just a so called "heathen" Hindu belief, while in truth it is also a Christian belief. Many scholars believe that the idea of reincarnation was a generally accepted belief in Jesus' time and that Jesus took it for granted. Several Biblical passages lend credence to this idea:

Matthew 11:14: "and if you are willing to accept it, he (John) is Elijah who is to come." Jesus was speaking about John the Baptist's ministry and referring to the prophecy of Malachi 4:5 which prophesied that Elijah would return as a forerunner to the Messiah.

Matthew 16:13-16: Now when Jesus came into the district of Caesarea Phillipi, he asked his disciples, "Who do men say that the Son of man is?" And they said, "Some say John the Baptist, others say Elijah, and others Jeremiah or one of the prophets." He said to them, "But who do you say I am?" Simon Peter replied, "You are the Christ, the Son of the living God." This passage seems to take the idea of reincarnation for granted. This belief was so commonly held by the people in Jesus' time and area that Jesus didn't teach it specifically—he didn't need to.

John 9:13: As he passed by, he saw a man blind from his birth. And his disciples asked him, "Rabbi, who sinned, this man or his parents, that he was born blind?" Jesus answered, "It was not that this man sinned, or his parents, but that the works of God might be made manifest in him."

The disciples refer to karma in this passage. They ask whose karma was responsible for the man's blindness—his own or his parents'. Jesus' answer here makes the point that we choose certain circumstances for spiritual growth that may not have a direct karmic connection. It reminds us not to judge people and their situations. We can't know why they experience what they do—it is their soul's business, not ours.

In 325 A.D. The Council of Nicea banned the concept of reincarnation. The leaders of the Roman Catholic Church felt it was corrupting the people because they would not take the Christian doctrine so seriously in this life if they thought they had other chances. The concept of reincarnation weakened the church's power over people. Obviously, if the church banned the idea, it must have been quite strong and powerful at the time or the church would have simply ignored it instead of making an issue of it.

One of Unity School of Christianity's most popular textbooks was entitled Adventures in Truth. Lesson 9 of that text states: "Reincarnation is the gospel of the second chance. Life has been compared to a school where we come to learn lessons. In school we do not expect to get a higher degree in one term of kindergarten. Just so with life. How many times we cry out, 'Oh, if only I had another chance!' Reincarnation is God's loving answer to that universal cry of the human heart. It is not punishment; it is the mark of God's forgiveness.

It is a providential means whereby, if through mistakes and missing the mark of Perfection (called "sin" in theology) we lose the body, we may be reclothed with another body so that we may try again to complete the great work that our Creator has given us to do:

"Death is but an open door,
We move from room to room.
There is one life, no more,
No dying and no tomb."

I believe the concept of reincarnation helps us in our spiritual progress. It helped me to realize that God does not pick on us and that we are not helpless victims of fate. If we've had difficult times, and most of us here in earth school have experienced difficulty, it's because we set up the lessons for ourselves. (We lose conscious memory of this when we re-enter earth life.)

We can break the pattern of negativity in our lives by understanding that we must forgive and release the past and start to love right here and now. We begin to see that there is ultimate love and justice. Rocco Erico, a well known Bible scholar says: "Life isn't always fair, but it is accurate."

Edgar Cayce, who died in 1945, was a simple religious man who found that, while in trance, he could diagnose illness and outline medical treatment for people who were up to hundreds of miles away. Thirty thousand cases have been documented and can be studied at the A.R.E., Association for Research and Enlightenment, in Virginia Beach, Virginia. In the course of helping people with their physical problems, he began to come up with reasons for the physical problems which were often traceable to past life events. At first this disturbed Cayce because he believed that the idea of reincarnation wasn't Christian or Biblical.

After a thorough investigation of his own, he decided otherwise. Cayce had the ability to travel in consciousness, while in trance, to the Akashic records (the book of life) for a soul. He gave many past life readings which helped people understand their current lives. Many excellent books have been written about Edgar Cayce and reincarnation.

During a visit to Virginia Beach in 1975, I heard Hugh Lynn Cayce, Edgar's eldest son, tell the following story: When Hugh Lynn was in college at Washington and Lee in Virginia, he had a red-headed roommate. Their relationship was intense and included much hostility. Yet, they were drawn to each other. Hugh Lynn was Protestant, his roommate Catholic, and they made nasty remarks about each other's religion.

One Christmas Hugh Lynn received a beautiful ring from his parents. He came back to his college room to find his roommate playing cards with some friends. Hugh Lynn proudly showed off his new ring and everyone admired it. His roommate said he wanted to try it on and started to take it off Hugh Lynn's hand. Hugh Lynn resisted this and they pushed and pulled until a deep bloody gouge appeared on Hugh Lynn's finger. At this point, they stopped, cleared the room and had a talk. They decided they would like to find out what was behind their desire to needle and hurt each other. Hugh Lynn asked his father to do a reading of past lives for the two of them.

Edgar Cayce discovered in the reading that these two souls had been antagonists for several lifetimes, always on the opposite side of every cause. During the Middle Ages one had been a Christian crusader, the other a Moslem fighting on the other side. During the Inquisition one had been condemned to death by the other. Edgar Cayce saw the lesson for them was to forgive the past and to learn to love and accept each other.

The two young men took this advice seriously and from that time on the roommate was a frequent guest in the Cayce home and became a true friend to Hugh Lynn and the family. The name of that red-haired friend is Thomas Sugrue, the author of There Is a River, the biography of Edgar Cayce that has sold millions of copies.

I'd like to share some of my own journey into exploring and then embracing the idea of reincarnation. Up until I was teaching Composition and Literature at Ferris State College in Michigan, I hadn't given the idea any thought. I had a vague idea that it was a Hindu belief that in no way had anything to do with Christianity or with me.

At the end of the Spring Quarter in my Composition classes, I assigned a written and an oral book critique based on a non-fiction book of the student's choice. A bright and articulate student named Becky Schaffer stood in front of the class and announced that her book was Here and Hereafter by Ruth Montgomery and that it was an investigation of reincarnation.

My first thought was, "oh this is going to be a lot of baloney," but I was teaching the students to not close their minds while they investigated new concepts. So, I sat there trying to be open-minded or at least pretending to be. However, I became interested in spite of myself and thought that

I might at least take a look at the book if I ran across it. A couple of days later, I was in the student bookstore, and this book was featured in a rack right at the front entrance. I picked it up with the idea that I'd get around to reading it some rainy day.

As fate would have it, that rainy day at home came the very next week. I had been searching for years for some kind of answers to life and why innocent people suffer. I often felt like a victim and that I did not deserve the traumatic events in my life. About halfway through the book, after example after example, explanation after explanation, and stories of how psychologists all over the world had age-regressed patients who flipped back into former lives, I surrendered my resistance.

Something loosened in my chest and I knelt down with my face in the recliner I'd been sitting in and began to sob. My prayer was, "Thank you God! There just might be some sense in the universe after all!" The book had repeatedly stressed that our purpose in life is to grow spiritually and the best way to do that is through meditation. Therefore, I sat on my bed and looked out the window at the pine trees and tried, but with absolutely no idea how to go about it.

I spoke with my office mate, Shannon, about this, and she said that I might like the kind of meditation she was doing and offered to take me to a TM Lecture. I signed up and learned TM. I noticed a difference right away. I felt more calm; I got along better with my 13 year old daughter; and best of all I had a new lease on life. After that I began to attend conferences on spirituality and at one conference I noticed the beautiful presence of two women singing and playing the piano. "Those are Unity people," I was told. Unity? Never heard of it, but stored the name in my memory.

Skipping over a lot of time and details, I attended the Unity Church in Grand Rapids, Michigan shortly after I first heard about Unity. Four years later, I left my tenured faculty position and began Unity Ministerial School. Meanwhile, I had a past life reading, which I made sure I took with a grain of salt; yet, at the same time it made sense and helped me to forgive and release my ex-husband. The reading stated that in a former life with him, I was the man, he the woman. I was an army general and quite cold and indifferent to my wife. The men who served under me went about raping women. While I did not do this, I did not stop them from doing it. After reading more books on reincarnation, I was ready to believe that there was definitely some karma between me and my husband.

Karma is leftover business and relates to sowing and reaping and the fact that "life is a boomerang." What we put out we get back in some form sooner or later. We have been male and female, black, white, red and yellow, rich and poor, in every conceivable situation over multiple lifetimes. With my childhood abuse and the tremendous difficulty with my ex, and other men, I opened to the idea that I'd been male in former lives and that I needed to experience the other side of the coin.

In this reading I also asked why my son Robert and I had suffered so much over his illness. Had we done something terrible in another life? The answer was basically the same one that Jesus gave to the disciples when they asked him who had sinned, the blind man or his parents. The answer given to me was that Robert and I signed up for this experience to progress spiritually and to grow in love and forgiveness.

It took me about five years of exploring to be able to say with no hesitation: "Yes, I do believe in reincarnation." This was underlined by the experience I had while on a trip to the Mediterranean. We were in Ephesus, the buried Biblical town in Turkey. The guide was talking about the beautiful tiles on the street and invited us to look down at them.

As I looked down, I broke into sobs. I felt detached from myself; the sobs were coming from somewhere inside me that I had no idea about. It was like a reunion with something I loved and missed. The sobs were sobs of recognition and joy. This experience was brief, but very powerful and one I will never forget. We went on to the next historical site, and I wondered, "What in the world just happened?" Nothing like that has happened since, but it was enough to convince me that I was definitely there before.

Edgar Cayce taught that when we are in more than a casual relationship with anyone, and especially in families, it is a karmic situation, an opportunity to come together to work out unfinished business—which is to ultimately bless, love and forgive, with no exceptions. The Course in Miracles teaches us that our job here in earth school is to love and forgive. It seems like the majority are not into that. They are more into conflict, war, and getting ahead at the expense of others.

That is why I was mad at God and the unfairness of life. The idea of reincarnation helped me let that bitterness and anger go. I began to trust that in the end, Divine Justice and Divine Order prevail, and that it is not my job to judge, but to forgive and love. I have come to understand that those who seem to do us the most harm are actually our teachers. It is through and because of our pain that we search for answers and truth. Once we bless the pain, forgive those who seemed to cause it, and decide that the spiritual path is the only sane path, we are free.

I'll close with a short poem from the wonderful poet Kabir who lived in the 1400's in India.

I Had To Seek The Physician

I had to seek the Physician (God)
because of the pain this world
caused me.
I could not believe what happened when I got there—
I found my Teacher.
Before I left, he said,
"Up for a little homework?"
"Okay," I replied.
"Well then, try thanking all the people
who have caused you pain.
They helped you come to me."

And so when we can come to the point where we bless every painful experience knowing that it has led us to open to a higher view of life, led us to a spiritual path that leads to ultimate love, peace, and joy, we can only be grateful for the love and Grace of God.

Sweet Surrender

The most difficult challenge we can possibly face
is the act of surrender, the unconditional
acceptance of what is. This is releasing control.
The journey home is one of surrendering,
undoing, and unlearning.
—Sanchez & Viera

Trust is a pre-requisite to surrender. Our egos resist trust and surrender and strain to maintain control. Surrender comes only when all of our best ego efforts fail. Believe it or not, this is the best thing that can happen to us. When as a result of our fear and ignorance, we are about to drive off a cliff and we run into an insurmountable roadblock, we need to give thanks, not curse the world for not giving us what we think we want. A Course is Miracles reminds us, "We do not know our best interests."

Therefore to trust our Higher Power, the Spirit of God in us, and to surrender to that instruction and guidance makes all the sense in the world. But because we have lived countless ego based fearful lives, it is not always so easy to let go of our old habits. That's why we appreciate teachers, leaders, books, instructions, and road maps. All the world's great religions provide the same basic road map. Love, forgive, trust, listen to the higher authority which is the spirit of truth within, undo the human level ego. This certainly includes a process of discerning which inner voice is ego and which inner voice is that of Holy Spirit.

Thankfully there is a simple test. Is the voice a voice of love or a voice of fear? Spirit's voice is always of love; ego's voice is always one of fear. Most of us have yet to overcome our fears—to accomplish this we must trust and surrender. I have found that in the midst of fear, if I can find the strength and courage to somehow trust in spite of it all, I am always fine. We can learn to trust and surrender; we can learn that we will be fine even when we can't see the end result. We can trust the words of the Dalai Lama when he said: "When everything is falling apart, something else is trying to be born."

Some lines from the lyrics of John Denver's song *Sweet Surrender:* "I don't know what the future is holding in store; I don't know where I'm going; I'm not sure where I've been. There's a spirit that guides me, a light that shines for me. My life is worth the living; I don't need to see the end." And then the recurring chorus: "Sweet, sweet surrender, live without care—like a fish in the water, like a bird in the air." And he made his transition while flying like a bird in the air—and I trust that his spirit is still flying high.

In the end, surrender is a decision to turn it over, to let go and let God, lay it down, shrug it off; laugh it off; trust Spirit to handle it and then to follow the instruction of Spirit about where to go, what to do, what to say, and everything else. Surrender is letting go our judgments, aggravations, worries and what ifs about the future. It is letting go our attempts to fix others and our complaints.

What's the payoff of sweet surrender? Peace, serenity, more energy. We waste a lot of energy being aggravated and resisting what is. When we truly surrender, everyday life becomes a joy. A Course in Miracles: "Be happy and give the power of decision to Holy Spirit." All of this makes sense, but on the human level, we still resist and struggle to keep control.

The Beloved sometimes wants
To do us a great favor:
Hold us upside down
And shake all the nonsense out.
But when we hear
He is in such a 'playful drunken mood,'
Most everyone I know
Quickly packs their bags and hightails it
Out of town.

We 'hightail it out of town' when we ignore the voice of Spirit and distract ourselves with all the toys of the outer world we can get our hands on. But then in the end, sooner or later, we will give up and listen. Sometimes willingly, sometimes kicking and screaming.

Ram Dass has always been a teacher for me. I remember listening to his tapes over and over again in the 70's when I first became aware that I wanted to be on a spiritual path. He has taught many people the lessons of acceptance, love and forgiveness. I had the pleasure of hearing him speak at the University of Florida in Gainesville a few years ago.

He was in a wheelchair and his speech was slurred as a result of a stroke; yet, he was in a state of sweet surrender. He shared that the stages of his life were like different incarnations. At one time he was a good golfer, a cellist, easily traveled the world and owned a sports car with a stick shift. Since his stroke he is in a new incarnation. He said: "This stroke has been my teacher. It has humbled me; I have let go my former incarnation and wring the sponge of each moment in this incarnation completely dry." He was smiling and joking throughout his presentation, obviously at peace.

There was recently a TV interview of a severely wounded soldier in a rehab hospital. He had only one leg; his jaw was held together by wire; he had only part of his tongue. What he managed to say brought me to tears: "I'm having fun in therapy. Nothing else to do. Might as well make the best of it." He was not fighting reality. He was experiencing a state of sweet surrender.

If we want to experience the joy of living in spirit, we must make peace with what is, no matter what it is. We must ignore the ego voice that says, "I'll enjoy life when everything is just the way I want it to be." We can't control everything, but we can give spirit control over our minds. Then we can choose to experience hope and joy even on the so-called downside of life. Helen Keller said: "Thank God for my handicaps, for through them I have found myself, my work, and my God."

When we can sincerely pray the serenity prayer, which is a prayer of sweet surrender, the situations we face are transformed and blessed: "God give me the strength to accept the things I cannot change; courage to change the things I can, and the wisdom to know the difference." Whenever we run away from what we cannot change by refusing to accept it, we keep meeting the situation again and again until we finally decide to surrender. There is a French proverb that says: We meet our destiny on the road we take to avoid it.

The solution is to meet life straight on, walking with Holy Spirit, surrendered and guided. Whenever we feel that God is turning us upside down and shaking us, let us bless the experience instead of hightailing it out of town. Let us surrender sweetly and find peace. Words from the Unity hymnal:

> Have Thine own way Lord, have Thine own way.
> Thou art the potter, I am the clay.
> Melt me and mold me after Thy will,
> While I am waiting, yielded and still.
> Have Thine own way Lord, have Thine own way.
> Hold o'er my being absolute sway.
> Fill (me) with thy spirit till all shall see
> Christ only always living in me.

Trusting the Unknown

"We must be willing to get rid of the life we've planned
So as to have the life that is waiting for us."
—Joseph Campbell

Living with "I don't know," what ifs, the unknown, the unexpected is difficult. Life is what happens while we're busy making plans for how it should be. Most of our fear, anxiety and frustration come from the uncertainties of life. Have you ever felt as anxious as a long tailed cat in a room full of rocking chairs? Most of us know the feeling! The following piece lays out our dilemma: "That map you're making with such care-I'm sorry, you must abandon it. You will not find what you are looking for in the same place you found it yesterday—but only now. It's going to take courage."—(excerpt from a poem by Claire Dacey)

We often deal with our fears and anxieties by trying to control circumstances by following what we have mapped out for ourselves. We become perfectionists, judgmental rigid pessimists,—resistant to change and growth. We too often go through life fearful, expecting the worst, and whining a lot. The good news is that it does not have to be that way! No one I know has escaped spending time in fear of the unknown. Yet Jesus said: "Be not anxious for the morrow." He taught that we are pure Spirit, and as such, we are safe, invulnerable. There is a lesson in A Course in Miracles that I've worn out: "Trust would settle every problem now."

Whenever we find it difficult to live each day in trust, what can we do? It's a good idea to face our fears and anxieties head on. I do that by dividing a yellow legal pad into two columns. In the first one I list all my fears about the worst that could happen. In the second column I write about how I would handle the worst if it should happen. I have a written dialogue with God and ask for guidance in how to proceed. This has helped me get a grip instead of falling apart. And most of the time the worst never happened anyway. Good psychological and spiritual advice is to be found in the following:

Fearing Paris

Suppose what you fear could be trapped
and held in Paris.
Then you would have the courage to go
everywhere in the world.
All the directions of the compass open to you,
except the degrees east or west of true north
that lead to Paris. Still, you wouldn't dare
put your toes smack dab on the city limit line.
You're not really willing to stand on a mountainside
miles away, and watch the Paris lights
come up at night. Just to be on the safe side,
you decide to stay completely out of France.
But then danger seems too close
even to those boundaries, and you feel
the timid part of you covering the whole globe again.
You need the kind of friend who learns your secret and says,
"See Paris first."
—Marsha Truman Cooper

When we can find the trust and the courage to jump right into the middle of the challenge, all kinds of good things can come from it. On the limited human level, we can't always know what's best for us. Sometimes it is exactly what we don't want! On the other hand, have you ever wanted something, didn't get it, and then realized that it was a good thing you didn't get it? Sometimes not getting what we think we want is actually the best thing possible. It is actually Divine Order! Our task is to build a foundation of surrender and trust in Spirit. God can see the big picture. We need to learn to trust the dimension of Divine Order that we cannot grasp with our human understanding.

Many times in my own life something has happened and my response has been: "Oh, no! Not this!" But, with the passage of time, I often can clearly see that it indeed was divine order and for the best. I invite you to review your life and find those things that turned out for the best in spite of your pain or resistance at the time. The following is a great example of how we cannot know our best interests.

An old farmer in ancient China had one horse that ran away. He said, "O woe is me!" But then the horse came back with a wild horse and he said, "What good fortune!" While breaking the new horse, the son was thrown off and broke his leg and could not help in the field. Again the farmer said, "O woe is me!"

Then, the emperor's army came through conscripting every able bodied young man to fight in a war, but his son was spared because he had a broken leg. The farmer then celebrates his good fortune once again. That is, until the next unwanted thing happens!

Life is a roller coaster—up, down, we never know! That is why we need to be flexible. A tree that is flexible will weather storms; the rigid ones break. Just so with us. We end up wasting too much energy resisting what is. Recent popular sayings that show some growth in consciousness: It is what it is. What is, is. Now where do we go from there?

When we trust and make bold moves forward, the universe steps in and provides whatever strength and trust we may need to keep going. The following story is an example of this. Migrating geese fly all day, but find a pond to rest upon at night. There was such a pond near the Healing Center in North Idaho where I lived for a number of years. We saw hundreds of geese on their stopover at the nearby pond on their way south.

One night there was an uncommonly early freeze. In the morning we saw that the pond was frozen over and the geese's feet were trapped in the ice. As we were wondering what we might be able to do to free them, they began to flap their wings, making an effort to fly away. They seemed to be of one mind and one focus. They didn't give up; they just kept flapping their wings. Before long, they were airborne, but the pond was considerably lower. The geese had lifted up the layer of ice they were trapped in and were flying away with it! What a lesson for us!

When you and I feel trapped in outer circumstances what do we do? Do we give up or make a move forward? Can we trust beyond the appearance? Can we keep flapping our spiritual wings in an attempt to lift off to higher consciousness and keep at it until we move forward into freedom? The more we trust the spiritual truth we know, the more likely we will be to find the freedom of spirit we desire.

So, let's dedicate ourselves to love, trust, release, prayer, meditation, forgiveness. In the freedom of spirit we can live, love, laugh and be happy. Someone once said, "Life is short; break the rules, forgive quickly, kiss slowly, love truly, laugh uncontrollably." Let's give it a shot!

When Things Fall Apart—Disaster or Opportunity?

"Buddha left a road map, Jesus left a road map,
Krishna left a road map, Rand McNally left a road map.
But you still have to travel the road yourself."
—Stephen Levine

So much seems to be coming at us in the world today. Maybe we're beginning to feel that Chicken Little was right and the sky is falling. Or we feel like the butcher who backed into his meat grinder and got a little behind in his work. Yes, sometimes we feel like the world is taking a bite right out of our behind!

Perhaps our routine has been disrupted, our job is threatened or lost, our finances are going down the toilet, our aging process is getting scary; our health or the health of loved ones is a concern. In times such as this we often question our perception of who we are and what we are about. Perhaps we feel betrayed by life's circumstances. There are unending scenarios for our lives to fall apart and for us to lose our center of gravity. It's part of the earth school experience.

The truth is that no matter how spiritually advanced we think we are, there is always another layer—more work to do—more our soul would have us learn—a deeper commitment we need to make. When things fall apart, we are presented with an opportunity to reevaluate—to take another look—because when everything is going along smoothly, we have no motivation to look more deeply into ourselves, or to progress into a more spiritually awakened state.

When our escape options have run out and there's nowhere to hide; when no matter how hard we try, we can't change or manipulate the situation, what can we do? We can eat more, drink more, try drugs, watch television for endless hours, shop till we drop. We all have our favorite ways to distract ourselves. The problem is that sooner or later, it all catches up with us.

As we mature on our spiritual path, we become more open and less resistant. We begin to realize that the wisest approach just might be to go ahead and let it all fall apart and see what we can learn from the experience,—without running and hiding or distracting ourselves, but truly listening for the instruction and guidance of Holy Spirit.

New creative ways of dealing with life just might slip through the cracks of our fears. The problem is that when we face them bravely and head on, there is usually a period of "not knowing." The stew is cooking in the pot, and we don't know how it's going to turn out. The rug has been pulled out from under and we don't know where or how we're going to land. The potential for craziness is big here, but the potential for incredible growth is also here.

The off-center in between state is an ideal situation for the soul to grow in trust. Why? Because then we have been cracked open and forced to give up our specific expectations. I have a friend in Cincinnati who has lived through several life threatening situations and still can't be sure that he will be here tomorrow. (And of course none of us can be absolutely sure of that.) He tells me that he has never felt so free in his life. He has come to a place of truly "letting go and letting God", of experiencing his body falling apart, yet trusting that all is well and will always be well. Beyond the earth suit, we are invulnerable, ageless, deathless spirit, safe and secure in the mind and heart of God.

There was once a woman going through the experience of cancer who woke up one morning, looked in the mirror, and noticed she had only three hairs on her head. "Well," she said, "I think I'll braid my hair today." So she did and had a wonderful day. The next day, she looked in the mirror and saw that she had only two hairs on her head. "Mmm," she said, "I think I'll part my hair down the middle today." So she did and had a grand day. The next day she woke up, looked in the mirror and noticed she had only one hair on her head. "Well," she said, "I'm going to wear my hair in a pony tail today." So she did and had a fun day. The next day, she woke up looked in the mirror and noticed that there wasn't a single hair on her head. "Yea!" she exclaimed, "I don't have to fix my hair today."

There was a Dear Abby column quite awhile ago that has stuck in my memory. Its theme is one of wisdom, bravery and being able to see blessings in the midst of circumstances falling apart. A mother wrote about the shock she experienced when she gave birth to a child with Down's syndrome. She said it was like planning a wonderful trip to Italy, but when the plane landed, the pilot said, "Welcome to Holland."

In response, another parent wrote about her experience of finding herself where she had not intended to go. Her two daughters were both born with serious rare and debilitating birth defects. One daughter lost an arm above the elbow and the other a leg above the knee,—this from a skin condition of constant blisters and bandages. Yet both girls went through public schools and on to college. One became a state champion debater; the other competed in state choir competitions.

The mother goes on to say, "My husband and I tried to be faithful stewards of the precious lives God had entrusted to our care—binding up their wounds and shielding them from the assaults of the world. One daughter passed at age 50, the other at 42. We are grateful that we were able to bring up these two beautiful children, even if the journey was not like most parents would expect. To prospective parents, we wish you Italy, but if you land in Holland, you can make that beautiful too."

We may not be consciously aware of the plan our soul has laid out for us, but we can be sure that we have chosen it and that we can trust a higher purpose for our lives even when they seem to be falling apart. This takes wisdom and it takes courage, but we have the very Christ of God within us to lead us and to give us strength to face and overcome our fears, the strength to keep moving forward in our soul growth.

A great Buddhist teacher, Rinpoche, tells a story about traveling with his attendants to a monastery he'd never seen before. As his group neared the gates, they saw a large guard dog with huge teeth and red eyes. It was growling ferociously and struggling to get free from the chain that held it. The dog seemed desperate to attack them. As they got closer, they saw the dog's bluish tongue and spittle spraying from its mouth. They walked past the dog, keeping their distance, and entered the gate. Suddenly, the chain broke and the dog rushed at them. The attendants screamed and froze in terror. Rinpoche turned and ran as fast as he could—straight at the dog! The dog put its tail between its legs and ran away.

Facing our fears, facing the unwanted and the unknown, facing the falling apart circumstances of our lives is like running toward the ferocious guard dog. When we boldly face our fears and "put on the whole armor of God," the fear dissipates and we discover and experience the freedom of Spirit that is our Divine Birthright. We discover that we are safe in the mind and heart of God no matter where we are—in Italy where we expected to be—or in Holland presented with opportunities we never dreamed of.

St. Paul urged us to "die daily"—to stop the clinging of the fearful ego and to let Spirit rule our lives. Reaching our limit and falling apart is not punishment but an opportunity to embark upon an expanded experience of life and love. I'll close with wisdom from Rumi:

"Remember the deep root of your being,
the presence of your lord. Give your life to the one who
already owns your breath and moments."
—Rumi

Why We Need to Forgive

"Exempt no one from your love or you will be hiding
a dark place in your mind where the Holy Spirit is not welcome."
—A Course in Miracles

It is very difficult for our human level ego to let go of slights, hurts, grudges, resentments. It actually feeds itself on these things to stay alive. Whenever we are feeling victimized, we're feeding the ego a juicy steak! So how can we free ourselves from this insane predicament? First of all, we gather the courage and determination to open ourselves to love and truth; we become willing to admit that we have made mistakes in the past. We ask for help.

Every one of us has been hurt or disappointed by someone—or we have hurt and disappointed others. These things sink into our consciousness and become inflamed and festering wounds. We often cling to our grievances, blaming, pointing fingers and crime solving. We need to understand that unforgiviness is like drinking poison and expecting someone else to die. Course in Miracles reminds us that "Forgiveness is the only sane response."

There are three types of forgiveness we need to deal with: Forgiving others, (including forgiving others for not forgiving us),forgiving ourselves, and forgiving the world in general—many of us have felt at times that we were victims because the universe was unjustly picking on us. Yet, Wayne Dyer reminds us that "acute unhappiness can be a great awakener." I can honestly tell you that it was my misery that was the catalyst for my growth. I was desperate to find a better way. And by the grace of God a path opened to me—as it does for all of us when we get to that point. It is our Divine Destiny to get to that point and to awaken to the love peace, and joy of God. However, we have the choice to nurse our grievances and muck around in our misery or forgive and be free.

I certainly had no clue I was choosing misery at the time I was experiencing so much of it, but I learned to trust that I did choose and <u>continue to choose</u> and create my own experience. Luckily I did not create myself, God created me and I cannot be separated from Him. We are all prodigal sons who took our inheritance and left home to go it on our own. We will eventually realize we're in trouble and decide to return to our father, who welcomes us, who does not condemn us, and who loves us unconditionally.

In order for us to come home to the full experience of God's love, there is a prerequisite—we must forgive and release. Without forgiveness there can be no unconditional love. Love and forgiveness is the only path out of all misery and unhappiness. Harvard medical school did a study of the health effects of forgiveness. The conclusion was that practicing forgiveness resulted in reduced stress, better heart health, stronger relationships, reduced pain, and greater happiness. As our burdened hearts let go of our hurts and resentments, we are open and free to receive new blessings.

How do we do this? First we must see the benefit of forgiveness and be willing to put it into practice in our daily lives. We ask Holy Spirit, our Higher Self, our Christ self, God—to help us. A prayer I have been using is "Dear God, reveal what needs to be revealed and heal what needs to be healed." This prayer is very effective and Holy Spirit revealed to me that I was still condemning myself for mistakes and transgressions that happened years ago.

I was not conscious of this, but I was shown that indeed a part of me was still beating myself up and that I need to have mercy and compassion upon the unhealed person I was at the time of my transgressions. I went into a meditation asking for help and I received it. Shortly after, I had a very vivid dream about my son Richard and we hugged and cried and released as our hearts overflowed with love. It is important to ask for Spirit to help us release and heal what needs to be released and healed because our consciousness is like an iceberg—there is much more under the surface than we can consciously see.

That is why we need to be willing to honestly go deep within and can shine a conscious light upon our most closely held thoughts beliefs and opinions. We can't change our lives for the better if we remain unconscious of what we are holding. It is important to look honestly into ourselves, but equally important to look without self condemnation.

A photo taken during the Vietnam War of a little girl running down the road with her clothes burned off and her body scorched by napalm. The man who coordinated the raid that caused that horror was a 24 year old helicopter pilot named John Plummer. When Plummer saw the photo in the military newspaper Stars and Stripes, he was devastated. Even years later, he told a reporter: "It just knocked me to my knees." The guilt over the bombing raid became a lonely torment. He suffered nightmares of the little girl screaming and running. He could not forgive himself.

Meanwhile the young girl in the photo—Kim—survived seventeen operations, eventually relocated to Toronto and became an ambassador for UNESCO. Years later, John Plummer heard that Kim would be speaking at a Veteran's Day observance in Washington D.C., not far from his home and he attended that event. He heard her say, "If I could talk face to face with the pilot who dropped the bombs, I would tell him we cannot change history, but we can try to do good things in the present."

Plummer wrote her a note from the audience which said: "I am that pilot." After the talk, he pushed his way through the crowd until they were face to face. She opened her arms to him and he fell into them sobbing, "I'm so sorry, I'm so sorry." She responded, "It's all right. I forgive. I forgive." After that day, they became friends. This is a beautiful example of The Course in Miracles statement: "The holiest spot on Earth is where an ancient hatred has become a present love."

In spite of the fact that there is so much hatred, vengeance and darkness in the world, there is also light, love and forgiveness. It is our assignment to be bearers of the light and agents of forgiveness. Gandhi said—"if we don't move past an eye for an eye and a tooth for a tooth, the whole world will be blind." We do have important work to do, starting with ourselves and our commitment to love and forgive. This is doing our part in saving the world. All our acts of love and forgiveness touch the whole.

It's always inspiring to look around and see past the hatred and violence to the forgiveness and love that still goes on in spite of everything. And it is possible to forgive quickly when we know the healing power of it. The following are two moving examples: Amy Beal went to Africa to help people, loved them, and taught them. During an uprising, she was killed. Her parents, instead of hating and seeking revenge, went to Africa and continued her work there. They explained, "Amy lives through us by our sharing her work."

Nicholas, a young boy, was on vacation in Italy with his parents. They were driving a rented car down a highway and Nicholas was asleep in the back seat. Bandits chased them and shot into the car, killing young Nicholas. The parents, in an incredible act of love and forgiveness, donated his organs so that other young children in Italy might live. Both these cases are triumphs of the Spirit. It is not our place to seek vengeance. It is our task to love and be free. I offer you an opportunity to begin this process now in the following meditation:

Allow your consciousness to drop deep within and align with your higher and more expanded self—Move into the core and center where all beings dwell in Light and Oneness. As you breathe in and out, become aware that you are part of the tide of life. Dive deep into your center, into the chamber where all life meets, to the inner core where all things are and evermore will be—a place where all is completion and perfection. Find a place of unity in your heart where you can forgive all those who knowingly or unknowingly caused pain in your life. Ask spirit to bring into your mind in this moment who or what you need to forgive and release. Take a few moments to honestly evaluate this.

Spirit is with you now and your heart is open wide enough to forgive and embrace all that have knowingly or unknowingly hurt you. Spirit is with you now opening your heart to yourself that you may forgive and bless yourself. There is only mercy, compassion and the grace of God flowing through you—take a moment to feel and accept this.

It is your path now to continue to move forward and to embrace your Divine Destiny, your sacred soul contract upon the earth. Stay open to the voice of Holy Spirit. You will be shown how to continue to expand your capacity to forgive, release, and love. God loves you; God is within you; you are sustained by the love of God, now and forevermore and you are safe and secure in the mind and heart of God. And so it is. Amen

SECTION FIVE

Happiness, Joy and Laughter

"God is ecstasy. God is as high as it gets.
If you want to be close to God,
Learn to be joyful."
—Michael Singer

Can We Laugh Ourselves to Enlightenment?
Choose to be Happy
Embrace Joy—It's Spiritual!
Make Joy Your Dance Partner
The Door to Happiness is Wide Open

Can We Laugh Our Way to Enlightenment?

"Joy is the infallible sign of the Presence of God."
—Teilhard de Chardin

"Puritanism is that haunting fear that somewhere,
somehow, someone is happy."
—H. L. Menken

Can we laugh our way into enlightenment? The answer is no. However, our experience on the way to enlightenment can be made a happy one if we pave our path with light heartedness and laughter. The Course in Miracles tells us that "God loves a happy learner." The characteristics of Spirit are love, peace, and **joy.** The psalmist declares: "The joy of the Lord is my strength." Unity co-founder Charles Fillmore was a happy joyful person who said: "We all should practice delightful, happy, joyous states of mind. Such thoughts open the way for the ever-present Divine Mind to pour out Its splendid resources into our mind and into our life."

Why do we find it so difficult to live in joy? The culprit is our human ego that thinks it is separate from God and often feels victimized by circumstances. Its goal is to lead us into hopelessness, bitterness and despair. This is the far country of the prodigal son, and when we tire of it, we are ready to embark upon a journey in consciousness that leads us back to our true joyful home in God.

Freedom of choice is the greatest freedom we have, so we can choose to see our lives differently, choose love over fear, and happiness over misery and self-pity. Fun and laughter change our perspective. When we learn to laugh at our mistakes, we've come a long way toward forgiving and releasing them, which in turn enables us to forgive and release the errors of others.

Whenever my friend Ione and I presented workshops, we tried to introduce an element of fun and laughter. One exercise we found most helpful was "singing our opera". We asked people to make a list of their wounds and miseries and then make up an opera on the spot and sing it. If it sounded terrible, so much the better! We of course did this for ourselves as well. My opera song was "woe is me; my husband is drunk; oh woe is me; my prince is not charming; alas and alack, what is to become of me? What shall I do?" You get the idea. This exercise can be done alone at home, but it's even more fun in a group.

I recently moved into my own apartment after six months of renting two rooms from my friend Ray who is a joker and loves to tease. Not a day went by without some laughter and good natured teasing. I enjoyed all this because it reminded me of growing up with three brothers who loved to have fun and tease. I once said to my mother, "Don't the boys like me? They are always teasing me." Her answer: "Of course they like you, if they didn't like you, they wouldn't tease you." Everything went along much more smoothly after that conversation! I could even, at least in retrospect, laugh about the day my brother Earl hid behind a tree with a garden snake and chased me down the street, me screaming at the top of my lungs all the way!

I believe we can be passionately serious about our spiritual life and love to laugh at the same time. I don't skip my time of meditation and quiet spiritual reading and contemplation. I have found that the deeper I get into the spiritual life, the more joy there is in my heart. I have learned that while I learned many valuable lessons as the result to my earlier difficult years, my life does not have to continue to be difficult now in order for me to learn and progress spiritually. It's wonderful to know that we can learn in joy as well as in sorrow.

Laughter and joy are healing on all levels, releasing stress and tension and helping us to see a bigger picture. Laughter and joy make our human life a better and happier life—and remember "God loves a happy learner." A Frank and Ernest cartoon had them climbing up a mountain saying to the wizard at the top: "Oh we attained enlightenment about the nature of reality a long time ago; now we're looking for loopholes." Of course, that is what we do on the human level all the time. We look for a loophole that will allow us to become enlightened without doing any work, without changing our attitudes, without forgiving everyone and forgiving everything we think someone might have "done unto us."

I love good quotes and here are a few regarding our choice for happiness. I have given the source if I have it: Don't let the rain on your parade drown your soul.—Yesterday's tears can water today's seed for tomorrow's roses.—You grow up the day you have the first real laugh at yourself. (Eleanor Roosevelt).—We are growing serious, and let me tell you, that is the very next step to being dull. (Addison).—Nothing is so exhilarating as to be shot at without result. (Winston Churchill)—Sometimes you have to be a little crazy to keep from going insane.—First cross the river, and then insult the crocodiles. (Confucius)—

Personally, I love silly therapy—just getting together with friends and laughing about everything we can think of. One reason I loved living at the Holo Center in Idaho with Ione and Masil was that we laughed a lot and enjoyed each other's company, and we had lots of visitors who also loved to laugh. We actually make a laugh tape—just laughter and giggles—we would look at each other and start all over. This went on for several minutes. And then we played it back and laughed some more! Invite some friends over and try it!

I would be amiss if I didn't include some Swami Beyondananda's guidelines for Enlightenment:—"Be a Fundamentalist—make sure the Fun always comes before the Mental. Realize that life in Earth School is a situation comedy that will never be cancelled. A laugh track has been provided. Have a good laugh-sitive twice a day, and that will insure regular-hilarity. If you're looking to find the key to the universe, I have some bad news and some good news. The bad news is—there is no key to the universe. The good news is—it has been left unlocked."

There are three religious truths:—Jews do not recognize Jesus as the Messiah.—Protestants do not recognize the Pope as the leader of the Christian faith.—Baptists do not recognize each other in the liquor store or Hooters. (unknown source) Harvey Cohen came up with the following admonition to "Lighten Up."

So you've dabbled in the occult, burned candles, gave up sex.
You've traveled to Sedona to visit the vortex.
You've meditated, visualized, affirmed with love and grace.
You've forgiven all your irritants till you're blue in the face.
You've been est-ed and you've tested tarot and astrology.
You've met your guides from the other side and did past-life therapy.
So you've been Rolfed and hypnotized, there's nothing you've avoided.
You've tried acupuncture, heavy breathing, even been Sigmund Freuded.
You've chanted mantras and you've om'ed, and journeyed near and far.

You've seen many of the channels and taken every seminar.

You burn incense in the afternoon, and sometimes reflex your feet.

You've become a vegetarian and seldom cheat.

You gave up salt and sugar and your diet's really pure.

Although at times you still get gas, just why you are not sure.

You drink herb tea until you see the best in all,—at last.

Your kundalini's straightened, and no longer at half-mast.

You've had your aura cleaned and your chakras lubed and tuned.

You've seen ET at least four times and two times for Cocoon

You go to sleep with crystals and you wake up with a tape

which subliminally instructs you to get your mind in shape.

You're gone here and there and everywhere, tried everything you know.

That path that called Enlightenment is such a busy show.

But after all that's said and done and all the things you've tried,

There's a truth that you should know while you're on your ride.

The Light you see that seems to be coming from things you do

is only as bright as the Light that radiates from within you!

So, dear friends, let us determine to Celebrate Life by remembering to pave our path with smiles and laugher as we passionately pursue an ever more intimate relationship with the God within us. And let us take inspiration and comfort in the words of Jesus when he said, "I have spoken these things to you, that my joy may be in you, and that your joy may be full."

Dear Mother-Father God, We rejoice always and celebrate that you dwell in us, as us. We open our hearts and minds to the joy that is your great gift to us. We are grateful and we know that we demonstrate our gratitude for your gifts with smiles, joy and laughter.

Choose to be Happy

"Happiness is uncaused."
—Sanchez and Viera

Happiness is uncaused. I have been chasing that thought around for days to squeeze the meaning out of it. Is that true, or not? It's probably safe to say that most of us have always believed that happiness is caused by something good, lovely, exciting, and desired coming to us from the outside, such as the perfect mate, circumstance, job, weather, outcome, and on and on.

So how does "happiness is uncaused" fit into the scheme of things? Could it even be possible to be happy no matter what? Could happiness actually be a decision we can make? Abraham Lincoln said, "Most people are about as happy as they make up their minds to be." A Course in Miracles reminds us: "When you are sad, know this need not be. Depression comes from a sense of being deprived of something you want and do not have. Remember that you are deprived of nothing except by your own decisions, and then decide otherwise."

So it looks like happiness is a decision we can make. We_can_decide to be happy "no matter what." At the same time it is essential that we call upon the right help. If we depend on the human ego to help us, we are destined to fail. The ego's goal is to continually seek happiness by striving for something outside itself and then never being satisfied with whatever it gets.

The story of King Midas illustrates that perfectly. He wanted more and more gold and was never satisfied. He ended up asking that everything he touched would turn to gold. Oh, Oh—he could not eat gold—and a gold bed would be quite hard to sleep on—and if everyone he touched turned into a gold statue, he's going to get lonely really fast. Our ego is like King Midas; no matter what it has, it wants more and it's never enough. We can't trust it as our guide.

The guide that will work is Holy Spirit, the voice that is nearer than breathing and closer than hands and feet. That voice needs a happy learner who is willing to unlearn the ego's lessons so that we can learn the joyous lessons of Spirit. If we are going to truly tap into the secret of happiness and claim it for ourselves, we must be very clear and disciplined.

We need to be willing to question every negative, dispirited, sad, victimized, angry, unforgiving and vengeful thought. If we are not willing to do this, we can forget about true happiness. We have made the choice to suffer. Paul Ferrini wrote: "I don't have to be a saint. I just need to realize that I'm unhappy when I'm not loving you." And we mean "you" with no exceptions. Unconditional, uncaused happiness comes from unconditional love of life and everyone and everything in it. Kipling reminds us to "treat triumph and disaster, those two imposters, just the same."

We shoot ourselves in the foot every time we allow circumstances to dictate how happy or sad or depressed we will be. We can't live in uncaused happiness by using the same yardstick we've always used to measure how we're doing in life and basing our happiness or unhappiness on that measure. We must indeed "be transformed by the renewing of our minds," as Saint Paul exhorts us to do in the New Testament.

The state of our collective minds is reflected in our world. It's a mixed bag. Someone once said that Earth is the insane asylum of the universe. And author Graham Greene said: "The lunatics have taken control of the asylum." It surely seems that way some days, does it not? However, we, each of us, have charge over our own choices; we have the freedom to choose how we want to feel. That is liberating news. I used to believe that I had no choice over my moods or how I felt. Not so. We can choose and we need to take the responsibility for it.

The great secret of happiness is that we can choose to be happy. Henry Miller said: "It's good to be just plain happy; it's a little better to know you're happy." There's a Unity joy song that goes, If you're happy and you know it clap your hands, stomp your feet, say amen and so on. I agree with Miller—it's great to be happy <u>and</u> know you're happy!

When we make the joy of the Lord our strength, we are strong indeed. Jesus is quoted in the gospel of John: "These things have I spoken to you that my joy may be in you and that your joy may be full." I have learned much over the years and a lot of it the hard way. I certainly have looked for joy and happiness outside myself in people and circumstances. Now, I can honestly say that whatever true joy and happiness I experience comes from choosing to open to, listen to, and be in harmony with the Holy Spirit within myself. When I am listening to Spirit, I love unconditionally, forgive, bless, and heed the instruction and guidance I receive. Then I am happy. Whenever I step away from those things, I suffer sadness and unhappiness and even depression.

Some things that distract us from listening to Holy Spirit are busyness, fear, living in the past and in the future, and of course the usual suspects: fear, anxiety, anger, nonforgiveness etc. It took me awhile to really grasp what being centered is all about because I was so accustomed to being scattered and pulled out into every situation and circumstance—rebounding, defending, surviving.

It takes a big leap to break out of old thought patterns and habits. If you find yourself saying, "that's just the way I am," know that need not be. You and I are the way we are because we don't know we have a choice, or if we know it intellectually we don't grasp it emotionally. Once we really get it and begin choosing happiness on a regular basis, wild horses won't be able to drag us away from it.

We'll be like the guy in the following story:

I used to work for John in the business of building towers, and sometimes he irritated me. He is always in a good mood and always has something positive to say. One day I confronted him: "I don't get it! How can you stay so positive?" He replied: "Each morning I wake up and say to myself, you have two choices today. You can choose to be happy or you can choose to be in a bad mood. I choose to be happy.

Each time something bad happens, I can choose to be a victim or I can choose to learn from it. I choose to learn from it. Life is about choices. In every situation there is a choice. You choose how you react to situations. You choose how people affect your mood. How you live your life is your choice."

I reflected on what he said. Soon thereafter, I left the tower industry to start my own business. We lost touch, but I often thought about him when I made a choice about life instead of reacting to it. Several years later, I heard that he was involved in a serious accident, falling some 60 feet from a communications tower. After 18 hours of surgery and weeks of intensive care, he was released from the hospital with rods placed in his back.

I saw him about six months after the accident. When I asked him how he was he said he was great and I could tell he truly was. I asked him how he managed to deal with his accident. "The paramedics were great," he said. "They kept telling me I was going to be fine. But when they wheeled me into the ER and I saw the expressions on the faces of the doctors and nurses, I got really scared. In their eyes, I saw 'he's a dead man.' I knew I needed to take action."

"What did you do?" I asked. "Well, there was a nurse shouting questions at me; she asked if I was allergic to anything. 'Yes, I replied." The doctors and nurses stopped working and waited for my reply. I took a deep breath and yelled, 'Gravity!' Over their laughter, I told them, 'I am choosing to live. Operate on me as if I am alive, not already dead.'" He lived, thanks to the skill of his doctors, but also because of his amazing attitude. I learned from him that every day we have the choice to live fully or give up.

So let us not forget that our greatest freedom is freedom of choice. The only thing we don't have choice over is our innate divinity, our innate goodness. We just have a choice about when we're going to get around to recognizing and expressing it and being very happy all the time as a consequence. We have a choice to embrace and express the joy and happiness of life or grumble our way through it chasing after things that can't really satisfy us in the long run.

We can choose to align ourselves with the busy frantic world of getting and spending and never being satisfied or we can recognize there is a better way and then we can choose it. There is much wisdom in the following poem:

Slow Dance

Have you ever watched kids on a merry-go-round?
Or listened to the rain slapping on the ground?
Ever followed a butterfly's erratic flight?
Or gazed at the sun into the fading night?
You better slow down. Don't dance so fast.
Time is short. The music won't last.
Do you run through each day on the fly?
When you ask how are you, do you hear the reply?
When the day is done do you lie in your bed
With the next hundred chores running through your head?
You'd better slow down. Don't dance so fact.
Time is short. The music won't last.
Ever told your child, "We'll do it tomorrow?"
And in your haste, not see his sorrow?
Ever lost touch, let a good friendship die
Cause you never had time to call and say, "Hi?"
You'd better slow down. Don't dance so fast.
Time is short. The music won't last.
When you run so fast to get somewhere
You miss half the fun of getting there.
When you worry and hurry through your day
It's like an unopened gift—thrown away.
Life is not a race. Do take it slower.
Hear the music before the song is over.
—David L. Weatherford

Have a happy day dear beautiful child of God, and choose a happy life!

Embrace Joy—It's Spiritual!

"We need to stop waiting for the world to change
so that we can enjoy ourselves."
—Michael Brown

How much joy are you willing to allow into your life? Do you get uneasy when you feel joyous? Do you fear that maybe it won't last so you don't allow yourself too much of it so you won't be disappointed when/if it fades? The truth is: Joy IS our birthright. Our natural state is God expressing joy through us. We need to know that indeed the joy of the Lord is our strength. The Bible has a lot of positive messages about joy:

Psalms30.5: Weeping may tarry for the night but joy comes in the morning. Isaiah55: For you shall go out in joy, and be led forth in peace; the mountains and the hills before you shall break forth into singing and all the trees of the field shall clap their hands. John 15: (Jesus speaking to disciples): These things I have spoken to you that my joy may in you and that your joy may be full." Living a life of joy is not sinful—it's Biblical and spiritual!

Whenever the Christ consciousness is born and reborn in us, we feel joy. Let's clear away any doom, gloom, sadness, sense of lost direction and get down to the real bedrock of our true selves—which is the joyful Christ of us—that is where we find the true and lasting joy of life. Let us develop our passion for joy; our passion for being right here, right now, standing on holy ground, expressing the one presence and power, radiating love and light.

David Hawkins: "Just one instant in a very high state can completely change a person's orientation to life as well as his goals and values. It can be said that the individual who was, is no more, and a new person is born out of the experience. That is what being born again really means—born into a new and higher state of consciousness. It often happens after near death experiences or after we are introduced to life changing ideas. This is when we see higher possibilities for ourselves and choose to passionately and joyously pursue them."

The key words here are passionately and joyously! Too often we pursue things in a state of anxiety and fear that we might not find what we want. We too often end up with confusion and busyness. Do you think you deserve joy? Do you realize that you can experience joy in the midst of whatever it is you're doing?

Story: An American businessman was at the pier of a small coastal Mexican village when a small boat with just one fisherman docked. Inside the small boat were several large yellow fin tuna. The American complimented the Mexican on the quality of his fish and asked how long it took to catch them. The Mexican replied, "Only a little while senor."

The American then asked, "Why didn't you stay out longer and catch more fish?" The Mexican said he had enough to support his family's needs. The American then asked, "But what do you do with the rest of your time?" The fisherman replied, "I sleep late, fish a little, play with my children, take siesta with my wife Maria, stroll into the village each evening where I sip wine and play guitar with my amigos. I have a full and busy life, senor."

The American scoffed: "I am a Harvard MBA and could help you. You should spend more time fishing and with the proceeds, buy a bigger boat. With the proceeds from the bigger boat, you could buy several boats. Eventually you would have a fleet of fishing boats. Instead of selling your catch to a middleman, you would sell directly to the processor, eventually opening your own cannery. You would control the product, processing, and distribution. You would need to leave this small coastal fishing village and move to Mexico City, then LA, and eventually New York City where you will run your expanding enterprise."

The Mexican fisherman asked, "But senor, how long will this all take?" To which the American replied, "Fifteen or twenty years." The Mexican asked, "But what then senor?" The American laughed and said, "That's the best part. When the time is right, you would announce an IPO and sell your company stock to the public and become very rich. You would make millions." The Mexican replied, "Millions? But then what?"

The American said: "Then you would retire, move to a small coastal fishing village where you would sleep late, fish a little play with your kids, take siesta with your wife, stroll into the village in the evenings where you could sip wine and play guitar with your amigos." I don't even have to explain the moral of this story! Relax! Enjoy simple pleasures and enjoy the blessings in your life right now. Wise is the person who experiences joy right here and now, regardless of circumstances. Once we sincerely claim our birthright of joy, no one or no thing can take it away. Poet Naomi Nye shares her experience:

> It is difficult to know what to do with joy.
> With sadness there is something to rub up against—
> a wound to tend with lotion and cloth.
> When the world falls in around you,
> You have pieces to pick up.
> Something to hold in your hands,
> Like ticket stubs or change.

But—joy floats.It does not need you to hold it down
It does not need anything.
Joy lands of the roof of the next house, singing
and disappears when it wants to.
You are happy either way.

As spiritual beings we are called upon to wake up to our birthright, claim it and then share it right now, right where we are. Please don't settle for anything less. Don't give up if you're in the middle of a depression or if life is not behaving as you might like right now. Open and stay open to help and healing. Do what is yours to do and know that it is not only possible to experience joy, but the Christ of you, your higher power, your guardian angel and every advanced being in the universe is ready to help you whenever you are ready to accept that help.

It has been my experience as I've moved out of my soap opera and into a much more symphonic existence that whenever my heart yearns for more advancement, for more love peace and joy, the perfect teacher comes along in just the form I need. It may be a person, a book, a chance remark,—whatever encourages me and spurs me on.

Sometimes it can even be in the form of a person who seems to be giving me a hard time, or in the form of circumstances that seem difficult—because that is just what pushes my growing edge! And when that difficult experience is over, and I am blessed to learn something valuable—that brings me joy. Remember: Joy is the infallible sign of the Presence of God—and God is always nearer than breathing and closer than hands and feet. Joy is waiting to bless us. All we need do is open our arms and embrace it! Please take a moment to hug yourself right now and affirm: "I embrace the joy of the Lord, and it's my birthright! Thank you God! Amen."

Make Joy Your Dance Partner

"People need joy as much as clothing.
Some of them need it far more."
—Margaret Collier Graham

Tip of the day from real age.com: "Laugh yourself young." A daily dose of laughter is one of the best remedies of all. Normal Cousins experience with laughing himself well from a so called incurable disease is legendary. Now, laughter as therapy is being taken seriously. It relaxes the body by reducing muscle tension and blood pressure—improves the immune system—stimulates the production and release of endorphins which relieve pain and stress. So, we even have scientific reasons to welcome laughter into our lives.

I love to be silly and quote silly things such as, "The ideal state is to be born old, gradually get younger and finally disappear. Charles Fillmore, co-founder of Unity said: "We should all practice delightful, happy, joyous states of mind. It is such thoughts that open the way for the ever-present Holy Spirit to pour out its splendid resources into our mind and into all our affairs."

It is Important to claim joy first. So often we feel that our joy is limited by present experiences of illness, lack, or disharmony—and that if we can only straighten out these conditions, then we will feel joyous. But the opposite is true: find joy first and then outer circumstances improve. Our Bible is full of references to joy: some examples: "Make a joyful noise unto the lord, all the earth; break forth into joyous song and sing praises! Sing praises to the lord with the lyre, with the lyre and the sound of melody.

With trumpets and the sound of the horn, make a joyful noise! Weeping may tarry for the night, but joy comes in the morning. The joy of the Lord is my strength."

Jesus said: "These things I have spoken to you that my joy may be in you and that your joy may be full." Why aren't we joyous more of the time? We get caught up in our problems; we allow our egos to take over and glorify our misery; we lose our trust in God and spiritual solutions. Joel Goldsmith said, "Fear is atheism." Actually any emotion that is not the love, peace and joy of God is atheism because we have left God out of the picture. One of my favorite Course in Miracles quotes is: "Trust would settle every problem now."

The Course also teaches us that: "To heal is to make happy. The light that belongs to you is the light of joy. Radiance is not associated with sorrow. To be wholehearted you must be happy. Fear and love cannot co-exist—it is impossible to be wholly fearful and remain alive—the only possible whole state is that of love. There is no difference between love and joy. Therefore, the only possible whole state is the wholly joyous. God's holy children are worthy channels of his beautiful joy. Joy calls forth a willingness to share it."

Our problem in general society is that we glorify suffering and victimhood. Our human ego feeds on misery and discontent. It wants us to seek and never find—that's how ego stays alive. There was a Gary Larson cartoon that featured a frog Country Western band singing, "I got the Greens, I got the Greens, really bad." We get the Blues, (or Greens if we are frogs), when our main focus is placed on outer problems and circumstances. Then, we're living life backwards, from the outside in. We can fine joy and live in it when we learn to live from the inside out while we put our trust in God and develop an inner state of spiritual love, peace and joy no matter what circumstances may swirl around us.

Too often put too much emphasis on our earth suit and its conditions. The Course gives us clear guidance in clearing our minds and making room for the joy that is ours by divine right: "When you are sad, know this need not be. Depression comes from a sense of being deprived of something you want and do not have. Remember—you are deprived of nothing except by your own decisions,—so decide otherwise. Choose peace instead of this. Choose love instead of this. Choose joy instead of this. When you are anxious or sad, realize that it comes from the capriciousness of the ego and know this need not be.

So next time you get the Blues, or the Greens, choose again. Change your mind. Read something uplifting, find the humor in circumstances and events—meditate, watch a funny movie—go for a walk, call a friend. If necessary make an appointment with a counselor or spiritual advisor. Take action to move to higher ground. I think it was Maxine who proclaimed: "Life should not be a journey to the grave, just existing without joy, but rather the goal is to skid in sideways, champagne in one hand—chocolate covered strawberries in the other, life thoroughly lived, and screaming—Woo-Hoo—what a ride!"

The Door to Happiness is Wide Open

"Once in awhile it really hits people that they don't
actually <u>have</u> to experience the world
in the way they've been told to."
—Alan Keightly

Movies have always been one of my favorite things. Through all the traumatic ups and downs of childhood, I could escape into the movies. My brothers used to tease me when I would cry in a sad movie. My response was, "Oh be quiet; I'm getting <u>my</u> money's worth!" I still love most movies, but I've become somewhat discriminating. I have even walked out of a few and distanced myself from others while watching.

But what might happen if we attended a movie theater that has it all. In addition to big screen and surround sound, headphones are supplied that allow us to taste what the characters are eating, smell what they smell, and even have the sensations of touch and feel the same emotions. Instead of watching the movie, we would be totally absorbed in it. There would no longer be an independent part of us that decides, "I don't like this movie; I want to leave." We would be totally sucked into the drama.

Our predicament in life is that we are so identified with our personal drama that we find it challenging to separate ourselves from it; we are caught in our personal dramatic movie. Sometime it takes quite awhile for us to realize that we are stuck in our own movie and that we might want to find a way out. Actually there are many exit signs in the theater of life, but we are so absorbed in our own experience, it's difficult for us to see them. That's why we need teachers and methods.

In our everyday movie life we try to find the culprits—those we can blame for our messes: Husband, wife, children, workplace, neighbors, and circumstances such as job loss, divorce, and death of loved ones. Which one is responsible for messing up our lives? The right answer is none of the above; there is no thing or no one to blame. So how in the world are we going to escape? How can we find the happiness we yearn for?

We need to recognize our dilemma, and then be willing to be open and receptive to actually using the methods that will free us. If we will open our eyes, we can discover the exit signs that will lead us out of our mind traps. A Course in Miracles says that we are too confused to recognize our own hope. Sometimes we are not open and receptive unless and until we become so miserable and uncomfortable that we cry out, "There has to be a better way!" By the love and grace of God there is a better way and by the grace of God we are destined to follow it.

In lucid dreams we realize that we are dreaming and that we can take charge of the dream. This happens when we dream of flying and a part of us is aware that we are dreaming, and we observe ourselves having the experience in the dream. This same experience can happen in everyday life once we can stand back and watch our thoughts and feelings as our life unfolds. We can cultivate awareness back of our anger that watches, that can say to us, "you're out of control right now—why don't you calm down?" We are not totally absorbed and taken over. Developing the habit of self-observation strengthens us psychologically and spiritually.

Our ability to watch and detach can be greatly enhanced by journaling—writing down our thoughts and feelings and then observing them. Writing down our thoughts keeps them from circling around in our mind going nowhere. When we stop our thoughts by writing them down, we are in a better position to see clearly and act wisely and skillfully. Actually having conversations with God is not only the prerogative of Neal Donald Walsh; we can have our own conversations and dig ourselves out of muddy emotions and thoughts just by writing them down and then listening for guidance from Spirit and writing those answers as well. I know this works well because I have worked my way out of many a muddy situation with this method.

Meditation is the most powerful path of all because in meditation we watch our thoughts go by without becoming attached to them. We are aware that we are aware. We plug into IS-ness, the Divine Hum, pure Being. The whole point of meditation is not meditation itself, but what it leads to: a wholly different peaceful and aware state of consciousness in every area of our lives. We begin to wake up to What we truly are—spiritual beings in earth suits.

It is possible to live most of our life in meditation—not just the few minutes twice a day or an hour a day. We can constantly be the Watcher, The Observer, without getting pulled into our everyday dramas and traumas. We can be so plugged into the Infinite Loving Presence that we just naturally extend it because we have become One with it. Then we see that we are Spiritual Beings watching our human dramas rather than becoming lost in them.

In a sense we die to our old problem riddled selves, and out of the silence of meditation, pure awareness and freedom results. Some wise words about freedom from the Persian poet Rumi:

Your way begins on the other side.

Become the sky.

Take an ax to the prison wall.

Escape. Walk out

like someone suddenly born into color.

Do it now.

You're covered with thick cloud.

Slide out the side.

Your old life was a frantic running

from silence.

The speechless full moon comes out now.

The more we are willing to just let the world be something we're aware of, something we watch and observe, the more it will let us be who we are—Awareness itself behind all the appearances. A wonderful example of seeing the truth of our soul's freedom, beyond all appearances, is the following poem, written by Robert Meyer who was confined to a wheel chair and lived in a nursing home in Iowa:

Never Left the Ground

At times upon the wings of thought my mind will soar.

I'll trade salutes with lofty clouds in air so pure.

I'll fly and whisper with the wind of life and love

in air so rarefied so high above.

I circle all the troubled trains of thought

that crisscross on the glistening tracks so far below.

I climb and climb and climb.

I feel no fright of upward flight.

I've scratched the ceiling of the sky and sat on stars.

Horizons know how far I've flown and shared with me

this other side.

I glide and glide and glide.

Look up! That's me, that speck you see so high.

Yes, Me!

I'm free. So fleet am I, I'll swoop and prove to you

that such movements of the mind are not confined to

sleepy dreams.

I wish you'd let me take you with me for a ride,

To dive and soar and climb and glide,

to fly upon the wings of thought to regal heights.

My eagle flights have taken me the world round.

And I have never even ever left the ground.

Wise teachers from cultures all over the world have some common advice. Let go all sense of being an unfairly treated victim. Love, forgive, meditate, observe, feed upon & think about the good, the true and the beautiful. Serve others. Each one of these things is an exit door into freedom and happiness beyond measure. We have a choice. We can make for the exit to freedom and happiness or remain stuck in the theater of the absurd and suffer. It amounts to choosing bondage or freedom, Heaven or Hell. On the 4th of July we celebrate the freedom of our country, but no matter what the date on the calendar, we can celebrate our own freedom of Spirit!

SECTION SIX
How Can We Help?

"If our relationship to one another is pure,
We want nothing from anyone but the opportunity
To work, share, or in some way be an instrument of blessing."
—Joel Goldsmith

Courage, Compassion, Commitment

"There is no more blessed place to stand than
in the center of a life experience dedicated to
Unconditional love and service."
—Michael Brown

This message is inspired by a true story told beautifully in the fifties film *The Scarlett and the Black* starring Gregory Peck. It is a story of courage, compassion and commitment during the Nazi occupation of Italy during World War II. The following poem sets the stage for what I'm going to share with you:

A Time for Heroes

It's not an ordinary time, not an ordinary time at all.
It's a time for heroes—Those who can face facts
Though they sear like a red-hot iron from the heart of a Pittsburg furnace.
Come close you who dare, but unless there are some who have courage
To come close, what hope oh world?
"Business as usual," is the cry of most,
as they draw the blinkers more tightly
around their eyes,
shielding themselves from the heart of the flame, clinging
desperately to whatever remains of a familiar world.
—unknown author

Father Hugh O'Flarity held a high position in the Vatican and was close to Pope Pius XII. Although the Germans occupied Italy, the Vatican held a neutral position and provided a safe haven for Jews and British and American escapees who managed to make it there. O'Flarity was deep into helping these refugees find safe places to hide and providing them with food—and in the end over 4,000 were saved, most of them making it safely to Switzerland. O'Flarity would dress in regular business clothes and rent apartments all over the city. Money was donated from wealthy sympathizers; when they had parties, O'Flarity was invited and money slipped to him. All this worked quite well until Himmler appointed Colonel Koppel to come to the area and tighten up the security.

Before long the Colonel's spies knew the role O'Flarity was playing and kept a strict watch on him. During this time Colonel Koppel called the leading Jews of the area into his headquarters and assured them that there were no death camps and that they were perfectly safe. Actually, the Colonel had personally supervised the removal of Jews to these camps. Koppel demanded 100 pounds of gold that he said would guarantee their safely.

When O'Flarity heard about that, he joined with the Jews and solicited gold jewelry and other items from Jews as well as Catholics and others. They were able to collect the gold. As soon as Koppel had it, he began raiding the Jewish quarters to take people away. Of course, this incensed O'Flarity and he renewed his efforts to help people escape. All the while the Nazi's knew what this priest was doing and they demand that he stop. When he refused, the Nazi's painted a white line around the Vatican and posted guards. Koppell told O'Flarity that he would be shot on sight if he stepped across the line.

Because of the vast scope of the work he was doing, O'Flarity knew that if it were to continue, it would be essential that he get out and make his contacts. That's when he donned many different disguises, including a nun, a street sweeper, and a street vendor. But his most daring disguise and escapade involved his wearing an SS uniform and going right inside a prison cell to administer last rites to a fellow priest who had been caught helping the underground. The priest was badly beaten, had been tortured and still he had refused to give up information. He was sentenced to face a firing squad the next day. Before he was taken away, Father O'Flarity was able to offer comfort to his fellow priest and administer the last rites. O'Flarity managed to drive away undiscovered.

Near the end of the war when Koppel knew it was over for him, he had one of his men disguise himself as a priest, go into the Vatican and kidnap O'Flarity. He was brought to the Coliseum for a private meeting. Koppel's wife and two children were living with him in Rome, and he feared for their safely after the people would be freed. He asked O'Flarity to arrange safe passage for them to Switzerland. When O'Flarity vehemently refused to help him, Koppel fell apart, obviously broken. He cursed God and screamed, "Fake! Fake! There is no God!" O'Flarity walked away, not disguising his contempt for this man who had harmed so many.

When the allies took over Rome amid much joy and celebration, Koppel was taken prisoner and questioned. The interrogator asked, "What group or individual was responsible for arranging the escape of your wife and children to Switzerland?" He insisted that he did not know. Up until that moment he had no idea what had happened to his family, but of course he did know who helped them.

End of story? Not quite. O'Flarity received the praise of the Pope and was given several humanitarian awards. Koppel was sentenced to life in prison for war crimes. End of story—not quite yet. Father O'Flarity visited Koppel in his prison cell every month until Koppel died there, a convert to Catholism.

I believe impactful true stories such as this can teach and inspire us. Why was O'Flarity willing and able to do what he did? Certainly he was a hero who demonstrated courage, compassion and commitment. It's been said that courage is the daring of the soul to go farther than it can see. Helen Keller said, "Life is either a daring adventure—or nothing." O'Flarity had the courage to constantly risk his life to help many others. He had every reason to give it up and stay safe with the Vatican walls, but he chose to keep on until the end, committed to do what his strong faith demanded, willing to surrender even life itself for his high cause.

Obviously he had tremendous compassion for all those in fear of losing their lives, and he did everything he could to help them. In the end, he even had compassion for his worst enemy. More lines from A Time For Heroes: "The hero sees a way through the inferno, a way through the desert, A way through famine, war, and earthquakes—a hero's way. Not a way of survival, but a way of life, a way of strength and effectiveness, a way of assurance and calm, born of his unwavering love for and commitment to, the One who still even in these turbulent times, especially in these turbulent times, is Lord of Heaven and Earth. The hero goes quietly to work, needing no chariot, no spear, no audience, no praise, and no reward."

Here in this Earth School there is always a need for spiritual heroes to show up and inspire us. I think The Dali Lama, Nelson Mandela, Bishop Tu Tu, and many other modern heroes qualify. The bottom line for you and me, and the question for all of us is, "What is *ours* to do?" First we need to attend to our own psychological and spiritual business of healing what needs to be healed inside ourselves. This often takes courage—personal and spiritual growth work can be very scary, but it is the best thing we can do for ourselves, and then we can extend love and healing out into our world. We can't extend love and compassion if we can't feel it for ourselves. Once we do, we can become heroes in our own arena.

Our work will take on diverse forms, depending on our individual circumstances, but we will receive opportunities if we cultivate courage, compassion and commitment to be open and receptive to the guidance and instruction of Spirit. The conclusion of A Time for Heroes and a challenge for us: "Let our arena be the circumstance where we are, and into that arena, pour ourselves, awakening our own indomitable courageous spirit. This is the building block of a true spiritual awakening. Our old world will crumble under the pressure of our courage, compassion and commitment. Out of confusion and darkness, a new world will appear filled with miracles of love and light."

Let us stand up and show up with courage, compassion and commitment in the arena of our current circumstances. There is enough work for all of us. And the most important work of all is spiritual awakening. Once we make that our priority, everything else will be revealed to us and our path will be clear.

Closing Prayer:
Dear Father-Mother God: We want to see clearly, love unconditionally, and act wisely and skillfully. We want to do what is ours to do, and so we commit to the higher way, the higher choices, and we move forward in faith and trust in Your Presence and Power, now and forevermore. Amen.

A Life That Matters

"Stand up and show your soul."
—Clarissa Pinkola-Estes

A story with a moral: A mouse looked through a crack in the wall to see the farmer and his wife opening a package. "What food might it contain?" He was devastated to discover that it was a mousetrap. Retreating to the farmyard, the mouse proclaimed the warning: "There is a mousetrap in the house!" The chicken clucked and scratched, raised her head and said, "Mr. Mouse, I can tell this is a grave concern to you, but it is of no consequence to me. I cannot be bothered by it." The mouse turned to the pig and said, "There is a mousetrap in the house!" The pig sympathized but said, "I'm so very sorry, Mr. Mouse, but there is nothing I can do about it but pray. Be assured you are in my prayers." The mouse turned to the cow. She said, "Wow, Mr. Mouse. I'm sorry for you. But it's no skin off my nose." So the mouse returned to the house, head down and dejected, to face the farmer's mousetrap alone.

That very night a sound was heard of a mousetrap catching its prey. The farmer's wife rushed to see what was caught. In the darkness she did not see that it was a venomous snake whose tail the trap had caught. The snake bit the farmer's wife. The farmer rushed her to the hospital and she returned with a fever. Now everyone knows you treat a fever with fresh chicken soup, so the farmer took his hatchet to the farmyard for the soup's main ingredient. But his wife's sickness continued, so friends and neighbors came to sit with her around the clock.

To feed them, the farmer butchered the pig. The farmer's wife did not get well. She died, and so many people came to her funeral the farmer had the cow slaughtered to provide enough meat for all of them. So next time you hear that someone is facing a problem and think that it doesn't concern you, remember that when one of us is threatened, we are all at risk. In the book of Genesis, Cain asked God: "Am I my brother's keeper?" I do believe we are our brother's keeper and that we need to understand that what we think, say and do does matter.

Bottom line—every life matters because we are all one. What each of us puts in the pot of consciousness does matter. We live in a sea of consciousness, connected in every way. Matthew 25: 35-40 reads: "For I was hungry and you gave me food; I was thirsty and you gave me drink. I was a stranger and you welcomed me; I was naked and you gave me clothing; I was sick and you took care of me; I was in prison and you visited me." Then the righteous questioned him, "Lord when was it that we saw you hungry and gave you food, or thirsty and gave you drink? And when was it that we saw you a stranger and welcomed you, or naked and gave you clothes? And when was it that we saw you sick or in prison and visited you? And Jesus answered: "Truly I tell you, just as you did it to the least of these, you did it to me."

Why is this so? The Christ consciousness inhabits us all—God leaves no one out. Yes, it is true that a heavy veil of ego hangs heavy over much of the world's population, hiding the light, but again we all live in the same sea of consciousness. David Hawkins postulates in his books "Power vs. Force" and "The Eye of the I" that human consciousness is measurable and that he has been able to do it. The highest calibration that a human body could carry is 1000. This is the level of Jesus, Buddha and other avatars, the level of light, love and wisdom. The basic level of truth and integrity is 200. Until the 80's the collective human consciousness was 190; then it jumped to 207 in 1985. Yet, 78% of the world's population is still under 200. The higher the consciousness, the purer the power and love that person radiates. Lower levels are fear, hate, anger, and all forms of darkness and negativity.

Hawkins believes that the light counterbalances the dark. He says that one person such as Jesus calibrating at 1,000 counterbalances the negativity of the entire human race. If this were not so, we would have destroyed ourselves by now. Each person calibrating over 200 serves as a counterbalance for those below. It is very important to raise our consciousness because every degree over 200 in the collective contributes to the enlightenment of the whole.

A Course in Miracles tells us: "Our function is to work together because apart from each other we cannot function at all. God has joined all his sons with himself." So we can ask ourselves, "In every encounter, in every interaction, in every connection, am I making the world better or worse? Am I contributing to the light or to darkness?

So do we live a life that matters? Yes! Is changing the world for the better too tall an order? No! We cannot improve the consciousness of the world by war and force. We can improve it by putting energy into it that is above 200—the energy of forgiveness, understanding, love and service. We can allow ourselves to be embraced by the love of God and then extend and radiate that love. We can focus upon extending love to the world instead of feeling defeated and angry because of its insanity. Remember that light dissipates the darkness. Be light. Be love.

Author Clarissa Pinkola-Estes: "We know that it does not take everyone on earth to bring justice and peace, but only a small, determined group who will not give up in spite of continuing storms. One of the most calming and powerful actions you can do to intervene in a stormy world is to stand up and show your soul. Soul on deck shines like gold in dark times. To display the lantern of the soul, to fiercely show mercy towards others are acts of immense bravery and greatest necessity. Struggling souls catch light from other souls who are more fully lit and willing to show it."

I have been incredibly blessed by those lit up souls who touched my life with their teaching, their presence, and their wisdom when I was in the valley of darkness and despair. One of the most important things they taught me is that life was not meant to be miserable. As Joel Goldsmith wrote, man was not born to cry. We were born to reflect and participate in the love peace and joy of God. Unity taught me that as a child of God my natural inheritance is love peace and joy. And beyond that Unity and other spiritual teachings gave me all kinds of tools and teachings that have helped me allow God to lift my soul above all those trials and tribulations of my earlier life.

I see clearly now that we all live a life that matters and that we can be beacons of light and truly helpful teachers. We are sent out into the world to visibly uplift the people we encounter. Every action is a holy encounter—an opportunity to extend love. From A Course in Miracles: "When you meet anyone, remember it is a holy encounter. As you see him you will see yourself. As you treat him you will treat yourself. As you think of him, you will think of yourself. In him you will find yourself or lose yourself."

The poet John Donne wrote: "No man is an island, entire of itself; every man is a piece of the continent, a part of the main. Never send to know for whom the bell tolls; it tolls for thee." So turns out we all live a life that matters very much. We may at times feel as if we don't matter, but what we think or do does indeed matter. So let us go forth today and every day and let our light shine. Let us summon the wisdom and courage to stand up and show our soul!

Love Changes Everything

"Love is patient and kind." St. Paul
"Kindness is my religion." The Dali Lama

An elderly woman and her little grandson, whose face was sprinkled with bright freckles, spent the day at the zoo. Lots of children were waiting in line to get their cheeks painted by a local artist who was decorating them with tiger paws. "You've got so many freckles, there's no place to paint!" a little girl in line said to the little boy. Embarrassed, the little boy dropped his head. His grandmother knelt down next to him. "I love your freckles. When I was a little girl I always wanted freckles," she said, while tracing her finger across the child's cheek. "Freckles are beautiful." The boy looked up, "Really?" "Of course," said the grandmother. Why just name me one thing that's prettier than freckles." The little boy thought for a moment, peered intently at his grandma's face, and softly whispered, "Wrinkles."

I love the following Helen Stiener Rice verse: "Tis the human touch in this world that counts, the touch of your hand in mine that means far more to the fainting heart than shelter or bread or wine. For shelter is gone when the night is over, and bread lasts only a day, but the touch of your hand and the sound of your voice live on in my heart always." Jesus in A Course in Miracles asks us to "teach only love, for that is what you are." And "without extension there can be no love." In other words we must demonstrate love by expressing it which means to give loving kindness, service and support to others. Jesus also says, "The whole glory and perfect joy that is the Kingdom lies in you to give. Do you not want to give it?"

When we tune into and accept the great love of God for us, we naturally want to share that love with others. The moment we are willing to accept God's love, we open ourselves to its full expression in and through our life. There's a joy song in the Unity hymnal that includes the words: "Love is something if you give it away, you'll end up having more." Love is meant to be shared without limit and when we do so, we are affirming our own identity as extensions of the living, loving God.

Remember this truth: There is nothing we have ever done that could cause God to love us less; there is nothing we have ever done that could cause God to love us more. Why? Because we are totally, completely and unconditionally loved by God. We need to accept that love and allow God to love through us. God's love is greater than anyone or anything. God's love is so great that it fills all time and all space. It is instant compassion, constant tenderness, and transforming forgiveness. The love of God delights to bless us, and as we accept this blessing, we are delighted to bless our brothers and sisters.

I received a U-Tube story in my email awhile back that melted my heart as tears ran down my cheeks. A very talented portrait and nature artist, a crusty older woman named Kasiah, lives by herself on a goat ranch in Utah and is able to command thousands of dollars for her works of art. Somewhere along the way, she fell in love. She painted the portrait of a soldier who had been killed in battle. As she painted and studied the face in the photo, he became alive to her and she felt the love of a mother, a sister, a wife flowing through her. She packaged and shipped the portrait to his parents, refusing to charge for her work or the shipping.

Thus began her labors of love. She has completed and delivered hundreds of portraits of military men and women who lost their lives in service to our country. The spirit of love and kindness expresses through her and it is obvious that she is experiencing the joy of being a channel of loving kindness. She is able to capture the spirit of the men and women whose portraits she paints, and the next of kin who receive them are blessed by her sharing. What was so moving to me was seeing and hearing her talk to the subjects she paints as if they were right there in the room with her. She carries on a running conversation with them as she paints. And I'm sure they actually are there in spirit.

You and I may not be in a position to give on such a grand scale as Kasiah, but every act of loving kindness counts. The accumulation of all those acts, great and small is what will bring more light into the world. Those are the Miracles that A Course is talking about. The purpose of the Course is to remove the blocks to our experience of God's love. We are to teach only love for that is what we are. We are to behold the Christ spirit in our brothers and sisters. We are to forgive quickly so as not to accumulate grievances.

A seminary professor who liked to teach by object lessons brought a large dartboard and lots of darts to class. He told his students to think of anyone they would like to throw darts at, those who had angered them or done them wrong. The students picked up the darts and really got into it, laughing and teasing and putting lots of energy into the game. Finally the professor called a halt. He took the dartboard down and removed the covering with the target pattern. Underneath was the face of Jesus the Christ—poked full of holes, including the eyes.

Would you and I be so quick to throw the darts of anger and resentment, so ready to attack the basic divinity of others if we realized that we were indeed throwing darts at the Christ? In our fear and defensiveness, we forget who we are and who others are. We get into the games of attack, defend and get even. Our task becomes to forgive our enemies, to behold the Christ in them, to see beyond appearances, to recognize that God lives in all.

You may be thinking: Am I just supposed to allow people to abuse me, to run over me? I believe that it is appropriate to disallow inappropriate or abusive behavior. It may be wise to move away from a dysfunctional or abusive situation. It is important to honor the Christ in ourselves and not allow others who are in fear to throw darts at us. However, we can still love and bless them, forgive them. The truth is that we are all one in Christ and we can't throw a dart at anyone else without hurting ourselves. We need to understand that the offender is wearing a mask and underneath the mask is the Christ spirit.

Jesus taught us to love and bless our enemies to pray for those who despitefully use us. In other words we need to stop making anyone, even our so called enemies a dart board target. When we throw darts of anger and hate at anyone we also throw them at ourselves. Jesus said: "The measure you give will be the measure you get." In modern language we say, "What goes around, comes around."

The 15th century poet Kabir wrote: "Are you looking for Me, God? I am in the next seat. My shoulder is against yours." A woman named Mary Beth Sammons was riding the train home from a downtown Chicago courtroom following the finality of her divorce. She was alone in her seat, sobbing as she stared out the window, hoping that no one would notice her. Her 16 year marriage had ended and she felt an overwhelming sadness; she felt frightened and totally alone.

All of a sudden a hand appeared—the tiny manicured hand of a woman. She leaned forward and gave Mary Beth a small white envelope, then smiled and disappeared. The message was: "I know you don't know me, but I was watching you there crying, and my heart goes out to you. Know that though I am only a stranger to you, I care. It may not seem that way, but the sun will shine again, and you will see the rainbow. Signed-Someone Who Cares.

Mary Beth never saw the woman again, but the effects of her kind words remain deep inside her heart. On what seemed like the saddest, loneliest day of her life, a stranger's gesture of kindness reminded her that she was not alone, and that God, often through the actions of others—in this case a stranger—is always there to help and comfort her. She says that through the woman on the train, God poured love into her wounds and gave her hope that joy would someday come again. The woman on the train taught her that one small act of kindness really can make all the difference in someone's world.

I feel so very grateful for the many instances of loving kindness in my world, even in the midst of some extremely difficult situations in my younger years, instances of loving kindness gave me hope and faith that things could get better and that when all is said and done, the love of God changes everything. My goal is to allow God's love to flow in and through me to bless, love and heal. I strive to "teach only love, for that is what I am." When we are in the love mode, we are in a forgiving and understanding consciousness that allows us to trust in the love of God—despite all appearances. In that consciousness we are indeed radiating centers of Divine Love and Light, mighty to attract our good and to radiate good to others.

Let us have complete faith in ultimate Divine Love and Justice. Let us strive to see beyond the appearances of the world of the ego. Let us trust that as we give our best to the world, the world will give its best back to us. Let us strive to know beyond a shadow of a doubt that indeed Love Changes Everything.

Sacred Service

"Until he extends the circle of his compassion to all living
things, man will not himself find peace."
—Albert Schweitzer

"The truly helpful are invulnerable
because their helpfulness is their praise of God.
—A Course in Miracles

We perform sacred service when we offer the best of who we are and what we have for the benefit of one another. We all know the Bible story of the Good Samaritan. The Samaritan helped a man that others passed by because he was guided to extend his compassion beyond the concept of "our own." What we're talking about is not being "do gooders" from duty, fear, or obligation—not buying our way into Heaven. It is not something we do for those "poor unfortunates who are "less than."

Sacred service means serving the Christ in ourselves and others because we are tuned into the love of God and there is nothing else to do. It is to know that we play on a level field here in Earth School; we are all one in spirit. Joel Goldsmith reminds us: "There never has been a mortal and all that appears as mortal is the Christ incorrectly seen." Jesus said, "Inasmuch as ye do it unto the least of these, ye do it unto me." We can take this truth into every area of our endeavor. I believe that the following poem captures the spirit of how we can "work for God" no matter what we're doing:

Working For God

I will acquire divinely deep, God-given
Concentration, and then use its unlimited
Power to meet all demands of my life.

I will do everything with deep attention:
My work at home, in the office, in the
World—all duties great and small will be
Performed well.

On the throne of silent thoughts, the God
Of peace is directing my actions today.

After contacting God in meditation I will
Go about my work, whatever it may be,
Knowing that God is with me, directing me
And giving me power to bring forth that for
Which I am striving.

I will use my money to make the world
Family better and happier, according to the
Measure of my ability.

—Paramahansa Yogananda

There are a myriad of possibilities to extend ourselves in love and service every day if we will just open our eyes to see those possibilities. Too often we don't understand how important every act of caring, love and kindness can be. We think: "What can just one person do? What can someone like me do?" I learned a valuable lesson about that when my son Richard died. At the time I was not tuned into spirit and felt great pain. I discovered that every small thing, every word of comfort that people extended was helpful. Knowing that people cared touched my heart. Before that experience I didn't think that I could comfort anyone in pain; after that experience, I didn't hesitate to send a card, make a visit or phone call. I came to realize that we are all connected and it is important to show people that we care.

Whatever we do with love counts—makes an impact—changes things. The following true story from Nursing Management Magazine illustrates the point: Dr. Frank Mayfield was touring Tewksbury Institute when on his way out he accidentally collided with an elderly floor maid. To cover the awkward moment he started asking questions. "How long have you worked here?" She answered, "Almost from the beginning." Dr. Mayfield asked, "Can you tell me something of the history of this place?" The floor maid replied that she'd like to show him something.

She led him down to the basement under the oldest section of the oldest building and pointed to what looked like small prison cells, their iron bars rusted with age. "That's the cage where they used to keep Annie," she said. "Annie was a young girl brought here because she was incorrigible. She'd bite and scream and throw her food at people. Doctors and nurses couldn't even examine her. I'd see them trying to examine her while she was spitting and scratching at them. I was only a few years younger than her myself, and I used to think, "I sure would hate to be locked up in a cage like that." I wanted to help her, but I didn't know what to do. If the doctors and nurses couldn't help her, what could I do?"

I decided to bake her some brownies and brought them to her cage and said: "Annie I baked these just for you; I'll put them right here where you can get them if you want." I got out of there as fast as I could because I was afraid she might throw them at me. But she didn't. She actually took the brownies and ate them. After that she was nice to me when I was around. I started talking to her and even got her laughing.

One of the nurses noticed, and she told the Doctor, and he asked me to help with her. So every time they wanted to see Annie or examine her, I went into the cage first and explained and calmed her down and held her hand. That's when they discovered that Annie was almost blind. About a year later, the Perkins Institute for the Blind opened. Annie went on to study there and became a teacher herself.

Annie came back to Tewksbury to visit and to see if there was something she could do to help out.

The director had just received a letter from a man who had written about his daughter; he said she was unruly, almost like an animal. He'd been told she was blind and deaf and deranged. He was at his wit's end, but he didn't want to put her into an asylum. So he wrote to ask if there was anyone—any teacher—who would come to his house and work with his daughter.

And that is how Annie Sullivan became the lifelong companion of Helen Keller. When Helen received the Nobel Prize, she was asked who had the greatest impact on her life and she said: Annie Sullivan. But Annie said: "No, Helen the woman who had the greatest influence on both our lives was a floor maid at the Tewksbury institute. History is changed when one person asks,"What can someone like me do?"

What we do matters. What we give matters. What we contribute matters. What you do matters; it sends ripples that extend to infinity. We can't even know, and we actually should not be concerned with the details or results of our extending love and service. We are keeping our sacred commitment to serve one another by just extending the love we are to every person and every situation that presents itself to us. May we make the prayer of St. Francis an ideal for our own sacred service:

Lord, make me an instrument of thy peace.
Where there is hatred, let me sow love;
Where there is injury, pardon;
Where there is doubt, faith;
Where there is despair, hope;
Where there is darkness, light;
And where there is sadness, joy.
Oh, divine master, grant that I may not so much seek
To be consoled as to console;
To be understood as to understand
To be loved as to love.
For it is in giving that we receive;
It is in pardoning that we are pardoned;
And it is in dying that we are born to eternal life.
Amen

Teach Only Love

"Teach only love, for that is what you are."
—A Course in Miracles

What is the greatest commandment? Jesus' answer: "Love the Lord your God with all your heart and with all your soul and with all your mind. This is the first and greatest commandment. The second is like unto it: Love your neighbor as yourself. All the law and the prophets hang on these two commandments." (Matthew 22:37)

The apostle John tells us in his first letter that God is Love and that there is no fear in love because perfect love casts out fear. The question we might ask is, "How do I teach only love?" I believe, we teach it one thought, one choice, one decision at a time. We teach it by choosing to forgive ourselves and others. We teach love by living it. The Dali Lama states: "Loving kindness is my religion."

One of my favorite Unity ministers, who was a loving light to so many in Unity when he was the Senior Minister at Unity Village Chapel, wrote the following:

I tried to conquer the universe
and it defeated me—
I tried to understand the universe
and it outwitted me—
I tried to capture the universe
and it eluded me—
So, clumsily, hesitantly, I tried to

love the universe—and it embraced me!
—Sig Paulson

Let's look at some ways we can love the universe by opening to loving one another. That is how we teach love. In truth there are many ways to express love, and because we are unique individuals inside our innate oneness, we have different preferences when it comes to expressing love and receiving it. Our partner, child, or friend may respond differently, and have different preferences when it comes to giving and receiving love.

Michigan poet Theodore Roethke's tongue in cheek poem is all about love's preferences:

To an Amorous Lady

The Pensive Knu, the staid Ardvaark
accept caresses in the dark
The bear, equipped with paw & snout,
would rather take than dish it out.
And snakes, both poisonous and garter,
in love, are never known to barter.
But my dear, when amorous arts we would pursue,
You can with pleasure, bill or coo—
You are indeed one in a million
At once Reptilian and Mammalian.

So let's look at various ways we can teach love. We can teach love by affirming one another. Mark Twain once said: "I can live for two months on a good compliment." We all want to be acknowledged and appreciated.

It motivates us to do and give more. A carrot works much better than a stick for most of us.

The opposite of that is verbal abuse which demonstrates the speaker's lack of love for himself and others. The wise Solomon said: "The tongue has the power of life and death." and "An anxious heart weighs a man down, but a kind word cheers him up." Sincere compliments, encouraging words, and kind words such as,"You can do it! You've got what it takes! What a beautiful job that is!" are ways of teaching love. Jesus constantly affirmed the truth of us: "You are the light of the world. You are the salt of the earth. Let your light shine."

Another way we show love to ourselves and others is to carve out quality time. Quality time is giving undivided focused attention to listen and fully hear another. We give quality time to ourselves when we take time in the silence to commune with spirit. Jesus often went apart alone. He also often went apart with his disciples, giving them quality time. Because we get too involved in being busy, quiet time and quality time are too often neglected.

Quality time is an important way to express love to our partners, husbands, wives, children, grandchildren. Make a date. Go somewhere and talk. Nothing to talk about? Read the same book or article or attend a movie together and discuss it afterwards. We all have observed couples who are obviously together, but not talking to one another. And we see people who talk, listen, and make eye contact, sharing quality time. A great way to get closer to our children and grandchildren is to make special dates to take them out one at a time to lunch, movie, park, zoo or museum. The idea is to give undivided attention. People who do this love the results.

Giving and receiving gifts is a way of making love visual. They don't need to be expensive or 'store bought'—we're not talking about bribes. Some of the most prized gifts come from our young children: dandelion bouquets, drawings, handmade crafts made in school. Perhaps the best giving of all is done naturally and spontaneously to someone in need whether we know them personally or not. The following story is about a poor boy who was given a gift of kindness and love.

A Glass Of Milk.

One day, a poor boy who was selling goods from door to door to pay his way through school, found he had only one thin dime left, and he was hungry. He decided he would ask for a meal at the next house. However, he lost his nerve when a lovely young woman opened the door. Instead of a meal he asked for a drink of water. She thought he looked hungry so brought him a large glass of milk. He drank it slowly, and then asked, How much do I owe you?" You don't owe me anything," she replied. "Mother has taught us never to accept pay for a kindness. He said, "Then I thank you from my heart."

As Howard Kelly left that house, he not only felt stronger physically,but his faith in God and man was strong also. He had been ready to give up and quit. Many years later that same young woman became critically ill. The local doctors were baffled. They finally sent her to the big city, where they called in specialists to study her rare disease. Dr. Howard Kelly was called in for the consultation. When he heard the name of the town she came from, a strange light filled his eyes. Immediately he rose and went down the hall of the hospital to her room. Dressed in his doctor's gown he went in to see her. He recognized her at once. He went back to the consultation room determined to do his best to save her life. From that day he gave special attention to her case. After a long struggle, the battle was won.

Dr. Kelly requested the business office to pass the final bill to him for approval. He looked at it, wrote something on the edge, and the bill was sent to her room. She feared to open it, for she was sure it would take the rest of her life to pay for it all. Finally she looked, and something caught her attention on the side of the bill. She read these words: "Paid in full with one glass of milk"—Dr. Howard Kelly. Tears of joy flooded her eyes and she prayed: "Thank You, God, that your love has spreads through human hearts and hands."

As that story demonstrates, we can definitely share and express love through service to one another. First John 3:19: "Let us not love with only words or tongue, but with actions and in truth." We show love when we ask, "How can I help?" "What do you need?" When we serve we are spreading bread upon the waters and often reap rewards in amazing and unexpected ways, like the woman who gave the hungry boy a glass of milk.

Physical touch is also important for human survival. When love and attention in the form of physical touch and speech is withdrawn from babies, they cannot survive. They wither and die. We all need touch. We have heard of or experienced therapeutic massage, or perhaps a program nurses utilize called Touch for Health. There are many kinds of loving touch besides sexual touch that we can share with others. A pat on the back, a touch on the arm, hugs. I have the best job in the world because I get many hugs every Sunday. I love to both give hugs and receive hugs. I'm like the lady in Theodore Roethke's poem. I'm both Mammalian and Reptilian!

I'll close with some more ideas about how to teach only love: Go forth and mend a quarrel; sincerely forgive; search out a forgotten friend; write a kind note; share some treasure; keep a promise; relinquish a grudge; apologize if you were wrong; try to understand; examine your demands on others; appreciate; be gentle; laugh a little more; express gratitude; praise God; take pleasure in the beauty and wonder of the earth; regard every person as a beloved brother and sister; set a holy intention to be an emissary of love, mercy, and generosity to everyone you meet; speak love, and teach love,—for that is what you are.

The Treasure of Teachers

"Life is no brief candle to me. It is a sort of
Splendid torch which I've got hold of for the moment.
I want to make it burn as brightly as possible
Before handing it on to future generations."
—George Bernard Shaw

This message is dedicated to teachers everywhere whose greatest challenge is to see the potential in their students—to see past appearances and circumstances—to inspire and encourage the next generation. Many can't believe we make much difference in the overall situation of the world. However, we are all teachers and learners, all keepers of the vision for future generations. Everything we think, say, and do matters not only to ourselves but to everyone around us. Emerson said, "Be an opener of doors to such as come after thee and do not try to make the universe a blind alley."

Jesus was a master teacher in his many encounters. He saw potential in Matthew the tax collector and called him down from a tree to become a disciple. He saw potential in all the disciples. They were simple, regular people and looked down upon by the scribes and Pharisees. Jesus looked at their hearts and potential, not their status in the society of the time.

We all might want to ask ourselves, "How many people do I dismiss from my life because I am not willing to look beyond their status, their age or their appearance? How many people in this world do I discount because I don't look for the qualities that may not be readily apparent?" We too often dismiss people from our lives because they are different from ourselves.

I invite us all today to be more mindful of the Biblical advice: "Do unto others as you would have them do unto you." You are reading about what to do, but the challenge is to go forth and use the information and inspiration. The Bible tells us: "Be doers of the word and not hearers only." Start by reaching out to others; there is never a lack of opportunity to give love and encouragement to those around us. Teachers and grandparents have a unique and wonderful opportunity to do that—but in truth we all can find our own opportunities to reach out.

There is a moving teacher's story that has become an urban legend. Originally written as fiction, it keeps being retold as if it were true by such people as Paul Harvey and Wayne Dyer. I think this is because it captures the very essence of the spirit of good teaching. Who knows how many teachers it has inspired to become more caring and compassionate and thus better teachers? Here is the story:

Many years ago an elementary teacher named Mrs. Thompson stood in front of her 5th grade class on the very first day of school an told the children a lie. Like most teachers, she looked at her student and said that she loved them all the same. But that was impossible, because there in the front row, slumped in his seat, was a little boy named Teddy Stoddard. Mrs. Thompson had watched Teddy the year before and noticed that he didn't play well with the other children, that his clothes were messy and that he constantly needed a bath. And Teddy could be unpleasant. At the school where Mrs. Thompson taught, she was required to review each child's past records and she put Teddy's off until last. However, when she reviewed his life, she was surprised.

Teddy's first grade teacher wrote, "Teddy is a bright child with a ready laugh. He does his work neatly and has good manners. He is a joy to be around. His second grade teacher wrote, "Teddy is an excellent student, well-liked by his classmates, but he is troubled because his mother has a terminal illness and life at home must be a struggle. His third grade teacher wrote, "His mother's death has been hard on him. He tries to do his best but his father doesn't show much interest and his home life will soon affect him if some steps aren't taken. His fourth grade teacher wrote, "Teddy is withdrawn and doesn't show much interest in school. He doesn't have many friends and sometimes sleeps in class."

By now, Mrs. Thompson realized the problem and she was ashamed of herself. She felt even worse when her students brought her Christmas presents wrapped in beautiful ribbons and bright paper, except for Teddy's. His present was clumsily wrapped in heavy brown paper from a grocery bag. Mrs. Thomson took pains to open it in the middle of the other presents. Some of the children started to laugh when she found a rhinestone bracelet with some of the stones missing and a bottle that was one quarter full of perfume.

But Mrs. Thompson stifled the children's laughter when she exclaimed how pretty the bracelet was, putting it on, and dabbing some of the perfume on her wrist. Teddy Stoddard stayed after school that day just long enough to say, "Mrs. Thompson, today you smelled just like my Mom used to." After the children left she cried for a long time. On that very day, she quit teaching reading, writing, and arithmetic. Instead, she began to teach children.

Mrs. Thompson paid particular attention to Teddy. As she worked with him, his mind seemed to come alive. The more she encouraged him, the faster he responded. By the end of the year, Teddy had become one of the smartest children in the class and, despite her lie that she would love all the children the same, Teddy became one of her "teacher's pets. A year later, she found a note under her door, from Teddy, telling her that she was still the best teacher he ever had in his whole life.

Six years went by before she got another note from Teddy. He then wrote that he had finished high school, second in his class, and she was still the best teacher he ever had. Four years after that, she got another letter, saying that while things had been tough at times, he's stayed in school and would soon graduate from college with highest honors. He assured Mrs. Thompson that she was till the best and favorite teacher her ever had.

Then four more years passed and yet another letter came. This time he explained that after he got his bachelor's degree, he decided to go a little further. The letter explained that she was still the best and favorite teacher he ever had. But now his name was a little longer. The letter was signed, Theodore F. Stoddard, M.D. The story doesn't end there. There was yet another letter that spring. Teddy said he's met this girl and was going to be married. He explained that his father had died a couple of years ago and he was wondering if Mrs. Thompson might agree to sit in the place at the wedding that was usually reserved for the mother of the groom.

Of course, Mrs. Thompson did. And guess what? She wore that bracelet, the one with several rhinestones missing. And she made sure she was wearing the perfume that Teddy remembered his mother wearing on their last Christmas together. They hugged each other, and Dr. Stoddard whispered in Mrs. Thompson's ear, "Thank you Mrs. Thompson, for believing in me. Thank you so much for making me feel important and showing me that I could make a difference." Mrs. Thompson, with tears in her eyes, whispered back. She said, "Teddy, you have it all wrong. You were the one who taught me that I could make a difference. I didn't know how to teach until I met you."

I want to share a story about a teacher who tremendously influenced my life, Mr. Richard Blanchard. When I was in high school in the very small town of Clare, Michigan, my father's alcoholism worsened and he often staggered down the main street on his way to or from the local bar. I felt shame and embarrassment about this and tried to make up for it by trying to prove my worth by achieving as much as I could. Mr. Blanchard was a speech, drama and Latin teacher who treated every student with dignity and respect and called us Mr. or Miss. So he always addressed me as Miss Ireland.

In the speech and drama class, Mr. Blanchard had all of us read a favorite poem and made a contest out of it. I won first prize in this poetry reading contest by reading John Keats' poem *Ode on a Grecian Urn.* I was especially honored when he asked the top three students to read their poetry a second time so that he could record them. My first prize was a beautifully illustrated copy of the Rubaiyat of Omar Khayyam, which is still a prized possession. Mr. Blanchard and his wife had a baby son Richard, and I was delighted to be asked to baby sit for them several times. Mr. Blanchard was only at my school through Junior year, but I never forgot him. I named my first born son Richard after him. My philosophy of teaching was based on what he and other wonderful teachers had passed on to me: Look for intrinsic worth, talent, beyond any appearances, and treat students with dignity and respect.

When teaching at Ferris State University in Michigan, I thought about Richard Blanchard and that I would really love to look him up and thank him and let him know how much he had influenced my life and my teaching style. But all I knew was that he was originally from New Hampshire and had moved back there. I thought about writing an article in a teacher's journal with hope that he might see it.

About that time there was a teacher's conference in Boston which I attended along with three other faculty members. We decided to extend our time and take a short trip through New England while we were there. I told my friends about Mr. Blanchard and my desire to somehow find a way to thank him. Someone suggested that since New Hampshire is not heavily populated; why not look in the phone books of the biggest cities we pass through? The second time of searching produced a great result. During a rest stop outside Concord, I looked in a phone book, and lo and behold, a Richard Blanchard was listed!

I called the number, and the son Richard that I used to baby sit for gave me his dad's number. When we got to our hotel, I called and left a message and awhile later the return call came, and Mr. Blanchard's first words were: "Well, Julie May Ireland, how are you?" He remembered me and my brothers and invited me and my three friends to his home for lunch the next day. During that brief luncheon, I did my best to convey to him how much he had influenced me and how much I appreciated him.

When the lunch ended, he invited me into his study. "I have something for you," he said and handed me his recording of the poem I had recited in class all those years ago. My God, what a gift! The recording—surely—but more important was the fact that he kept it all those years and was able to give it back to me! We kept in touch for awhile after that and he sent me a clipping of his receiving the Teacher of the Year Award from the state of New Hampshire. He has passed on now, but his spirit and his teaching stay alive in me still today as I've moved into another facet of teaching through my ministry.

A lesson for us all is that we can pass it on, and it is our duty to pass it on. Pass what on? Love, respect, interest; we can let people know they matter without regard to where they may be in society's pecking order. When we do so, we inspire them to become more than they might have otherwise and to then pass the inspiration on to others. Because I was given that gift of respect by Richard Blanchard and many other teachers, I have always been committed to teaching others their own value and potential.

In Unity terms it boils down to: "I behold the Christ in you. Here the life of God I see. I can see a great peace too; I can see you whole and free. I can see God's love expressed; I can see you full of power. I can see you ever blessed; see Christ in you hour by hour. I behold the Christ in you; I can see that perfect one, blessed by God in all you do; I can see God's work is done." (From Unity hymn entitled, I Behold the Christ in You, lyrics by Frank B. Whitney.)

Triumph Beyond the Holocaust

"We ourselves feel that what we are doing
is just a drop in the ocean.
But the ocean would be less
because of that missing drop."
—Mother Teresa

The following is a story taken from a book that I co-authored with Ione Jenson entitled *Emerging Women—The Widening Stream*. We interviewed fifty women from all walks of life who displayed strength and courage and rose above adverse circumstances to help others. The book is now out of print (but still available on Amazon.com.). One of the most moving stories is that of Holocaust survivor, Alicia Appleman Jurman, and I include her story in this book because it is an outstanding example of strength, courage, and motivation to help others.

As the attractive smiling woman in red walked to the podium after her introduction, the nearly 1200 high school students in the North Idaho Community College auditorium clapped and cheered. They had read her book, and they were eager to hear more from her personally. With a warm and open demeanor and obvious affection for her audience, Alicia Applemen-Jurman began to speak.

We too had read her book *Alicia: My Story*, and had been deeply moved by the account of how a courageous young Jewish girl managed to survive the Holocaust and save many others. However, the most inspiring element of her story was that Alicia, in the midst of unspeakable horrors, which included the murders of her father, mother, and three brothers, never gave up her spunk, her spirit, her will to live, and her desire to be a complete human being. Alicia herself came close to annihilation a total of six times, "but they never touched my soul," she passionately testifies.

Alicia wrote her book and now speaks to students for two reasons. First, she swore on her brother Zackery's grave that she would tell the story so that her family and other silenced young people might live through the pages. Secondly Alicia loves and respects students and wants them to know the truth of what happened and what could happen again if people allow hatred and scapegoating to take over their lives.

She makes it clear both by her words and by her loving actions that she refuses to hate. She wants her work to serve as a stimulus for humankind to be more humane. "I tell the story of individuals," she says, "because it is difficult for people to relate to six million corpses, but they can relate to individuals." Perhaps that is why *Alicia: My Story* is being approved by an ever increasing number of Boards of Education in the United States and Canada for use as a textbook in history and Holocaust study classes.

Alicia's dedication and sincerity is illustrated by the fact that she does not accept fees of any kind for her work in the schools. Alicia's passion to tell the story drove her to write six days a week, up to thirteen hours a day for three years. She believes that the angels kissed her book, because five publishers wanted it, and then during the editing process, the only changes or corrections were for grammar and punctuation.

In the course of her writing, Alicia traveled back into her past, becoming the little girl whose sheltered and serene life with her family was shattered. The reader sees how the strength and values she gained from her early childhood carried her through the grueling ordeals of her teen years. Alicia recalls: I was a proud Jewish girl. When the oppressors called the Jews terrible names, I didn't believe them. I had studied Jewish history and knew that we had built an advanced civilization while our persecutors were still living in caves.

Alicia's strong will and sense of self-worth led her to defy first the Russian and then the German occupiers of her Polish hometown. The Russians began by taking all Jewish civil rights away, including the right of children to attend school. But Alicia loved school and her teacher, and she was determined to continue learning. A tree outside her former classroom window overlooked the teacher and the blackboard. For several days, Alicia walked to the school before daylight, climbed the tree, and then made herself as comfortable as possible in the branches. Through the open window, she heard the day's lessons, then climbed down the tree after everyone had gone home. Alicia laughs as she remembers the day the teacher wrote a math problem on the board and asked for answers. Alicia forgot herself, raised her hand, and slipped down the tree. The teacher came outside and made it clear that she must stay away from the school.

"Maybe that's why I love being in schools now," she tells her audience. "You students need to know that one of your greatest gifts is to be able to enter a classroom and to say, 'here' when the teacher calls your name. Sometimes people ask me how I can stand being in noisy schools, and I answer, 'What noise?' The voices of the children are beautiful to me; they are the voices of children with a future.

As Alicia speaks to the adults and students in the auditorium, everyone is spellbound, and many quietly cry. After the presentation, Alicia receives a standing ovation and the gift of a bronzed apple from the students. The next day we are invited to spend time with her as she talks with groups of students at one of the local high schools. In these small and informal sessions, Alicia sits on the desk, relaxed and obviously delighted to be here. In turn, the students show interest and respect as they ask thoughtful questions. Because they've read her book, many want to know what eventually happened to some of the specific people whose stories she so eloquently recounted. The students sound more than just curious. They seem to care.

A student asks why more of the Jews didn't fight back. Alicia makes it clear that the Jews did not all submit like sheep to slaughter. Alicia says:

Many Jews fought back; my brother Zackery was hanged for fighting back after they killed the girlfriend he loved and her two little sisters. Children can be brave and maintain values in the midst of horrors. We fought the murderers by building and digging hiding places in order to save as many people as we could. Wearing an apron with hidden pockets, I took dirt far away from our yard so it wouldn't reveal our secret activity.

Once while bathing in a creek with my mother, I became aware of my pitifully skinny body and asked, "Will I ever be a woman?" She replied, "You are a woman already." She taught me to make decisions and to be responsible, and her teaching was an important element in my survival. I loved her with all my heart and protected her and my brothers in every way I could.

However, there was no way that Alicia could stem the tide of horrors. She saw soldiers shoot off the faces of babies and young children. She herself was stomped on by a soldier, thrown in prison, given drinking water laced with typhus germs, stomped on once again and left for dead. She was buried while the Germans watched, but was then miraculously dug up again by a Jewish gravedigger who had felt her feverish body and realized she was still alive. He hid her under the straw of his wagon, took her home, and nursed her back to health. A student asks Alicia how she deals with people who deny that the Holocaust ever happened, and she responds:

I don't even bother to answer adults who are so foolish. But a 14-year-old boy in another school told me his uncle believes the Holocaust never happened. I asked the boy if he had a mother and father, sisters or brothers, grandparents. He said "Yes." Then I replied, "They don't exist, you don't have them, never had them." He burst out, "That's crazy!" "That's right!" I said. And people who deny the Holocaust are telling me that my father, mother, brothers, neighbors, friends, and countless others never existed. The boy then exclaimed, "That IS really crazy! I'd better have another talk with my uncle."

Another student asks about hate groups such as skinheads, and Alicia answers:

Not long ago two of them sat in the front row, ready to mock me. I spoke directly to them. "I understand your loneliness, but this group is not the answer. You will destroy yourself with hatred. Don't let these hatemongers use and abuse you." One of the boys walked out, but the other stayed and listened. This is also what I say to gang members, "Why allow anyone to destroy you with hatred?" Once after a talk, a young German came up to me sobbing, asking for my forgiveness. I held him in my arms and told him there was nothing to forgive, that I did not hold him responsible for what his ancestors did.

After the war, Alicia continued her work, again risking her life to save Jews by helping to smuggle them into Israel. Later, she herself emigrated and served two years in the Israeli navy. In 1950 she married an American construction engineer who had come to Israel to help build the country. They later moved to the United States and became the parents of three children.

Between 1982 and 1985, Alicia recorded her experiences in the book her children asked her to write. During the process, she often found herself reliving the horror, many times laying her head down on her typewriter and crying bitter tears. But the catharsis was important. The pain needed to be drained. Alicia now talks to other Holocaust survivors before they interview with Steven Spielberg, who is preserving their stories for history. She gently draws them out and helps them to deal with their pain in such a way that they are then able to coherently speak about their experiences.

When a student asks Alicia why, after all she'd seen, she still decided to bring children into the world, she replies: I had two major surgeries in order to get pregnant for the children I so desperately wanted. I trusted in the goodness of God, of the people in this country—I trusted life. I don't hate. I believe in God. People let God down when they decide to kill each other. I don't blame God. It's a human disgrace. I decided not to hate because I wanted to do something that could cause God to believe in us.

It is coming to the end of the period, and a student asks, "What is the most important thing you'd like us to remember?" Alicia replies: You young people possess strengths within yourselves in time of need. You can be brave and resourceful and hang on to your dignity, no matter what, even when the world seems to be withholding it from you. I trust that you will not forget what we learn from each other here today. Hatred can destroy a human being, a group of people, a country. It is important to face ourselves to not blame and scapegoat each other. To do so is to put our country in danger. You have your page in history yet to write. You are the children of the future. Please make a pledge to work for the freedom of everyone. Love, be happy, celebrate life.

The session ends with hugs and time for autographing books. We are amazed at the energy of this vivacious woman in her sixties, who doesn't look a day over 50. She invites us to sit and chat awhile. We learn that in December of 1994 she had a serious heart attack and then complications from surgery. The doctors had given up hope. What was supposed to be a five day hospital stay extended into seven weeks. But her work on earth was not finished. "The good Lord has always made the decisions about my life." She ends our encounter by sharing the following experience.

When I was in school in Israel after the war, we didn't pick the oranges in the orchard during the day because Arab snipers would shoot at us. One day, I couldn't wait for the taste of a juicy orange and went outside to pick one. An Arab bullet went through a branch, burned a path across my blouse, and fell at my feet. That bullet is in my jewelry box now. It reminds me that as long as God has work for me to do, I'll be around to do it.

SECTION SEVEN
Ask Reverend Julie

"The fact that I can plant a seed and it becomes a flower
share a bit of knowledge and it becomes another's,
smile at someone and receive a smile in return,
are to me continual spiritual exercises."
—Leo Buscaglia

I am here only to be truly helpful.
I am here to represent Him Who sent me.
I do not have to worry about what to say
Or what to do, because He Who sent me will direct me.
I am content to be wherever He wishes,
Knowing He goes there with me.
I will be healed as I let Him teach me to heal.
—A Course in Miracles

Ask Reverend Julie

Hello everyone,

In church this morning, people handed in their questions and I answered spontaneously. I will answer some of the same questions, which won't be a carbon copy, but I hope helpful to you in some way. Although individuals ask these questions, it's amazing how they apply to us all in some way.

Question one: **"How can we experience peace in the midst of chaos? How can I handle my anger and rage about the world's injustice and inhumanity?"**

I believe that before we can come to peace and before we can get a grip on our anger concerning injustice, we must first see if we can find some sense in the whole mess. I have experienced angst, anger, and rage about the seeming unfairness and cruelty of life on this planet. Someone once said, "Earth is the kindergarten of the universe!" Maybe so. There is no argument that life can be difficult and frustrating.

I will share the solutions I have found for myself in hope that they may be helpful. I spent the early years of my life feeling victimized by life's seeming unfairness. After all, I just wanted to love and be loved. Why did it have to be so difficult? The first answer that made any sense to me came to me from a student in one of my classes who introduced a book on reincarnation which had a clear explanation of how it works. I'm sure most of you reading this already are familiar with this, but I'll do a short explanation for those who may not be familiar with the idea.

First of all, it is not a "heathen" belief. Evidence supporting this was removed from the Bible around 312 A.D. by the Council of Nicea. Yet, they didn't get it all and we can still find Biblical support. Basically, no one "gets away" with anything. Whatever we put out comes back. Simple example: murder someone this life; get murdered yourself the next. Be an uncaring man in this life, a frustrated woman in the next. You get the idea. For me much frustration came because I thought the bad guys were getting away with so much. It might look that way, but no one "gets away" with anything. Everyone must account for their thoughts, words and deeds. No matter what it looks like, there is ultimate justice, and because we cannot see the big picture, it is not up to me and thee to judge anyone. Our job is to upgrade our own consciousness to that of love and forgiveness and trust.

How do we do that? The book on reincarnation stated that we are all here to learn and grow spiritually and that the one way to that is meditation. I sat on my bed and stared out the window at the pine trees and decided I needed help with this! By the grace of God, my office roommate was into Transcendental Meditation and took me to a lecture. I loved it, started meditating and my life was changed. Shortly after, I found Unity and my life took on a whole new meaning and purpose. I left frustration and bitterness behind. I'm not saying this can be done easily. It can be done, but it takes passion for the project! I had suffered enough and had a mighty passion to tune into a higher and better way and thankfully every step ahead on the spiritual path fed my soul.

As a result I left my tenured teaching position and went into the ministry because I have much compassion for people who suffer and want to help them be able to experience the peace and joy of Spirit. Take the first steps of opening your mind and heart to spiritual literature and learn to meditate. It will change your life.

Now for a couple of questions I didn't get to this morning;

Question two: **"Rev. Richard Lynch in 'Knowing Thyself' says for prayer to be effective, that we have to go beyond our 'self.' What does that mean to you?"**

I believe that means we have to get past our human ego and its jabbering bad advice and self-pity. That self we must get beyond is the self that believes it is separate from God, that judges by appearances and lives life reacting to it from the standpoint of being a victim. We can get past and beyond this self with meditation and reading—feeding upon—higher spiritual reading and hanging out with others on the path.

Question three: **"What advice can you offer to someone who has trouble controlling their emotions? I care too much. I'm too happy or too sad or angry or whatever. It's not acceptable. Help!"**

I can relate to what you are asking because before I began meditating, my emotions were all over the place as well. Help came to me in the form of Meditation. It has put a stable floor under extreme emotions. Please seriously consider learning to meditate. Depending on how out of control you feel, you might want to see a counselor to find out if you are bi-polar and need medication. I suspect we all are bi-polar to some extent because we all have mood swings to some degree. The question is how wide is the swing? It's good and healthy to care and to feel, but we can get out of balance and there is no shame in asking for help. Please remember: We are one with God and we are loved and blessed on our path, even when we don't know it. God Bless you all.

Ask Rev. Julie

"On the human level my life
is unmanageable; I need help."
—Master Mind Prayer

Dear Reverend Julie,

I am struggling. I have been doing some inner child work and feeling the pain. I am having a spiritual tantrum and asking God such questions as: Why, if You are a loving God who smiles upon my life, did You watch this happen when I was little child? How sick are You that You allowed a child to be hurt so badly! How can I believe in You! How can I trust anymore?" I need help.

—Stephanie in San Francisco

My Dear Stephanie,

I speak to you as a friend and as your former minister. I cannot ever claim to wave a magic wand and fix your problems, but I can speak words of Truth and pray that you hear them and take them to heart and use them to facilitate your own healing. You know that I too experienced a childhood that was quite bleak and traumatic until the age of nine. This included neglect and sexual abuse. I lost my son at age nine and another son has endured much pain as a result of meningitis. I too railed angrily at God asking "what did I ever do to deserve this?" I understand where you are coming from with these questions.

Now, I know that you know some Truth but it falls away when we allow our ego to get caught up in our own drama. It is not enough to just revisit and feel past pain—that may be a start because we need to face it.

But then it is imperative to move on. We must get above the level of the problem to solve the problem. We must look at the big picture. We are not here in Earth School to have our own way. We are here to expand our consciousness, to grow spiritually, to forgive and love unconditionally and to discover Who we are in Truth—expressions of God.

I believe we actually choose what we need to experience before we come into this life. God is not up in the sky pulling our puppet strings. This is Earth School and we are here to learn that we have a body and we have experiences here, but that is not who and what we are. We are spiritual beings and as such, no matter what happens *to* us, our true spiritual identity cannot be taken away. It is our Divine inheritance.

Please understand that it is possible to forgive everyone and everything in your life. It is the path to peace and joy. Without it we can't move forward. We don't condone the hurtful actions of others, but we can come to a place of understanding and compassion. If we are treated with less than love and respect, we can know the person is fearful and unhealed. I began forgiveness work on my childhood molesters at first for a very selfish reason. I knew that to not forgive meant continued pain and misery for me. So I willed to forgive and prayed visually. I put them in a light and whenever a thought of them and their actions arose I said, "I call upon the presence and power of the Christ. I forgive you."

This went on for quite some time because we go down through the layers of pain, shame, resentment, whatever needs healing. The issue can come up again and again and we go through the forgiveness process again and again until we know we're done. We will know that when we can actually, from our heart, send love to those who out of their own unhealed consciousness seem to harm us.

When I was in ministerial school, I was still working on these things and counseled with a dear lady, Rev. Martha Guidici. The healing words she said to me and words that I want to pass on to you: "Because you have experienced these things, you are going to be able to help others heal and move on." That was a huge turn around for me. Dear heart, I know you, and I do believe you have the potential to do the same. When we have wandered in the wilderness, when we have been in Hell and know what it's like, and when by the Grace of God we find healing and a way out, we are in a position to truly help others.

Please know that right now I am praying with you, holding you in the light and beholding your true spirit. You are not having a spiritual tantrum; you are having an ego tantrum. The ego wants you to keep suffering because it gains energy from that. You have a choice. Reach up and reach in to your true Spirit. Entertain truthful thoughts, not the lies of the human ego.

I know you are capable of this and I know that you know where and how to find the help you need. Do you have the will to move forward? In the Bible Paul said: "I believe—help my unbelief." On the human level we have moments of doubt, anger, fear, but we can know that we can let all that go and move on. I hope this helps you and others who may be going through challenges.

Ask Reverend Julie

"Thy will be done on earth
as it is in Heaven." Lord's Prayer

Dear Reverend Julie,

What is God's will anyway?

Wondering in Memphis

Dear Wondering,

In spite of the fact that this question has worried and confused people for a very long time, the answer is not all that complicated. God's will for us is to awaken to the truth of who and what we are: Sons and Daughters of the living loving God—innocent, eternal spirit—One with God our Creator.

I quote from A Course in Miracles: God did not will the destruction of His creations, having created them for eternity. His Will has saved you, not from yourself, but from your illusion of yourself. He has saved you *for* yourself.

Ego tries to convince us we're unworthy, but we cannot make ourselves unworthy because in truth we are God's treasure. God does not hide his will from us; we hide it from ourselves because our ego does not want to know it. The ego gets its energy and juice by convincing us we should doubt and fear God's will.

God wills only that we awaken to love and union by forgiving and opening ourselves to the guidance and instruction of Holy Spirit within us, nearer than breathing and closer than hands and feet. Jesus' teaching in the New

Testament and in A Course in Miracles show us how to join with God's Will, which is also our own true will.

We make the mistake of buying into the delusions of our ego when we believe we are separate from God and His will. God wills that we live in eternal love, peace, and joy (Heaven) because our Reality is one with the God of Love. Ego wants us to live in drama, struggle, pain, misery doubt and fear (Hell). If we are living in hell, we can, like the prodigal son, decide to return to the Father, Our Creator, The Source—and we will always be welcomed Home.

Dear Wondering, I hope this helps you see more clearly. I hope it gives you peace to know that you are always safe and secure in the mind and heart of God, even while you dream of wandering elsewhere.

Ask Reverend Julie

"The only true disability in life is a bad attitude."
—Scott Hamilton

Dear Reverend Julie,

Many spiritual teachers including you say that we choose our experiences before we come here. What do you feel "bad" experiences are for and why would we choose them?—Inquiring in Iowa

Dear Inquiring,

These are good questions to consider because just about everyone who ever comes to Earth School asks the same thing. We need to keep in mind the ultimate goal, which is to transform our consciousness from earthly to heavenly. We are here to learn to wake up to and embrace the spirit of God within us, the love and light we truly are. To do this we must learn to see past the ego that seeks to edge God out of our consciousness so that we live in fear and darkness—hell.

Our goal of Enlightenment may take thousands of years and lifetimes, but it can also happen in an instant as it has to someone like Eckhart Tolle or David Hawkins—and many others too numerous to name here. You and I can know that we are still "in process" if we are still working to rise above the battleground of our lives. Yet, being in process IS making progress! Once we begin to understand why we're here and what we need to be doing, we're on our way even when we stumble and slide back occasionally.

So, what are those so called bad and painful experiences for? Why would our soul choose them? Because we need to learn to utilize every one of them in order to make progress toward our goal of enlightenment. We are here to learn forgiveness and unconditional love for ourselves and all others—which leads to the love, peace, and joy of God—Enlightenment.

Each of us has our unique life and experiences. Yet, just below the surface we are all seeking the same thing. We want love; we want God; we want Enlightenment. How do we go about this? We must start where we are and deal with and heal what is in front of us, which includes all unhealed and unresolved issues from our past. Author and spiritual teacher Byron Katie asks, "How do we know something should be happening (or should have happened)?" And she answers, "Because it happened or is happening!" We must begin from where we are and move forward.

Many of you have read my history in *From Soap Opera to Symphony*. I detail my journey from shame, despair, and hopelessness to experiencing the love, peace and grace of God. I don't pretend to be enlightened yet because I do not feel love, peace, and joy every minute of every day. However, I can say that I feel it to a degree I never would have thought possible earlier in my life. I have come to see clearly why my soul chose a childhood of neglect and abuse. I can see why I chose an alcoholic father and husbands, why I made a soul agreement with my sons—Richard who died suddenly—and Robert who has endured serious difficulties. I needed to make peace with my life and truly forgive everyone and everything.

An athlete who trains for the high jump keeps raising the bar that he learns to jump over. As our soul seeks to elevate itself toward enlightenment, we set the bars, the hurdles, higher and higher. This is the way our souls grow. Yet, I believe that there are those lifetimes where we decide to take a breather. I used to wonder, "why me?" So many around me seemed to be living the charmed life I always yearned for. I have learned that ultimately, we each have our own soul's business and that we need to focus on that. Byron Katie reminds us that we have only three kinds of business—yours, mine, and God's. We have enough to do to tend to our own. It is a waste of time and energy to judge or try to fix what is not our own soul business.

A while ago, I was in Memphis as a guest speaker at Unity. A classmate from Unity ministerial school, Colleen Brown, lives in town and it was great to spend some time with her. Her response after reading my Soap Opera book was, "I had no idea, no idea, what you went though. You seemed so together and happy with your friends." I take this as a great compliment because I had already made great progress in moving beyond considering myself a victim. I was indeed feeling very happy and fulfilled and delighted to be where I was.

Another touching encounter at Memphis Unity was with Rev. Thelma Hembroff, a former minister who experienced a stroke in New Orleans during hurricane Katrina. She was between a walker and a wheel chair, her right arm paralyzed. Yet she is still as she always was, impeccably coiffed, made up, dressed—and smiling. I spent time with her and detected no sign of self-pity. She also wrote her life story, which is very full of challenges and overcoming and I said to her story: "I had no idea, no idea." that this smiling successful and put together woman had experienced so much challenge and trauma in her early life.

It's important to realize that our history is a record of our soul choices, but it is NOT our identity! Society does not make it easy for us to remember this. We are too often judged and categorized by our circumstances, but we must remember that any circumstance can be a hurdle, but it is not who we are. By the grace of God, we have a higher identity. We are spiritual beings at one with God and with one another, whether we currently know it or not. It is our Earth School assignment to wake up to this truth and to bless every experience along the way because every experience can help us wake up.

Ask Rev. Julie

"Be kind; everyone you meet is fighting a hard battle."
—John Watson

Dear Reverend Julie,

I can't get rid of occasional bad and sad days. I meditate and pray. I read uplifting books. In spite of that I just lose it now and then. I seem to forget what truth I know, and then I suffer. Can you give me some advice about how to deal with that? Do you have those kinds of times, and if so, what do you do?—Sad Sandra in South Carolina

Dear Sandra,

Yes, I do have "bad and sad days." Here's what I do. I use them. They are a signal, a message that I have more work to do, more forgiveness and release and healing. There is no need to feel shame about this. The need is to stop and examine what's happening. This can be done by journaling—writing about how and why you are feeling distress. Write about who or what triggered it. Ask Holy Spirit to be the guide, the presence during the process.

The human ego encourages our sadness, our sense of being victimized, and then feeds on our misery. As you know, we can dig ourselves into some very deep holes. It's important to turn it around as soon as possible. As soon as we get honest with ourselves, we gain a foothold and start to climb higher in consciousness. It can take an hour, a day, a week or even longer, but relief will come as soon as we begin a sincere process of self observation and become willing to see where the ego mind has misled us. The grace of God kicks in, and the darkness begins to lift. We can't dismiss the seriousness of these challenges. They can be rough. It feels like an ugly monster (ego?) is dumping a pot of thick warm glue over us, drowning us in misery, anger, and confusion, temporarily shutting down all the higher truth we know.

It helps to know that even highly "spiritual" people experience dark times. Saints such as Paul have described their temptations and dark days. Recently, some writings of Mother Theresa were released, revealing that even she questioned her own faith and activities and experienced her own very dark times. It seems that we need to become spiritual warriors. It has been said that old age isn't for sissies. Maybe so, but a full commitment to a spiritual life is not for sissies either! "Be kind: everyone you meet is fighting a hard battle," said John Watson. It takes courage and strength to look at ourselves honestly and to admit that on the human ego level, our lives are unmanageable and that we need help.

Humility takes spiritual strength; staying open and receptive to the guidance and instruction of Holy Spirit requires that we stay alert and pay attention to where our minds and emotions wander. There is a section in A Course in Miracles that I read often entitled This Need Not Be. (Text Chapter 4, section IV.) It leaves no place to run and hide and cautions us against voluntary dis-spiriting. I will share a few sentences here, and I encourage you to read the whole piece. This one section is worth the price of the book! The following is just a small sample:

"When your mood tells you that you have chosen wrongly, and this is so whenever you are not joyous, then *know this need not be*. When you are sad, *know this need not be*. Depression comes from a sense of being deprived of something you want and do not have. When you are anxious, realize that anxiety comes from the capriciousness of the ego, *and know this need not be.* Watch your mind for the temptations of the ego, and do not be deceived by it. It offers you nothing. Yet you are not sufficiently vigilant against the demands of the ego to disengage yourself. *This need not be.*"

I've discovered that I must say "no" to my ego. Just recently my mind started down a self destructive path, and I was able to say to myself, "Oh no you don't!" By the grace of God I was able to tune into a higher part of my mind that knows better. It still took awhile for the negativity to dissipate, but the important thing is that it DID dissipate before I dug a hole and fell in it.

So my dear Sandra, keep on keeping on with your spiritual work. Become a spiritual warrior. Meet the dark days head on, and do your soul work. As you do this, you will become stronger and continue to grow spiritually. Don't be afraid to share your experiences, your struggle and your methods of overcoming with others on the path. "Be an opener of doors for such as come after thee, and do not make the universe a blind alley," is advice given by Emerson that I have tried to follow as a teacher, minister and friend. Bless everything in your life, the darker learning times as well as the joyous times. There comes a time when you will realize that it is all good.

Ask Rev. Julie

"I tore myself away from the safe comfort
Of certainties; and Truth rewarded me."
—Simone de Beauvoir

Dear Reverend Julie,

If I am already perfect, why is it necessary to work so seriously on my spiritual growth? If I just accept my perfection, isn't that enough?
—Confused in Charleston

Dear confused,

If you could truly and deeply **experience** your perfection, that would surely be enough. The problem is that most of us know theoretically in our heads that we are indeed pure spirit, perfect sons and daughters of the living loving God; however we don't know it in our hearts so that we truly experience the love peace and joy of God in our daily lives.

Why is that? Seems that we have veils over the truth of our being and it can and does take diligent spiritual focus to begin to remove them. Where do these veils come from—how did they get there? Ah, that is the so called "fall of man"—a fall in consciousness from the state of innocence where the sense of separation from God (the human ego) was born.

One of my favorite spiritual authors and teachers David Hawkins in his wonderful book entitled "Eye of the I" has a great explanation I'd like to share with you. He answers the question: "Why is 'work' even necessary in spiritual endeavor?" Hawkins says, "The ego can be thought of as a set of **entrenched habits of thought** that are the result of entrainment by energy fields which dominate human consciousness. They become reinforced by repetition and by the consensus of society."

A Course in Miracles reminds us that the ego is very tenacious and tricky and loves to lead us down all kinds of side roads. As I observe myself honestly, I can see and feel those times when I am on an ego side road. Yet, by the grace of God, I also experience those wonderful peaceful, loving, joyful times when I am experiencing oneness with Spirit. Why can't I just stay tuned into Spirit and relax? Because I still have not totally risen above my ego—it's still with me enough that it I realize that I need to stay diligent in my spiritual work.

I have to take time to meditate, read and study higher spiritual teachings, and observe myself honestly so that when my ego wants to be fearful, angry and resentful, I can see clearly enough to choose differently. David Hawkins simplifies the problem with this advice: "In practice, then, one transcends the negative by merely choosing the opposite. With the internal discipline that stems from passionate commitment, the negative choices are no longer seen as options."

I personally do my spiritual work because I have a passion to truly experience my innate perfection in God, not just "know about it" mentally. But, there is another side of the coin. I have a plaque that says: "Angels can fly because they take themselves lightly." I don't think it's a good idea to make our spiritual life drudgery. We get in our own way when we do.

I have a good friend who does kitchen table philosophy with me. His idea is to just focus upon love and caring and serving others. He does not feel the need to wrestle within his spirituality. He's got a good point. In the final analysis, perhaps **Balance** is the answer. Relax, release, let go. The paradox is that sometimes we need to work, to wrestle with our ego to attain that surrender. Unless we are a bodhisattva (a totally enlightened being here to help others) we do most likely have at least some "work" to do. That work can be self-observation, spiritual study, prayer and meditation, and just day to day loving kindness.

Because the ego is so tricky, it will try to use even our spiritual endeavors to enhance itself with the thought, "I am more spiritual than you are." I think one of the best ego-busters is laughter. With the ego's encouragement, we take ourselves much too seriously. I've found that by laughing and even being silly, layers of self-righteous pompous viewpoints can be seen for what they are. They can then just dissolve by themselves. It is not our job to judge how others go about their spiritual business. We each have our ways, and if we have a pure intent and listen to our own inner guidance and take care of our own spiritual business that is all we need to do. So work as you are guided, relax, laugh and love and stop worrying about it. I hope this helps.

Ask Rev. Julie

"Be kind; everyone you meet is fighting a hard battle."
—John Watson

Dear Reverend Julie,

I can't get rid of occasional bad and sad days. I meditate and pray. I read uplifting books. In spite of that I just lose it now and then. I seem to forget what truth I know, and then I suffer. Can you give me some advice about how to deal with that? Do you have those kinds of times, and if so, what do you do?

Sad Sandra in South Carolina

Dear Sandra,

Yes, I do have "bad and sad days." Here's what I do. I use them. They are a signal, a message that I have more work to do, more forgiveness and release and healing. There is no need to feel shame about this. The need is to stop and examine what's happening. This can be done by journaling—writing about how and why you are feeling distress. Write about who or what triggered it. Ask Holy Spirit to be the guide, the presence during the process.

The human ego encourages our sadness, our sense of being victimized, and then feeds on our misery. As you know, we can dig ourselves into some very deep holes. It's important to turn it around as soon as possible. As soon as we get honest with ourselves, we gain a foothold and start to climb higher in consciousness. It can take an hour, a day, a week or even longer, but relief will come as soon as we begin a sincere process of self observation and become willing to see where the ego mind has misled us.

The grace of God kicks in, and the darkness begins to lift. We can't dismiss the seriousness of these challenges. They can be rough. It feels like an ugly monster (ego?) is dumping a pot of thick warm glue over us, drowning us in misery, anger, and confusion, temporarily shutting down all the higher truth we know.

It helps to know that even highly "spiritual" people experience dark times. Saints such as Paul have described their temptations and dark days. Recently, some writings of Mother Theresa were released, revealing that even she questioned her own faith and activities and experienced her own very dark times. It seems that we need to become spiritual warriors. It has been said that old age isn't for sissies. Maybe so, but a full commitment to a spiritual life is not for sissies either! "Be kind: everyone you meet is fighting a hard battle," said John Watson. It takes courage and strength to look at ourselves honestly and to admit that on the human ego level, our lives are unmanageable and that we need help.

Humility takes spiritual strength; staying open and receptive to the guidance and instruction of Holy Spirit requires that we stay alert and pay attention to where our minds and emotions wander. There is a section in Course in Miracles that I read often entitled This Need Not Be. (Text Chapter 4, section IV.) It leaves no place to run and hide and cautions us against voluntary dis-spiriting. I will share a few sentences here, and I encourage you to read the whole piece. This one section is worth the price of the book! The following is just a small sample:

"When your mood tells you that you have chosen wrongly, and this is so whenever you are not joyous, then *know this need not be*. When you are sad, *know this need not be*. Depression comes from a sense of being deprived of something you want and do not have. When you are anxious, realize that anxiety comes from the capriciousness of the ego, *and know this need not be.* Watch your mind for the temptations of the ego, and do not be deceived by it. It offers you nothing. When you have given up this voluntary dis-spiriting, you will see how your mind can focus and rise above fatigue (and other negatives) and heal. Yet you are not sufficiently vigilant against the demands of the ego to disengage yourself. *This need not be.*"

I've discovered that I must say "no" to my ego. Just recently my mind started down a self destructive path, and I was able to say to myself, "Oh no you don't!" By the grace of God I was able to tune into a higher part of my mind that knows better. It still took awhile for the negativity to dissipate, but the important thing is that it DID dissipate before I dug a hole and fell in it.

So my dear Sandra, keep on keeping on with your spiritual work. Become a spiritual warrior. Meet the dark days head on, and do your soul work. As you do this, you will become stronger and continue to grow spiritually. Don't be afraid to share your experiences, your struggle and your methods of overcoming with others on the path. "Be an opener of doors for such as come after thee, and do not make the universe a blind alley," is advice given by Emerson that I have tried to follow as a teacher, minister and friend. Bless everything in your life, the darker learning times as well as the joyous times. There comes a time when you will realize that it is all good. I surround you with a prayer of love and light and know with you and for you that you are a beautiful child of God and heir to untold love and blessings.

Ask Rev. Julie

"On the human level my life
is unmanageable; I need help."
—Master Mind Prayer

Dear Reverend Julie,

I am struggling. I have been doing some inner child work and feeling the pain. I am having a spiritual tantrum and asking God such questions as: Why, if You are a loving God who smiles upon my life, did You watch this happen when I was little child? How sick are You that You allowed a child to be hurt so badly! How can I believe in You! How can I trust anymore?" I need help.

Stephanie in San Francisco

My Dear Stephanie,

I speak to you as a friend and as your former minister. I cannot ever claim to wave a magic wand and fix your problems, but I can speak words of Truth and pray that you hear them and take them to heart and use them to facilitate your own healing. You know that I too experienced a childhood that was quite bleak and traumatic until the age of nine. This included neglect and sexual abuse. I lost my son at age nine and another son has endured much pain as a result of meningitis. I too railed angrily at God asking "what did I ever do to deserve this?" I understand where you are coming from with these questions.

Now, I know that you know some Truth but it falls away when we allow our ego to get caught up in our own drama. It is not enough to just revisit and feel past pain—that may be a start because we need to face it.

But then it is imperative to move on. We must get above the level of the problem to solve the problem. We must look at the big picture. We are not here in Earth School to have our own way. We are here to expand our consciousness, to grow spiritually, to forgive and love unconditionally and to discover Who we are in Truth—expressions of God.

I believe we actually choose what we need to experience before we come into this life. God is not up in the sky pulling our puppet strings. This is Earth School and we are here to learn that we have a body and we have experiences here, but that is not who and what we are. We are spiritual beings and as such, no matter what happens *to* us, our true spiritual identity cannot be taken away. It is our Divine inheritance.

Please understand that it is possible to forgive everyone and everything in your life. It is the path to peace and joy. Without it we can't move forward. We don't condone the hurtful actions of others, but we can come to a place of understanding and compassion. If we are treated with less than love and respect, we can know the person is fearful and unhealed. I began forgiveness work on my childhood molesters at first for a very selfish reason. I knew that to not forgive meant continued pain and misery for me. So I willed to forgive and prayed visually. I put them in a light and whenever a thought of them and their actions arose I said, "I call upon the presence and power of the Christ. I forgive you." This went on for quite some time because we go down through the layers of pain, shame, resentment, whatever needs healing. The issue can come up again and again and we go through the forgiveness process again and again until we know we're done. We will know that when we can actually, from our heart, send love to those who out of their own unhealed consciousness seem to harm us.

Julie Ireland Keene

When I was in ministerial school, I was still working on these things and counseled with a dear lady, Rev. Martha Guidici. The healing words she said to me and words that I want to pass on to you: "Because you have experienced these things, you are going to be able to help others heal and move on." That was a huge turn around for me. Dear heart, I know you, and I do believe you have the potential to do the same. When we have wandered in the wilderness, when we have been in Hell and know what it's like, and when by the Grace of God we find healing and a way out, we are in a position to truly help others.

Please know that right now I am praying with you, holding you in the light and beholding your true spirit. You are not having a spiritual tantrum; you are having an ego tantrum. The ego wants you to keep suffering because it gains energy from that. You have a choice. Reach up and reach in to your true Spirit. Entertain truthful thoughts, not the lies of the human ego. I know you are capable of this and I know that you know where and how to find the help you need. Do you have the will to move forward? In the Bible Paul said: "I believe—help my unbelief." On the human level we have moments of doubt, anger, fear, but we can know that we can let all that go and move on. I hope this helps you and others who may be going through challenges.

Ask Reverend Julie

"The only true disability in life is a bad attitude."
—Scott Hamilton

Dear Reverend Julie,

Many spiritual teachers including you say that we choose our experiences before we come here. What do you feel "bad" experiences are for and why would we choose them?

Inquiring in Iowa

Dear Inquiring,

These are good questions to consider because just about everyone who ever comes to Earth School asks the same thing. We need to keep in mind the ultimate goal, which is to transform our consciousness from earthly to heavenly. We are here to learn to wake up to and embrace the spirit of God within us, the love and light we truly are. To do this we must learn to see past the ego that seeks to edge God out of our consciousness so that we live in fear and darkness—hell.

Our goal of Enlightenment may take thousands of years and lifetimes, but it can also happen in an instant as it has to someone like Eckhart Tolle or David Hawkins—and many others too numerous to name here. You and I can know that we are still "in process" if we are still working to rise above the battleground of our lives. Yet, being in process IS making progress! Once we begin to understand why we're here and what we need to be doing, we're on our way even when we stumble and slide back occasionally.

So, what are those so called bad and painful experiences for? Why would our soul choose them? Because we need to learn to utilize every one of them in order to make progress toward our goal of enlightenment. We are here to learn forgiveness and unconditional love for ourselves and all others—which leads to the love, peace, and joy of God—Enlightenment.

Each of us has our unique life and experiences. Yet, just below the surface we are all seeking the same thing. We want love; we want God; we want Enlightenment. How do we go about this? We must start where we are and deal with and heal what is in front of us, which includes all unhealed and unresolved issues from our past. Author and spiritual teacher Byron Katie asks, "How do we know something should be happening (or should have happened)?" And she answers, "Because it happened or is happening!" We must begin from where we are and move forward.

Many of you have read my history in *From Soap Opera to Symphony*. I detail my journey from shame, despair, and hopelessness to experiencing the love, peace and grace of God. I don't pretend to be enlightened yet because I do not feel love, peace, and joy every minute of every day. However, I can say that I feel it to a degree I never would have thought possible earlier in my life. I have come to see clearly why my soul chose a childhood of neglect and abuse. I can see why I chose an alcoholic father and husbands, why I made a soul agreement with my sons—Richard who died suddenly—and Robert who has endured serious difficulties. I needed to make peace with my life and truly forgive everyone and everything.

An athlete who trains for the high jump keeps raising the bar that he learns to jump over. As our soul seeks to elevate itself toward enlightenment, we set the bars, the hurdles, higher and higher. This is the way our souls grow. Yet, I believe that there are those lifetimes where we decide to take a breather. I used to wonder, "why me?" So many around me seemed to be living the charmed life I always yearned for. I have learned that ultimately, we each have our own soul's business and that we need to focus on that. Byron Katie reminds us that we have only three kinds of business—yours, mine, and God's. We have enough to do to tend to our own. It is a waste of time and energy to judge or try to fix what is not our own soul business.

A while ago, I was in Memphis as a guest speaker at Unity. A classmate from Unity ministerial school, Colleen Brown, lives in town and it was great to spend some time with her. Her response after reading my Soap Opera book was, "I had no idea, no idea, what you went though. You seemed so together and happy with your friends." I take this as a great compliment because I had already made great progress in moving beyond considering myself a victim. I was indeed feeling very happy and fulfilled and delighted to be where I was.

Another touching encounter at Memphis Unity was with Rev. Thelma Hembroff, a former minister who experienced a stroke in New Orleans during hurricane Katrina. She was between a walker and a wheel chair, her right arm paralyzed. Yet she is still as she always was, impeccably coiffed, made up, dressed—and smiling. I spent time with her and detected no sign of self-pity. She also wrote her life story, which is very full of challenges and overcoming and I said to her story: "I had no idea, no idea." that this smiling successful and put together woman had experienced so much challenge and trauma in her early life.

It's important to realize that our history is a record of our soul choices, but it is NOT our identity! Society does not make it easy for us to remember this. We are too often judged and categorized by our circumstances, but we must remember that any circumstance can be a hurdle, but it is not who we are. By the grace of God, we have a higher identity. We are spiritual beings at one with God and with one another, whether we currently know it or not. It is our Earth School assignment to wake up to this truth and to bless every experience along the way because every experience can help us wake up.

Ask Rev. Julie

"I tore myself away from the safe comfort
Of certainties; and Truth rewarded me."
—Simone de Beauvoir

Dear Reverend Julie,

If I am already perfect, why is it necessary to work so seriously on my spiritual growth? If I just accept my perfection, isn't that enough?

Confused in Charleston

Dear confused,

If you could truly and deeply **experience** your perfection, that would surely be enough. The problem is that most of us know theoretically in our heads that we are indeed pure spirit, perfect sons and daughters of the living loving God; however we don't know it in our hearts so that we truly experience the love peace and joy of God in our daily lives.

Why is that? Seems that we have veils over the truth of our being and it can and does take diligent spiritual focus to begin to remove them. Where do these veils come from—how did they get there? Ah, that is the so called "fall of man"—a fall in consciousness from the state of innocence where the sense of separation from God (the human ego) was born.

One of my favorite spiritual authors and teachers David Hawkins in his wonderful book entitled "Eye of the I" has a great explanation I'd like to share with you. He answers the question: "Why is 'work' even necessary in spiritual endeavor?" Hawkins says, "The ego can be thought of as a set of **entrenched habits of thought** that are the result of entrainment by energy fields which dominate human consciousness. They become reinforced by repetition and by the consensus of society."

A Course in Miracles reminds us that the ego is very tenacious and tricky and loves to lead us down all kinds of side roads. As I observe myself honestly, I can see and feel those times when I am on an ego side road. Yet, by the grace of God, I also experience those wonderful peaceful, loving, joyful times when I am experiencing oneness with Spirit. Why can't I just stay tuned into Spirit and relax? Because I still have not totally risen above my ego—it's still with me enough that it I realize that I need to stay diligent in my spiritual work.

I have to take time to meditate, read and study higher spiritual teachings, and observe myself honestly so that when my ego wants to be fearful, angry and resentful, I can see clearly enough to choose differently. David Hawkins simplifies the problem with this advice: "In practice, then, one transcends the negative by merely choosing the opposite. With the internal discipline that stems from passionate commitment, the negative choices are no longer seen as options."

I personally do my spiritual work because I have a passion to truly experience my innate perfection in God, not just "know about it" mentally. But, there is another side of the coin. I have a plaque that says: "Angels can fly because they take themselves lightly." I don't think it's a good idea to make our spiritual life drudgery. We get in our own way when we do.

I have a good friend who does kitchen table philosophy with me. His idea is to just focus upon love and caring and serving others. He does not feel the need to wrestle within his spirituality. He's got a good point. In the final analysis, perhaps **Balance** is the answer. Relax, release, let go. The paradox is that sometimes we need to work, to wrestle with our ego to attain that surrender. Unless we are a bodhisattva (a totally enlightened being here to help others) we do most likely have at least some "work" to do. That work can be self-observation, spiritual study, prayer and meditation, and just day to day loving kindness.

Because the ego is so tricky, it will try to use even our spiritual endeavors to enhance itself with the thought, "I am more spiritual than you are." I think one of the best ego-busters is laughter. With the ego's encouragement, we take ourselves much too seriously. I've found that by laughing and even being silly, layers of self-righteous pompous viewpoints can be seen for what they are. They can then just dissolve by themselves. It is not our job to judge how others go about their spiritual business. We each have our ways, and if we have a pure intent and listen to our own inner guidance and take care of our own spiritual business that is all we need to do. So work as you are guided, relax, laugh and love and stop worrying about it. I hope this helps.

Ask Reverend Julie

"Thy will be done on earth
as it is in Heaven." Lord's Prayer

Dear Reverend Julie,
What is God's will anyway?
Wondering in Memphis

Dear Wondering,
In spite of the fact that this question has worried and confused people for a very long time, the answer is not all that complicated. God's will for us is to awaken to the truth of who and what we are: Sons and Daughters of the living loving God—innocent, eternal spirit—One with God our Creator.

I quote from A Course in Miracles: God did not will the destruction of His creations, having created them for eternity. His Will has saved you, not from yourself, but from your illusion of yourself. He has saved you *for* yourself.

Ego tries to convince us we're unworthy, but we cannot make ourselves unworthy because in truth we are God's treasure. God does not hide his will from us; we hide it from ourselves because our ego does not want to know it. The ego gets its energy and juice by convincing us we should doubt and fear God's will.

God wills only that we awaken to love and union by forgiving and opening ourselves to the guidance and instruction of Holy Spirit within us, nearer than breathing and closer than hands and feet. Jesus' teaching in the New

Testament and in A Course in Miracles show us how to join with God's Will, which is also our own true will.

We make the mistake of buying into the delusions of our ego when we believe we are separate from God and His will. God wills that we live in eternal love, peace, and joy (Heaven) because our Reality is one with the God of Love. Ego wants us to live in drama, struggle, pain, misery doubt and fear (Hell). If we are living in hell, we can, like the prodigal son, decide to return to the Father, Our Creator, The Source—and we will always be welcomed Home.

Dear Wondering, I hope this helps you see more clearly. I hope it gives you peace to know that you are always safe and secure in the mind and

heart of God, even while you dream of wandering elsewhere.

RECOMMENDED READING

(Some of my favorite inspirational books)

A New Earth—Eckhart Tolle

The Diamond in Your Pocket—Gangaji

A Thousand Names for Joy—Byron Katie

The Art of Spiritual Healing—Joel Goldsmith

The Art of Meditation—Joel Goldsmith

The Infinite Way—Joel Goldsmith

Man Was Not Born to Cry—Joel Goldsmith

Entering the Castle—Carolyn Myss

The Eye of the I—David Hawkins

Into the Light—John Lerma, M.D.

Many Lives, Many Masters—Brian Weiss, M.D.

The Mantram Handbook—Eknath Easwaran

The Prospering Power of Love—Catherine Ponder

There is a River—Thomas Sugrue (Edgar Cayce Biography)

Take Me to Truth—Sanchez and Viera (based on A Course in Miracles)

The Presence Process—Michael Brown

What We May Be—Piero Ferucci

Who Would You Be Without Your Story—Byron Katie

What is Mysticism?—Jon Mundy

The Unthethered Soul—Michael Singer

Your Soul's Plan by Robert Schwartz

The Illuminated Rumi—Coleman Barks

Thanks to Angels:

Jeanne & John Alderson

Joanne Abitabilo

Laurie Alexander

Ted Bruce

Cheryl & Jessie Burnett

Shelby Beckett

Tony Bare

Dan & Jean Boardwine

Jean Boyd

Dick Beene

Wilma Clark

Sharon Cook

Carolyn Cornelison

Charlotte Curtis

Ben Castelli

Cynthia Davis

Lori Ferguson

Buck Gotschall

Jeanette Grenette

Cheryl Gibbons

Larry Gross

Kathryn Hathaway

Elizabeth Hubbard

Pam Hitt

Margaret Ireland

Frank Johnson

Karen Johnson

Kathleen Jacobs

Connie King

Myra Kauffman

Nancy Lysen Kirtley

Susan Kolk

Alex Kruse

Jacquie Kennedy

Shannon King

Lou & Jennie Logan

Joanna Love

Carolyn M. Lawson

Jo Langston

Pat Locke

Lois Morton

Emily Millett

Vicki McManus

Sharyl McGrew

Lynn Montgomery

Jane Rae May

Janet Nah

Donna Newberry

Judy Pouncey

Julie Pestella

Bruce Pelham

Angela Rolle Polk

Annie Rolle

Aline Rundle

Geralyn & Andy Russell

Rick Swenson

Teresa Sumrall

Vicki Spray

Rebecca Sweat

Mary Shannahan

Jane Selman

Donni Sorrell

Mary Beth Seay

Barbara Sovereen

Walter Thomas

Glenna Trauets

Carol Trescott

Rosalie & Marv Witbeck

Constance & William Roberts

Mary Ruth Williamson

About the Author

Reverend Julie Keene has served several Unity ministries since her ordination in 1982: Coeur d'Alene, Idaho; Tallahassee and Gainesville Florida; Salt Lake City and St. George, Utah, and until October 2009, Cincinnati, Ohio. While a ministerial student she served as leader in Columbia, Missouri when they were first forming a group.

Julie lived and worked at the Holo Center in Idaho and traveled extensively presenting workshops with co-leader, psychologist Ione Jenson. They presented workshops to over 100 Unity and Religious Science groups all around the United States, including Hawaii. They also served a short period at Unity in Bermuda. Before entering the ministry, Julie taught Composition and Literature at Ferris State University in Michigan. She gave up tenure as an Assistant Professor to attend Unity Ministerial School in 1980.

Julie's goal is to be truly helpful and totally loving and compassionate as she speaks and facilitates workshops. She is dedicated to helping people live an expansive spiritually focused life. Because she has moved through challenges and obstacles in her own life, she is well equipped to help others on their journey to wholeness.

Julie currently resides in Tallahassee, Florida where she helps out at Unity of Tallahassee by doing the early 9:30 Sunday morning service and facilitates A Course in Miracles. (See schedule)

www.Jewelskeenespirit.com
Jewelskeene613@aol.com